D1200876

The Best of
Paddler Magazine

*Stories from the World's Premier Canoeing,
Kayaking, and Rafting Magazine*

The Best of
Paddler Magazine

Stories from the World's Premier Canoeing, Kayaking, and Rafting Magazine

edited by
Eugene Buchanan

Menasha Ridge Press

Published by Menasha Ridge Press

Distributed by The Globe Pequot Press

Cover design by Grant Tatum

Cover photograph by Chuck Wales / Amy Wiley, 1995

Text design by Erin Wright

Library of Congress Cataloging-in-Publication Data:

Best of Paddler Magazine : Stories from the World's Premier Canoeing, Kayaking,
and Rafting Magazine / edited by Eugene Buchanan
    p. c.m.
    ISBN 0-89732-330-0
    1. Canoes and canoeing. 1. Buchanan, Eugene. 11. Paddler (Fallbrook, CA)

GV 783.B48 2000
797.1'22—dc21   00-039445

Manufactured in the United States of America

10 9 8 7 6 5 4 3 2 1

First edition, first printing

Menasha Ridge Press
P.O. Box 43673
Birmingham, AL 35243
(205) 322-0439
www.menasharidge.com

CONTENTS

As well as being backed by the American Canoe Association, the oldest waterways conservation organization in the world, *Paddler* magazine is spearheaded by Publisher/Editor-in-Chief Eugene Buchanan, who has been with the publication since 1991. A former kayak instructor and sea kayak and raft guide, Buchanan—when he can find the time—also enjoys a successful freelance career, with articles published in the *New York Times, Men's Journal, Sports Afield, Outside, National Geographic Explorer, Adventure Journal, Ski, Powder, Bike,* and other national publications. An avid adventurer with several first descents to his credit, Buchanan's passion for traveling, writing, and paddling has taken him on assignments to six of the seven continents, from Africa to Australia, and South America to Siberia. "It's great being able to combine my two pastimes of writing and paddling," says Buchanan, recently featured in an Outdoor Life Network special. "And this gives me a unique perspective in helping our contributors do the same."

When I first took the editorial reins at *Paddler*, I set up shop in a two-bedroom apartment in Boulder, CO. Nurturing a love affair for both paddling and writing, I felt well-suited to the task. I had guided river and sea kayak trips in Alaska; guided rafts in Colorado; canoed the Boundary Waters and Canada; worked as a kayak instructor ("Keep your head down!"); and had just gotten off the Grand Canyon, where I met my wife, Denise. My writing background was equally varied, with stints at two newspapers and freelance pieces in publications as varied as the *New York Times* and *Men's Journal*. Still, when the boxes from the main office arrived on my doorstep, I was somewhat overwhelmed. Inside were stories and photos (some of the latter straight off peoples' refrigerators) from hundreds of contributors. How on earth do you dive into such a project? Naturally, I did what any other self-respecting river runner would do: ignored them and went paddling. Upon returning, I applied tools from river running to writing: supporting a door for a desktop with four empty rocket boxes (the height was perfect); turning an empty ammo can into a Rolodex; converting a drybox into a filing cabinet; and stacking coolers on top of each other as shelves for inherited books. It wasn't pretty, but voila! an office was born.

The publisher at the time was located in Southern California, and he was content with my satellite office (if you can use such a term to describe a drybox filing system)—especially since the previous editor had his office in Indiana. It took me a whole two months to realize the job could be done just as well—or even better—out of a mountain town with a river flowing through it as in the arid Front Range. So, I packed my drybags and headed for the greener pastures of Steamboat Springs, CO, where the magazine remains today. That was eight-and-a-half years ago, and a lot of water has passed by the office since then. Looking at where the magazine was then and where it is today, the change is as great as a snow-melt river from fall to spring. I now have a real desk with real legs—the rocket boxes are back in the garage where they belong—and eight full-time employees burn the midnight Coleman fuel to put out what we affectionately dub, "the world's number one canoeing, kayaking, and rafting magazine."

Just as the Colorado River needs tributaries to carve the Grand Canyon, *Paddler* also needs feeder streams. Ours come from two sources: contributors and previous publications. Back when our pay rates would barely put Top Ramen on the table, our contributors continued to send in stories, reviews, technique pieces, and accounts of exotic adventures. They still do so because, like us, they love the sport and love writing about it. If anything, this "Best Of" compilation is a tribute to them; like looking at the strata of a canyon cliff, this book represents a cross-section of their contributions over the years.

The other part of the equation comes from the publications that laid the groundwork for *Paddler*. Our tale starts in 1991 when California entrepreneur Jim Ellis got a wild hair and decided to buy a small publishing company whose primary title was an agricultural trade magazine called *Avocado Grower*. Though it's hard to fathom how a magazine like *Paddler* could grow from something like *Avocado Grower*, thrown into the package Mr. Ellis bought was an offshoot called *River Runner*, a whitewater magazine that had been around ten years. At first Mr. Ellis didn't know what to do with it. Combining the titles into *River Grower* or *Avocado Runner* didn't make much sense. Then an idea seeded: why not buy up other similar-sized paddling publications and twist them like a giant avocado roll into one larger magazine? He did just that, purchasing such titles as *Canoe Sport Journal, Canadian Paddler, Ocean Kayak,* and others to form *Paddler,* a magazine for boaters of all persuasions.

My involvement was rather serendipitous. A long time ago, while living my impressionable years in Telluride, CO, I attended the annual *River Runner* Rendezvous, a three-day festival drawing boaters to San Miguel County for friendly competitions (like the ammo-can tug-of-war), presentations, and general celebration. The then-editor of *River Runner* gave a presentation on freelance writing, and it hit me that he had the best job in the world. I took a job as sports editor of the *Telluride Times,* began freelancing, and eventually submitted a story to him. I heard back a few months later. "Uh, I like the concept, but it needs a little work. Maybe try to be the leaf circling in the eddy?" My idea was lame (some transcendental piece about watching twigs float around in creeks), and apparently, so was my writing. But I kept at it and eventually landed a column in the publication. I kept the column after moving back to Boulder to work as a reporter for the *Denver Business Journal.* Writing about foreclosures, however, wasn't nearly as much fun as writing about rivers. After burning my vacation time on an assignment to kayak in Ecuador, I tried the leave-of-absence angle to go on a similar trip to Peru's Tambopata. I was flatly refused, so I quit and went anyway. Upon returning, I switched to the PR side of things, taking a job as media director for the World Pro Mogul Tour, and continued to freelance. By then, *River Runner* had become *Paddler,* and when the ski tour brought me to California, I swung by the office and was offered the job left vacant by the passing of *Canoe Sport Journal* editor Harry Roberts. The rest, as they say, is history.

A lot of manuscripts have come and gone since then, some following the path of my leaf-and-twig story (straight into the trash bin) and some finding their way into *Paddler.* Naturally, some have been better than others. One of my first jobs was to edit a previously unpublished story by Ernest Hemingway on how to prepare for a canoe trip. Much as I wanted to change Papa's piece on paddling, I didn't touch a word (even though many of his suggestions were outdated). Though we've yet to publish a story from anyone near as famous—except, maybe, a story we ran by Harvey Bucklesnort from Boone, NC—contributors have continued to flood us with material. The best of these are compiled in what you have before you (as a cred-it to those selected, Hemingway's story didn't make the cut). Making the selection wasn't easy. With *Paddler's* average of 116 pages six times a year over ten years, it meant combing through nearly 7,000 pages for the best of the best. Granted, not all those pages are editorial. Some are devoted to advertising, some to photos, and some to letting our readers bellyache and whine about what they don't like. But it was still a formidable task. To help with the process, Bud Zehmer of Menasha Ridge Press found it in his heart to pay our Steamboat office a visit in the bowels of fall when the aspens were turning, fish were rising, and cool temperatures buffeted single-track mountain bike rides. With all those distractions, the process took a couple of days, each of us campaigning for certain pieces and rejecting others.

To make matters easier, we divided the stories into different categories, finding that—barring shorter pieces like Hotlines, Skills, and Eco—most of them could be placed into one of five broad-ranging categories: Humor, Profiles, Destinations, Reflections, and Expeditions. A few fit all of those at once; but those usually weren't even good enough to talk about on a bike ride. The real work began once we had a master list divided into the respective groupings. Some of the pieces, ahem, are mine (an editor's prerogative), and the rest come from an assortment of authors. It would be nice to think that everything we print is worthy of a "Best Of" book. In truth, that's far from the case (as much as I liked our noseplug review, it didn't fit into the line-up). We got eddied out a few times, and countless stories we would've liked to include had to be dismissed. But we're happy with the final result, as the stories are as varied as our readership. They run from a helmet's point of view on protecting its owner's head (Humor, if you couldn't guess) to an introspection on why a top extreme kayaker paddles Class V. Humor and Reflection stories were compiled by sorting through our Innuendos department; Profiles (a re-listing of our "Paddlers of the Century" story from Jan/Feb 2000) and Destinations came from their respective departments; and Expeditions surfaced from features and our First Descents section. What they all share are good, solid ideas; good, solid writing; and the feeling that the author had as much fun working on it as we did selecting it. Paddlesports have come a long way since the magazine was formed. Instead of a Perception Mirage on the cover, it's now a streamlined play machine. Instead of a wool-clad canoeist, it's, well, still a wool-clad canoeist. But *Paddler* has been there every step of the way, printing the sport's triumphs, disappointments, innovations and techniques. And as we enter our tenth anniversary in 2001, we hope to continue doing so as long as paddlers are plying waterways, tranquil or white. Now, if I can just find a filing cabinet to take the place of my drybox . . .

—Eugene Buchanan
Editor-in-Chief

HUMOR

Death of a River Guitar

by Eugene Buchanan

It happened on the Bruneau. Night three of a four-day trip through Idaho's southern desert. I still don't really know how it happened, just a blinding flash, a swift movement out of the darkness surrounding the campfire, and then *Kabong!,* a sound that echoes deep in the recesses of my mind.

Kabong! is about the only way to describe the sound of a guitar breaking over your head. And though the arc swung by the perpetrator wasn't sufficient enough to completely encase the instrument over my cranium, it was sufficient enough to serve its purpose: to stop the guitar's incessant twanging. One moment I was strumming a classic E, A, D progression and the next the arm of Norman Bates was raising over me straight out of Hitchcock's *Psycho.*

While the incident provided plenty of fodder for subsequent campfire conversations, it marked the end of an era for a river guitar with more mileage on it than most tub-floored Avons. Of course, this mileage showed itself in its tell-tale twang, which was largely responsible for its abrupt ending (as well as a fair-sized bump on my head).

Although he wasn't the one who perpetrated the crime, my friend Pete was the first to be pushed to the brink by the guitar's not-so-melodious wails. "You ought to burn that thing," he said when I sat down to play it around the fire that ill-fated night. "Come on, I'll give you another one when we get home. Just set it on the fire as a ceremony of sorts." Soon, everyone around the fire, many of whom had been subjected to its tortuous tones on previous trips, began chanting slogans reminiscent of a New England witch hunt. "Burn It! Burn It! Burn It!" the cries rang out.

Realizing the guitar's mortality was at stake, I quickly intervened much as a mother would to protect her offspring. After all, the guitar was a part of me and had seen more river camps than my wetsuit booties and toothbrush combined. "Okay, okay," I conceded, succumbing to the peer pressure. "But first let me play just one last verse of the Bruneau Blues (E, A, D, of course). It's the least you can do." As with a firin-squad prisoner asking for a cigarette, I was granted my last request and thereby proceeded to improvise lyric after lyric to the same three chords that had become the guitar's mainstay.

The lyrics flowed as readily as the Bruneau, whose lapping on the beach added background percussion. They recounted how I stole the three-quarter-size instrument from my sister before taking off for college. They waned about river sand spilling from its body onto my instructor's studio floor when I took my first lesson. They eulogized the piece of bark wedged under its bridge to elevate a string; the fishing line that served as an E string in a riverside pinch; the time it doubled as a paddle and rolled a kayak; the time it found itself strapped to the bow of a sea kayak to break waves for eight days in Glacier Bay; the time it made it down the Grand Canyon without a case, my lone song piercing its way into people's skulls for 18 days. All in all, it was a stirring performance. Whether the audience thought so or not, I'll never know. But I like to think that its last notes had some sort of effect on the listeners surrounding the fire. And in fact, I actually thought it was home free, that its last-ditch effort to redeem itself had saved it from a fiery death. But then came the dreaded *Kabong*.

In mid-lyric, the perpetrator sneaked out of the inky surroundings, grabbed the nylon-stringed wonder by the neck and swung it high overhead. Before I could shift to a D-seventh, it came crashing down over my head, just short of splintering. I like to think that some of the crowd sympathized with me; that some emotions had been awakened by its last fleeting tune. But the bottom line is that its illustrious career was cut short, that its time had come to go to that giant catgut factory in the sky. As with its strings' nine-lived namesake, it had escaped casualty in the past,

emerging unscathed, albeit a little damp, after countless flips and nights left out in the rain. It had even survived eight different cases that had long since returned to the earth as soggy cardboard. But it was not to escape El *Kabong*.

Whether I was blinded by emotion or the darkness of the Idaho night, I never got a good look at its infliction. And by the time I revisited the scene of the crime the next morning, it had already been stuffed inside the two trashbags serving as its case. Although I realized its days were now numbered, I still packed it with the same ginger care I always reserved for it, stuffing the trashbag-covered amoebae inside an orange drybag, throwing a smaller one over the neck, and tightening both down with a cam strap. It wasn't perfect, and would barely keep it dry if the oar guide sneezed, but it was a ritual that had worked in its healthier days and one I trusted would work now.

When I returned home, the bundled-up amoebae found its way into my basement, where it rested in peace until just last week. That's when, with remorse for not giving it a proper burial, I ventured down and unwrapped it from its trashbagged tomb. After unfastening the last twisty-tie, I pulled it out of its suffocating shell, letting it breathe for the first time since the Bruneau. Hesitating, I turned it over to look at its wound. There, on its back, was a crack and an indentation bearing a striking resemblance to the top of my head. But it wasn't a gaping hole, and more importantly, it didn't appear to be fatal. Could it really be? Could it be saved? Reaching into a nearby ammo-can, I pulled out a roll of duct tape and carefully applied a

4

bandage, bending the splintered ends back into place like a surgeon resetting a bone. "It's alive!" I cried, dropping to my knees like Dr. Frankenstein.

Then I began to play. First an E, then an A, and then a D. And then I realized—just like the Grinch at Christmas—that *El Kabong* didn't stop the guitar from playing after all. It didn't sound as good as the replacement guitar Pete (in keeping his word) had given me, but it still played. The tell-tale twang didn't sound any better, but notes and melodies were once again flowing freely from its duct-taped soul. Sitting alone in the confines of my basement, I strummed through my entire repertoire of songs to the ears of cement walls and a gravel floor. I've thought about breaking it back out of its grave, pulling it out of a drybag at another riverside fire. But better to let people think it went out in a blaze of glory. Better to let them remember its last song and the swift arc of *El Kabong*. And for my head's sake, better to stick with playing to an audience of concrete.

Loony Laws Concerning Canoes

by Eugene Buchanan

Prohibited from sitting in a canoe while reading comic books? Banned from using a feather duster to tickle a girl in a canoe?

These laws and more, which have been painstakingly researched by Tennessee historian Robert Pelton, are actual pieces of legislation that have been passed throughout the country over the past 200 years. And although most of them are archaic, many have legitimate safety reasons behind them.

"Nobody really knows how they came about," says Pelton, who recently published his first book, *Loony Sex Laws*. "Laws like these usually surfaced after someone did something the community didn't like and there wasn't a law for it. They're old and unusual, but no one ever bothered to take them off the books."

Pelton has been collecting funny laws about everything from sports to sex for 22 years by spending eight to ten weeks a year traveling around the country and poking his nose into newspapers and courthouses. In so doing, he has unearthed some juicy pieces of paddling legislation. "If you ask around, almost everyone knows of a funny law," he says. "Especially the old timers. But there's no way you can verify them."

Keeping this in mind, and perhaps keeping a few grains of salt handy, here are a few of the more ludicrous laws concerning canoeing. In Browns Mills, NJ, a law states, "Any person who shall wear in a canoe any device or thing attached to her head, hair, headgear, or hat, which device or thing is capable of lacerating the flesh of any other person with whom it may come in contact and which is not sufficiently guarded against the possibility of so doing, shall be judged a disorderly person." This might appear superfluous, but when you think about it, it makes sense. After all, who wants to go paddling with someone who has a chainsaw strapped to his head?

There's also a strange one from Rogersville, AL: "No female wearing a nightgown can be found riding in a canoe, and women must be fully dressed before they can legally be taken for a ride." Most likely, this was enacted to prevent hypothermia. Most nightgowns don't wick water away from the body easily. As for why men weren't covered in the legislation, it's anyone's guess. If you're a male and have a yearning to paddle in nighties, Alabama's your state.

While you're making your rounds, however, steer clear of Desbiens, Quebec, on Sundays. Here it's against the law for married men to canoe alone on Sunday. Even if you're in your nightie. Married women can, but not men. This is a tough one to figure. Probably has to do with making sure men spend enough time with their families. Speaking of Sunday canoeing restrictions, no one, male or female, in Needles, BC, is allowed to read the Sunday paper while sitting in a canoe while church services are in session. You can sit in a canoe, but you can't read the paper. If you have time for both, you probably have time for church. On the same line, it's against the law to read comic books in a canoe in Norwood, NC. This one might have stemmed from someone going over a waterfall just as Batman was about to apprehend the Joker.

If reading comic books puts you to sleep, think twice about doing so in Pine Falls, Manitoba. Here it's perfectly legal for a person to sleep in his canoe. But no person is to be found asleep in a canoe "after the sun rises in the morning." The sleuthing Pelton even dug up a canoeing law for tobacco chewers in Moran, WY. A law here prohibits a woman from chewing tobacco while canoeing without first having permission from her husband. Single ladies, apparently, can dip away to their heart's content.

But even if they're not chewing, don't think about making advances on canoeing gals in Iowa—at least if they're strangers. Here a municipal code states: "It is unlawful for any male person, in a canoe or other vessel on the Des Moines River, within the corporate limits of the city of Ottumwa, to wink at any female person with whom he is unacquainted." Legislators here were probably looking out for women who would be so taken aback at a stranger's wink that they might faint and topple the boat. You can

wink at your wife or sister all you want. Chances are they won't think twice about it. Just don't do it at strangers.

Other attention-getting tricks are also taboo. In Ambridge, PA, it's against the law to tickle a girl under her chin with a feather duster while she's riding in your canoe. You can tickle girls in other canoes with a feather duster and you can tickle a girl with a feather duster on other parts of her body. You can even tickle her under the chin with something other than a feather duster. But feather dusters and chins are off-limits. This one probably has something to do with not wanting to disrupt the paddler's vision and concentration.

Speaking of disruption, according to an old Revised Ordinance in Putnam, IL, "No person shall hallo, shout, bawl, scream, use profane language, dance, sing, whoop, quarrel, or make any unusual noise or sound while riding in a canoe or boat in such manner as to disturb the peace and quiet of others in the area." Other areas also crack down on disruptiveness. In Sterling, ID, you can be arrested for making "silly or insulting faces" at anyone cleaning or working on a canoe. By the same token, boisterous paddlers should also steer clear of Sanish, ND, where laws prohibit "laughing out loud" while riding in a canoe.

There are also several laws concerning canoeing fashion. Men with mustaches should stay away from Crutwell, Saskatchewan, where a local law bans men with hair growing over their upper lip from canoeing with females. If you're a female with a mustache you're okay. But you probably won't be able to find anyone to paddle with anyway. Women have their own fashion regulations. In Ballantine, SC, every woman in a canoe must "be found to be wearing a corset." In addition, a physician is required to inspect each female found in a canoe to make sure she is complying with this archaic law. There's also a rule regulating the heel length of women's shoes in a canoe in Edgemont, AR. Heels can measure no longer than 1.5 inches high.

Prejudices aside, there are also fashion laws affecting both sexes. In Lisco, NE, it's unlawful to operate a canoe on the North Platte River with untied shoelaces. In Clinton, MO, it's against the law to canoe while wearing a hat which "would scare a timid person." And here's a real fashion doozy. If you're a woman weighing over 200 pounds who likes to wear shorts in a canoe, beware of paddling in Albany, GA. It's a strict violation of the law for a woman here over 200 pounds and attired in shorts to ride in a canoe. And remember if you do wind up canoeing with a woman like this, no winking.

You also have to watch out for kissing. In Mobridge, SD, is an ordinance against kissing in a canoe for "longer than three minutes." As a further safety measure, canoe kissers are also required to "pause for breath" between smooches. You'll fare no better with your 200-lb. mate in Biron, WI, where a law prohibits kissing a woman in a canoe unless she's "properly chaperoned." If you can get your arm around her for a hug, don't do so in Chepachet, RI. An old law here says, "No man can place his arm around a woman without a good and lawful reason" while taking her for a ride in a canoe. Another law protects women in Burnsville, WV. No married woman here is allowed to go canoeing on the Sabbath unless she "is

properly looked after." How? Her mate must always be close behind. And he's also required to carry a loaded gun "over his left shoulder."

So the next time you're out canoeing in your nightie, trying to hold a three-minute kiss with a high-heeled, 200-lb., tobacco-chewing stranger, you might want to pause and think about what state you're in first—both emotionally and physically.

9

All in the Family

by Eugene Buchanan

For some reason, mothers seem to enjoy getting involved in the affairs of their offspring. David Letterman's mom proved this in the 1996 Olympics. My mom proved it this past summer when she decided to take up kayaking.

No matter that she is 59 years old. She just felt it might be a good way to get to know her son better and understand his preoccupation with paddling. As with ducks following a mother, however, nature usually passes down this type of knowledge from generation to generation, not the other way around. You don't often see a duckling chastising his mother over an ineffective ferry angle.

I had already broken with nature much earlier by taking her on a few overnight rafting trips. And she behaved admirably for a mom, sleeping on the sand and even joining in on a few spontaneous campfire lyrics. Having mom along didn't inhibit me or the group. Everything was more or less the same, from midnight sweat huts to crack-of-noon libations. The same held true last summer when she joined me on a five-day trip down the Yampa. She held her pee when going to the bathroom, helped haul gear to camp, and even helped organize the kitchen, just as she does whenever she visits our home.

In a way it felt good to repay the favor. After all, my first experience rafting came on the very same river on a commercial trip with my family when I was no more than seven. I don't remember much about it, except for picking some Indian paintbrush flowers and giving them to her in a bouquet. Unfortunately for my machismo, I did so in front of the guides. But I didn't mind my mama's-boy image. It was a small token of my appreciation for getting me out on my first river. But things are different now that she has taken up kayaking.

To find out why she decided to take up the sport, I called her. Interviewing her wasn't easy: "Hey mom, I was thinking about doing a story on you taking up kayaking and I . . . yeah, yeah . . . I washed behind my ears . . . but listen, I was wondering why you . . . yeah, yeah . . . I ate my vegetables . . . "

Eventually we got through the small talk and I weaseled an answer out of her as to why she decided to take up kayaking. "So I wouldn't have to ride in a raft with your father," she promptly answered. Next, I asked her what she liked and disliked about it.

"I don't like sitting at water level and wiggling around all the time."

"Wiggling?"

"Well, you know, the kayak always wiggles."

It was an in-depth conversation that shed a lot of light on why mothers meddle in the affairs of their offspring. So perhaps it would be better to start at the beginning. Last summer she called me up to see if I could swing a deal with a kayak school I had taught at in the late '80s. I tried to appease her by calling the owner, but I didn't have much bargaining power. Perhaps he knew my mom and knew what a hassle it would be. She signed up anyway for a three-day kayak clinic that started with a flatwater day on a local lake followed by two days on a Class I–II river.

At first none of the instructors knew she was my mom. In fact, at 5'2" and 105 pounds, her specs on the student roster made her sound rather appealing, especially since there wasn't a category for age. After fighting for the right to teach her, thinking she was a young, impressionable coed, the instructors were surprised when she showed up for class and increased the average age by about 30. And I can't say I envy whoever had to teach her. An ex-politician, she is used to having her way and sometimes has a little difficulty grasping simple concepts like "lean the way you fall" and "keep your head down when you roll." And I'm sure that whoever had the pleasure of teaching her reached the frustration point a little earlier than with younger 105-lb. students.

The next two days on the river involved more of the same and then some. During the first day's shuttle she insisted on riding on top of the vehicle's roof rack. Try as they might, the instructors couldn't persuade her other-

wise. They had just as tough a time on the water. Leaning into a turn and lifting your knee when crossing an eddy line did not come naturally. She did things her own way regardless of what the group was doing. But she made it through the course, learned the bow rescue, and even paddled upright through the Class II rapid at the end of the day. She was now hooked on rivers, and even joined a local club on a couple of outings to nearby waterways.

But she quickly began to carry her new-found skill a little too far, almost to the obsessive stage. I found this out when she told me that she had joined a new recreation center that boasted a kiddy pool connected to an adult pool by a little channel of flowing water. It didn't take her long to figure out that this bore some resemblance to a real river, complete with imperceptible eddies on the sides of the kiddy pool. Now all she needed was a boat. She figured this could be solved by sitting on top of one of the pool's blue kickboards. She also figured out that by strapping a water aerobics waist flotation belt underneath the kickboard and around her thighs, she could sit on the thing without falling off, allowing her to ride the current from the adult to the kiddy pool and practice her lean when she hit the eddy.

Upon hearing of her misadventures I cringed to think that I had ever been attached to her with an umbilical cord. Especially when she took it one step farther and tried to roll her kickboard in the shallows of the kiddy pool. As she learned in class, she would tip over on her kickboard and set up for her roll by reaching her hands out of the water. As on the river, however, she invariably brought her head up too quickly. This resulted in a fair amount of thrashing and air gulping, as well as the prompt, undivided attention of the lifeguard who hopped from his perch to save the lady from drowning in the kiddy pool.

She has been back to the rec center several times to practice, and now the lifeguards know her. They don't hide the kickboards and they don't put up the closed sign. As long as it doesn't hurt anybody, they let her do her thing. She hasn't been back on the river since, and most likely won't until I invite her along on another trip. The only thing I'm afraid of is that she might like her little kickboard more than she likes kayaking. If that's the case, it might not be such a bad idea to follow Letterman's lead and send her off to Norway.

The Helmet Speaks

by Jonathan Katz

Call me Protec. I'm a paddling helmet. And be sure you spell it right. It's T-E-C, not Z-A-C. Prozac is for the inside of your head. Protec is for the outside.

I took early retirement one Sunday last summer, at Bull's Bridge on the Housatonic. Now I can put my feet up, sleep late weekends instead of driving to the river, and write my memoirs. Mostly they tell the story of my relationship with my Head, which is attached to the body of a middle-aged boater with a family and a career, good balls, few brains, and primitive skills. His name is John "Zip" Locke, believe it or not a direct descendant of the famous English philosopher who gave us life, liberty, and the pursuit of happiness.

Zip started paddling in tandem Grumman. He and his partner shared a two-piece wetsuit. They wore orange Stearns lifejackets and no helmets, and paddled Class I, but called it Class II. Then Zip bought a plastic Discovery and he and his buddy began to run real Class II, using an air mattress and a boogie board for flotation. They were clueless and swam like Olympians. On one of these early runs Zip got religion and started to wear an old bicycle helmet. Then his partner enrolled in business school and quit boating. Zip was alone.

Zip and I met in a paddling shop in North Appalachia. I was hanging with other brain buckets on the wall in the back of the shop, between the cheap raft paddles and a magazine rack. The boys and I all look alike: shiny red with teardrop-shaped drain holes set above the corporate logo, black Fastex buckles and some Styrofoam on the inside. Why Zip picked me I'll never know. But he slipped me on and we fit like we were made for each other. I was his helmet. He was my head. He dropped two twenties on the counter and suddenly I had a job.

Zip started abusing me right away. He tossed me in his trunk to rattle around and freeze and bake with the rest of his gear, and I got to know the gang: Paddle, Rope, the Biner Twins and a fellow who changed his name from Life Jacket to PFD. All in all a good bunch of guys, who did what they could to keep Zip out of trouble—which was a full time job. Zip was solo open boating now, beating his shins, losing his equipment, and providing plenty of rescue practice for his paddling buddies.

I'll say this much for Zip. He never left me in his car when it was time to paddle. He never locked me in the shuttle vehicle by mistake. He never marooned me on some godforsaken river bank in the middle of nowhere. And he never backed his car over me, even when he was skunk-drunk and reeling. No way. When he was on the river, I was on his Head, where I belonged. Considering what happened, it was a damn good thing.

Which brings me to the issue of "foreseeable impacts." Back when I was very young I had a warning label stuck on my inside, written by a lawyer who got good money for writing it. My label said something like, "This helmet will not protect the user against all foreseeable impacts." Such as bullets. I have cousins made of Kevlar who might stop a bullet, but they mostly join the Army and don't spend a whole lot of time on rivers. And there are other foreseeable impacts. Like the time Zip saw this girl boater changing clothes and just couldn't stop staring at her. So she sashayed up and punched him square in the kisser. Totally foreseeable, but I have no face guard (unlike my football buddies) and there are times when I simply have to rely on the moron to duck. Another foreseeable time came when Zip got stiff on tequila and creamed his cranium on a beam in the men's room of a Mexican food joint. I was in the trunk gagging on exhaust fumes while Zip drank up the money he needed to replace his muffler, which he'd disemboweled driving shuttle earlier that day. This was back when he drove that foreign "sports sedan" with the negative clearance. Thirty thousand dollars for a car that would high-center

on painted lines. As for me, when I'm off his Head I'm off duty.

Zip kept on paddling, and we kept on doing rivers together. And boy did we meet some weirdoes. Like the German Army Helmet with a six-inch iron spike sticking out the top. I guess his Head used him to spear fish. Another had a plastic bullfrog glued on his earpiece and the word "Jeremiah" hand-lettered across the back. A third helmet's Head had even laminated a dead rat to him with epoxy resin. He said it only stank for a year. And of course we saw lots of those newfangled, blue-spangled squirt helmets, painted metalflake to match the boat; it looked like the helmets displaced more water than the boats did. We even saw an old, stout football helmet with full cage worn by a notorious boater from Boston. You meet all kinds of helmets in this sport, worn by all sorts of boaters, the good, the bad, and the awful.

Along the way I acquired noseclips and a visor, got my shine dulled and picked up my share of scratches. We call it "patina" and it's how us veterans stand apart. Zip would tap a rock now and again when he swam. He'd also sometimes bump into branches when he portaged. Once I even stopped a slushball Mark Chopper threw at him. On another cold trip his paddle iced up and slipped out of his top hand. It clipped him in the earpiece and would have bonked him good if I hadn't been there. Also, after an hour or two in his boat, Zip's balance goes. When he gets out on land he weaves around and bumps into things. I've seen other boaters do this when they first get out, before they get their land legs back. An inner ear thing. I call it "paddler's vertigo" and haven't seen it covered in any of the safety articles.

But after four years of open boating I still hadn't had a moment of glory. A helmet's sacred duty is to Protect the Head Within. So you sit around waiting for the One Big Shot which is your date with destiny, that upstream-pointed, rebar-studded, neck-breaking, skull-busting chunk of concrete just downriver from where your Head capsized. And you get no warm-up when it comes. Just step up to the plate, take your swing, and what you hit is what you get.

When Zip started kayaking, the action picked up considerably. For one thing, I got to meet Skirt. For another, Zip rolled often, and rolling on shallow Eastern rivers is like pulling the handle on a cosmic slot machine, mostly getting nothing but never knowing when your Head is going to hit the jackpot. And the granite at the bottom of a Class II river is just as hard as the granite beneath Class IV. Only the Class IV comes at you a little quicker. So Zip got nicked a little, and stayed lucky, and began to believe that he was good. And when Chopper invited him to paddle Bulls Bridge at two feet, he said sure.

The Bulls Bridge section opens with an insane Class V that the sane start below, then drops with no warm-up into the Flume, a eight-foot waterfall with a messy lead-in and a small, sticky, diagonal hydraulic at the brink. Zip had never run the Flume before, and he was tight and nervous. He watched Bam Bam McBride and Chopper clean the drop, and then sucked in his gut and followed their line. The little sticky hole rolled him like a cigar and dumped him over the falls upside down. Game time.

While Zip is falling, let me explain that I'm just a dumb chunk of polystyrene. I have no Brain of my own and must rely on Zip to do the thinking for us both. Zip is a fanatic for keeping records, and after 136 trips with him I've come to realize that his head is a bottomless pit of stupidity. He has an infinite capacity for dumb mistakes, bonehead moves, and other jerk-brained idiocy. Which makes being his Helmet an exercise in sheer sustained terror. So just this once, as Zip fell, I discovered that deep within the wasteland behind his eyes there is intelligent life and survival instinct which sent a rational message to Zip's overweight and underconditioned body. The message was one word: "Tuck!" And Zip tucked his head and body into a little round ball like a small boy hiding from the monster in the closet. Then BAP!! the back of his head slammed into a boulder. Game over.

The impact crushed a two-inch dent in me and drove my bottom edge into the back of Zip's neck like a karate chop. He made one weak roll attempt and wet exited. As he got trashed down the river he realized the good news: he was conscious and his limbs were moving. McBride and Chopper got him into an eddy and he floated his way onto a rock like a dying tadpole and lay there, shaking. My foam earpiece had come undone from its Velcro and was hanging in his eyes. So he took me off and saw the damage, the dent, the deep gouges in my plastic. He felt the back of his neck at the base of his skull where the river had delivered its punch. A big, swollen knot was rising fast. He wobbled to his feet, thought hard for a minute, and then canceled his river trip. McBride checked his eyes. The pupils appeared normal, and in any of McBride's friends that is a bad sign. Chopper picked me up, looked at me, fingered my deep dent, then turned to Zip and made the decision: "Any time you get hit that hard you go to the hospital and get checked out."

So we drove Zip and his stiffening neck to New Milford Hospital, where there was a good crowd in the emergency room on Sunday morning. The receptionist sat behind her computer terminal trying to sort out people's complaints and make sure the hospital had an insurance company to bill. Confronted with a wet, smelly, dazed kayaker she simply opened a new computer file and started from the top. She was in hot pursuit of Zip's major medical policy when McBride whipped me out and showed her the dent. Her eyes widened and she looked back to Zip. "You were wearing this helmet?"

Trying not to move his neck, Zip nodded. She showed me to the on-duty doctor, who got a collar for Zip and moved him to the front of the line. If you want good service in the ER, take me with you. They put Zip on a stretcher and wheeled him to X-ray. The technician spoke to him. "We're going to take one film, a cross-table lateral. If you have a broken neck it will show on here." Zip waited and stared at the ceiling. He thought that "cross-table lateral" sounded more like football than medicine. He thought about a broken neck, about his wife and kids, about Slim Ray's comeback, about how boring looking at the ceiling was and whether he'd have to get used to the view for the next six weeks or 30 years. He moved his fingers and his toes. He thought about quitting kayaking and being grateful for

the opportunity to take up golf. The time he spent on the stretcher, waiting for the doctor to read his film, was long and cold and scary.

The cross-table lateral and the rest of Zip's x-rays were normal. Zip smiled. He thought about retiring his Helmet, and he held me in his hands. He massaged my dent and felt my gouges and imagined taking the impact on his naked, fragile skull. He thought, helmets are good.

Zip is fine. He is back paddling again, and getting trashed again, and trying to become a better boater. I'm okay too. After a few days in the hot sun my dent popped out. The gouge marks are permanent, but at least I'm round and symmetrical again, like Zip's head. And we're back boating together. But he is looking to replace me with a heavier-duty model. The way he paddles, he better. That way, I can retire for good and finish my memoirs. No hard feelings. I've done my job.

Some Real Rodeo Announcing

by Eugene Buchanan

"Ride That Wild Thang!" and "Spur That Wild Pony!" are not phrases you're likely to find in the *Whitewater Rodeo Announcer's Handbook*. Nevertheless, they're attention getters that all rodeo announcing wannabes might want to include in their bag of vocal tricks. For proof look no further than last year's Yampa River Festival held in downtown Steamboat Springs, Colorado. I wish I could take credit for these phrases, but they're the brainchild of Chad and Kip, two unlikely rodeo announcers who are more at home on bucking broncs than bucking boats.

It all started three weeks before the festival at the weekly organizers' meeting. "Charlie's going to be gone," said organizer Pete Van De Carr, running down his lengthy To Do list in preparation for the festivities. "Looks like we're going to have to get someone else to announce." Charlie, in this case, is Charlie Taylor, who has held a firm rein on the Yampa River Festival's announcing post for the past 15 years. A coalminer-turned-actor, who has performed everywhere from L.A. to the local high school, Charlie has a flair for the job that has earned him the distinguished title of Yampa River Festival Announcer For Life. "He got the job because of his theatrics on and off the river," Van De Carr told me later. "He's a natural."

Unfortunately, he's also a natural river runner, meaning when the chance came to run the Grand during last year's festival, he wasted no time in packing his dry-bags and vacating the announcing throne. All eyes around the table landed on me as Charlie's natural successor. After all, I had some legitimate announcing experience under my belt, having once stumbled upon an announcing job in the ski industry for the World Pro Mogul Tour. Phrases like "Slicin' and a Dicin'!" and "Thumpin' and a Bumpin'!" might not translate directly over to kayaking, but they were close enough to work in a pinch. For the past two years I had even relieved Charlie when it came time to announce the festival's Crazy River Dog Contest. Apart from there being more canines in the audience than kayakers, it was the most experience anyone at the table had. Feeling obligated to volunteer for something, I took the job—not to upstage Charlie, but because it seemed the lesser of the volunteering evils. It was either announce, clean up the park afterward, or rise at 5 a.m. to blow the starting horn for the downriver race.

The announcing table was located above the "Rabbit Ears" hole, site of the festival's rodeo. I showed up fashionably late, as all Hollywood types do, just as the downriver race was nearing completion. The first few hours were pretty straightforward, involving little more than keeping people abreast of competitors' times and rattling off sponsors' names every other (Al's Tavern) word. Like Charlie, I even managed to farm out the announcing duties when it came time for the Crazy River Dog contest—allowing my vocal chords to rest for the rodeo.

I continued my multisyllabic blabbing, thinking I was God's gift to rodeo spectators, until two men in their early 20s—dressed in colorful flannel shirts and felt cowboy hats—came up to the stage. It was then that I realized my time in the limelight was dwindling. Kip and Chad were cowboys in town for a different type of rodeo, one held every weekend less than a block away at the Steamboat rodeo grounds. Their specialty was bronc riding. Festival Organizer Pete had bumped into them and convinced them to join me in the announcing stand. After the first few competitors went through their heats, I handed the mike over to Kip. "Well, what do you think, Kip? Is this a little different from the type of rodeo you guys are used to?" Those were about the last words I spoke during the entire competition. "Well Boy Howdy, I tell you what," he said into the mike. "These cowpokes are givin' it their all this evening ain't they?" Just then another competitor washed out of the hole and struggled to regain the eddy as time ran out. "Folks, let's give this here ol' cowboy a big ol' hand," drawled Kip, not missing a beat. "Cause that's all he's

gonna' get tonight." The crowd loved it, so I let him continue as soon as the next competitor eased into the hole. "Ride that Wild Thang!" Kip suddenly blurted out of nowhere. "Spur that Wild Pony!" chimed in Chad. By now it was hard to tell if the crowd was paying more attention to the competitor or the two cowboys who had suddenly taken center stage. When the contestant went for a 180-degree spin, Kip kept the analogy going. "Uh-oh folks, he's got 'em by the tail now! Com' on, nose 'em on in there and Ride that Wild Thang!"

Relegated to my new title of rodeo announcing assistant, I whispered in his ear whenever I thought I could be of assistance. "That's called a hole and that's an eddy," I whispered during a break in the action. "And those things around their waists are called spray skirts."

"Skirts?" he glanced back incredulously, forgetting to turn off the mike. "What the hell are them cowboys doing wearing skirts?"

The spectators heard every innocent word, and after their laughter subsided, I continued with the lesson. "When they go straight up it's called an endo," I whispered. "Sort of like what happens when a bronc bucks."

"Ride on that Wild Thang!" he suddenly blurted again out of nowhere as the competitor got spit out of the hole. "Whoa! Now say hello to Mr. Eddy!" The first contestant to get an ender was also rewarded with Kip's cowboy charm. "Whoa! Now hold on cowboy!" he yelled. "That bronc is a startin' to buck now. Com' on, climb back on that hoss' and Ride that Wild Thang!"

As is the case in equine rodeos, Kip was used to having the announcer get the crowd involved. And that's exactly what he was doing here, getting everyone to hoot and holler to get the competitors psyched up for their rides. The crowd loved every minute of it, and it made me feel guilty every time I grabbed the mike to say something halfway important like, "Next up Steve Louis in bib number 23." My style didn't hold a candle to Kip's, whose authenticity and naiveté made even the competitors laugh before their rides.

By now any thoughts I had about pursuing a rodeo announcing career were long gone. It might work if I could convince Kip and Chad to go along with me on the circuit, but that would mean forfeiting their careers in the saddle. It might also make it tough on the publishers of the *Whitewater Rodeo Announcer's Handbook*—they'd have to come up with a new edition every time the cowboy commentators hopped off their broncs and into the announcing booth.

Paddling Penance

by Eugene Buchanan

I should have known I was facing an upstream battle when the sheriff spelled kayak "kiyac" on the police report.

I also should have known, however, that any impulsive, two-in-the-morning decision to paddle a Class V run the next day was bound to lead to trouble. Trouble that could have easily earned my partner and me a high-profile position on the post office wall, with two helmet-haired mug shots below the words: WANTED FOR SECOND DEGREE CRIMINAL TRESSPASS!

The incident in question arose after being issued a summons to appear in court for such a violation—having learned the hard way that a popular put-in for the Colorado River's Gore Canyon was off limits. To get there all you had to do was drive on a county road through private property (perfectly legal), park your car within four feet of the road (also perfectly legal) and then hop a fence and cross the railroad tracks to get to the river (perfectly illegal).

Doing so saved you more than an hour of flatwater, but it didn't save you any embarrassment if you got caught. Everything was fine until we returned at the end of the day to complete the shuttle. Parked next to us was Buford T. Justice with one foot resting on his bumper and an open pad on top of his thigh. Next to him stood the irate rancher who ratted on us by saying we were trespassing on railroad property.

"This your car?" asked the sheriff, master of the obvious, rolling his eyes to the only car in miles. Had we known better, we probably could have simply lied and left. But being an honest representative of the paddling community, I said something to the effect of, "Officer Opie, I cannot tell a lie," much like the litterbugging vandals in Arlo Guthrie's *Alice's Restaurant*. Besides, with keys in our hands and sprayskirts still on, we weren't fooling anyone. It didn't take long for Officer Opie to weasel the truth out of us and get us to confess to the crime of crossing the railroad tracks to go "kiyacing."

Guerilla boating friends back home were quick to chastise us for being so brave and honest. "You shouldn't have admitted anything." said an anonymous kayak manufacturer who frequents the run. "Whenever that happened to me, I just said I was simply asserting my right to park on a county road." Since I'm not that quick on my feet and since I could not tell a lie, my next step was to visit my friend, Kris Hammond, an attorney with Steamboat Springs' Oliphant, Hammond, O'Hara, & Atwell LLC, and apprised him of the situation. It didn't take him long to put matters in perspective. He asked me if we admitted anything, and I said, "sort of." He asked me if I felt like we were free to go at any time and I said, "I guess so." Then he asked if we did it and I said, "yeah."

"Well, you're not making it easy to build a case," he said. "You're telling me all of the wrong things.

"Tell you what," he added. "Give me a $500 retainer, go in, and plead guilty."

I think he was joking. The only retainer I ended up giving him was a pair of river sandals. But I still had to go to court and I was still harboring a guilty conscience.

For the most part, kayakers are an honest bunch. They'd rather sit in front of bars than stand behind them. They might tell a little whitewater lie here and there by exaggerating the size of a drop, but they're floaters first and felons second. I carried this notion with me as I prepared for the pending court date.

Eventually the court date came up and Kris and I made the early morning jaunt for the disposition hearing in Hot Sulfur Springs. On the way we discussed our strategy. At first I thought I should probably plead insanity. After all, you have to be fairly insane to run Gore anyway. But Kris told me that might not work. At the courthouse he discussed the case with another lawyer friend, claiming that we might have a case because of something called Easement by Prescription, which basically says if someone goes over private land long enough, the law eventually gives the public the right to go over that land. Tom Sitz, an attorney for the Environmental Protection Agency who caught wind of the case and helped form the Gore Access Committee to help solve this problem, thought this might be worth a crack.

But not with me as a scapegoat.

"Using that summons to test the theory of adverse possession is a lot to ask of someone," he told me. "Whoever volunteers to do so is putting his butt on the line. And I don't even know if adverse possession would work in this context or not. But I'd be interested to find out."

As we were called into the courtroom, Kris's lawyer friend turned and said, "Good luck. Hope your defense holds water." Nothing like a little lawyer humor to settle your nerves before you have to face the Honorable Cecil Wayne Williams.

The guy taking the stand before me looked like he was clearly guilty of something. And it looked like Judge Williams realized this. Kris told me earlier that the judge liked to intimidate people. Not maliciously, but just to get them to take the law seriously. Just what I needed—someone to intimidate me for kayaking a run that intimidated me.

With palms more sweaty than they had ever been gripping a kayak paddle, I was finally called to the stand, my river sandals hidden by the podium. Peering over his eyeglasses, the judge studied my case and then asked for my plea.

As rehearsed with my attorney, I bellowed out. "No contest, your Honor." In a way, this seemed fitting because it echoed my chances of ever having a clean run through the canyon. And even though it was akin to pleading guilty, it made me feel better. The way I looked at it, running Gore washed me free of everything, including guilt, anyway. In the end I settled for a Deferred Judgement Sentence. My lawyer said this was nothing more than a sneaky device by which the guilty go free. It basically means that if I'm a good boy for six months, they'll throw the case away. I also had to cough up $98 in court fees, as well as a $50 donation to one of 12 charitable cases. Since American Rivers wasn't on the list, I gave it to a fund to stop game poachers.

The fine was originally set at $100. But with slick lawyer rhetoric, Kris struck a deal with the prosecuting attorney. "Listen," he said. "Can't we lower the fine if my client agrees to print something about the put-in being off limits? Isn't that providing a community service in itself?" Three years of law school and seven years of practice went into that statement, and it worked.

The DA agreed and here it is. The river-right put-in for Gore Canyon is technically off limits. There, I said it. I've paid my dues to society for my heinous crime. But as well as sticking to the end of the plea bargain, another reason I'm writing this is that just as in *Alice's Restaurant,* you too might someday find yourself in a similar situation. And if you do, there's not a whole lot you can do. Jumping up and yelling "Kill! Kill!" might have worked for Arlo, but it won't work on the Honorable Cecil Wayne Williams or this Officer Opie.

Still, society forgets easily, at least crimes that don't involve post office walls. The other day I even received a letter asking me to donate $20 to become an honorary member of the County Sheriffs of Colorado. Written by Sheriff Ed Burch, it began: "I am writing to you, Mr. Buchanan, because I believe you are a law abiding citizen."

Apparently he didn't realize I'm also a "kiyacer."

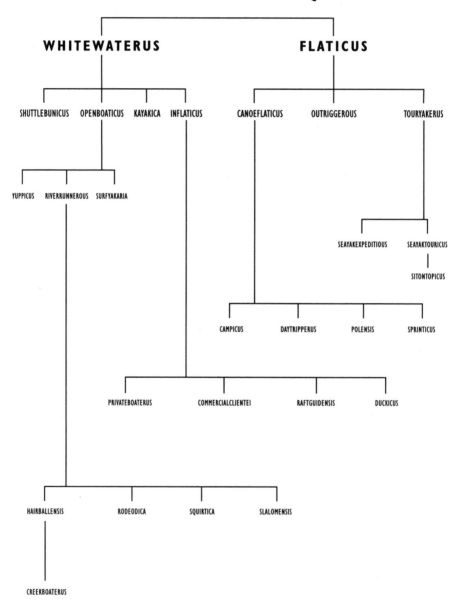

GENUS PADDLEAQUA

WHITEWATERUS

FLATICUS

SHUTTLEBUNICUS OPENBOATICUS KAYAKICA INFLATICUS

CANOEFLATICUS OUTRIGGEROUS TOURYAKERUS

YUPPICUS RIVERRUNNEROUS SURFYAKARIA

SEAYAKEXPEDITIOUS SEAYAKTOURICUS

SITONTOPICUS

CAMPICUS DAYTRIPPERUS POLENSIS SPRINTICUS

PRIVATEBOATERUS COMMERCIALCLIENTEI RAFTGUIDENSIS DUCKICUS

HAIRBALLENSIS RODEODICA SQUIRTICA SLALOMENSIS

CREEKBOATERUS

Evolution of a Paddle Species

by Eugene Buchanan (with Aaron Bible)

In the mid-18th century, Swedish botanist Carl Von Linne developed binomial nomenclature to give naturalists a common ground on which to classify and categorize organisms. This Latin system of biological classification has proven an invaluable tool in understanding life and its role on Earth. Well, the time has come to give the same order and common ground—or in this case, water—to the paddlers that have evolved on the waterways of North America. A formidable task, perhaps, especially since these organisms—canoeists, kayakers, and rafters—share many common traits. But their evolutionary success has given rise to highly differentiated species within a common genus, *Homopaddleaqua*.

Homopaddleaqua is a genus that derives pleasure from paddling, generally for reasons other than survival (although in some instances—see *H. hairballensis*—survival comes with the territory). Somewhere down the evolutionary line, however, the species diverged. Some began using one-bladed paddles, some adopted two-bladed paddles, some migrated to flatter environments, and some pushed Darwinism to the limit utilizing the laws of gravity. Although the point of evolutionary divergence is often blurred, and a fair degree of overlap exists between certain species, habitats dictate relative strengths and weaknesses.

Refer to the following, then, as a field guide and handbook for identifying the variety of species belonging to genus *Homopaddleaqua*. In order to facilitate this process, we've outlined certain distinguishable traits applicable to individual species: each possesses distinct features, referred to as Species Characteristics; and each favors certain ecosystems, referred to as Habitat. Also note that while some species are somewhat less evolved, others have further diverged into sub-species due to geographical isolation and innate biological drive. Use this species checklist to see how many specimens you can spot on the water.

gency rooms and banging on manufacturer's doors demanding warranties.

HOMOPADDLEAQUA HAIRBALLENSIS

Known in some regions as *H. hairboaterus*, *H. hairballensis* exhibits blatant disregard for Darwin's survival theory, with seemingly destructive behavior stemming from highly evolved adrenal glands. Most often seen in kayaks, but occasionally found in decked and open C-1s and inflatables. Demonstrates cool demeanor in potentially lethal environments.

Species Characteristics: Displays seasonal migration habits, often international in scope, and tendency to videotape antics for off-season entertainment. Lies dormant during droughts, but is active in spring, summer, and rainy seasons. High testosterone levels (and large testicles) in males ensures reproductive capacity—however, same trait also limits the gene pool of suitable mates. Digestive and urinary tracts evolved to process large amounts of water.

Habitat: High gradient drainage systems throughout North America, especially during peak flows. Migrates seasonally. May also be found in emer-

HOMOPADDLEAQUA CREEKBOATERUS

A peculiar offshoot of *H. hairballensis* adapted to paddle on rocks instead of water. Perhaps the most avian of all *Homopaddleaqua* in its boating behavior and fascination with flight.

Species Characteristics: If identification is suspect, look for multicolored plastic shaving tracks left on rocks. Also identifiable by protective shells on elbows and face. Frequently seen in highly rockered kayaks with bow indentations (look for bow caps, plastic welds, and duct tape), and may suffer from acute ankle disorders and inflamed lower vertebrae. Known for limbocapacity while dodging strainers, and rarely speaks without including such terms as "feet per mile."

Habitat: Any aquatic environment containing more rocks than water. Most active during and directly after rain storms. Prolific in the Southeast and on steep tributaries of tributaries of water-ways frequented by other *Homopaddleaqua.*

HOMOPADDLEAQUA RODEODICA

A new offshoot of *H. hairballensis* and *H. creekboaterus* that has acquired the innate ability to recreate in river features avoided by other *Homopaddleaqua.* Attempts to subsist on handouts from industry sponsors. Evolutionary traits include nasal passages adapted for frequent, high pressure douching; equilibrium adapted to withstand high centrifugal forces; and sinewy abdominal musculature showing marked resistance to torqueing.

Species Characteristics: High-pitched speech patterns resulting from water-clogged nasal passages; also displays frequent water emissions from nasal cavity during conversation (occasionally attempts to cure ailment through use of noseplugs). Nomadic lifestyle with fellow species creates behavior patterns illustrating lack of authoritative control. Capable

of subsisting on beer and Power Bars (as long as they're free), and known to mention "dude," "shred," and "cartwheel" at least once per sentence.

Habitat: Old RVs, campgrounds, Mexican restaurants, crowded motel rooms, and high-profile hydraulics throughout the country. Demonstrates summer migration pattern with flock of other *H. rodeodica, H. shuttlebunnicus,* and species groupies.

HOMOPADDLEAQUA SQUIRTICA

Known for propensity to be held underwater with apparent enjoyment, *H. squirtica* is amphibious in nature, paddling lowest volume craft of all *Homopaddleaqua.* Capable of performing maneuvers executed by *H. rodeodica* without benefit of hydraulics.

Species Characteristics: *H. squirtica* is easily identifiable once watercraft is stripped away. Most noticeable features include gangrenous feet and raw, red kneecaps. Also look for blue tint to face and cheeks. If dissecting specimen, identifying features include highly developed lung capacity and pressure-resistant eardrums.

Habitat: River bottoms through-out North America, particularly near squirrelly eddy lines and bottomless whirlpools. Often seen on shore repairing fiberglass boats.

HOMOPADDLEAQUA OPENBOATICUS

Result of interbreeding between *H. hairballensis* and *H. canoeflaticus.* Considers swimming Class IV–V fun, and often seems confused about paddles. Species has yet to propagate as readily as other *Homopaddleaqua.*

Species Characteristics: Enjoys kneeling in puddles for extended periods of time, creating prune-like wrinkles on kneecaps and feet. Thinks kayakers are wimps and often talks with Southern drawl. Often found out of breath from inflating float bags.

Habitat: Can be seen following kayakers down Southeastern waterways. Found in cafes serving day-old coffee and in campgrounds.

HOMOPADDLEAQUA SLALOMENSIS

A species known for its propensity for bumping into dangling pieces of wood, *H. slalomensis* is divided into three distinct sub-species: *K-oneicus, C-oneicus* and *C-twoicus.* Each is known for single-mindedness and focus bordering on obsession.

Species Characteristics: Identifiable by habit of making Class V moves on Class III rivers. Well-defined torso musculature contrasts sharply with species' pale, spindly, lower limbs. Can often be seen paddling upstream in strange training rituals. Generally mates within species.

Habitat: Town slalom courses, World Cup sites, anything with vertical poles dangling over river features. Most prolific spawning grounds centered on east coast. Can also be found in video rooms monitoring performance.

HOMOPADDLEAQUA SEAYAKTOURICA

The two-bladed cousin of *H. canoe-flaticus*, *H. seayaktourica* prefers paddling from point A to point B, often migrating to warmer climates in winter. Some members of this species are solitary, while others congregate in pairs (and in rare instances, trios). Each experiences difficulty turning and exhibits frustration from having water drip off paddle onto arms.

Species Characteristics: Displays foot dexterity evolved from rudder use, and chronically sore vertebrae from hoisting long, heavy boats onto shuttle vehicles. Frequently found with binoculars to eyes in search of birds and sea mammals.

Habitat: Densely populated maritime and lake regions. Often found at paddling symposiums.

HOMOPADDLEAQUA SEAYAKEXPEDITIOUS

Distinguishable by their craft's one-inch waterline, excess storage hatches, and large, bow-mounted compass. Decks frequently contain every paddling accessory known to man.

Species Characteristics: Often seen in company with *H. seayaktourica*, *H. seayakexpeditious'* most noticeable feature is plumage indicative of long migration patterns. Distinguishable characteristics include multi-ported hulls, spare paddles and other accessories strapped to deck, back-mounted hydration systems, wide-brimmed hats, lip-balm-on-a-necklace, waterproof maps and journals, and miscellaneous camera equipment. Seemingly unaffected by extreme water and air temperatures, *H. seayakexpeditious* occasionally sleeps at sea and attempts to solicit funds and gear from like-minded sponsors.

Habitat: Wanders well beyond its home range. Can also be found in map stores and camping on isolated beaches.

HOMOPADDLEAQUA SITONTOPICUS

A recently evolved variation of *H. seayaktourica*, easily distinguished by absence of skirt plumage. Displays notable claustrophobic tendencies when inside cockpits, and marked aversion to rolling. Boasts the tannest lower limbs of all *Homopaddleaqua*. Not to be confused with *H. surfskiei*, which uses *H. sitontopicus* skills for racing and lifeguard rescues.

Species Characteristics: Affinity for tropical climates and Class I–II whitewater. Paddle skills often sub-par to that of other *Homopaddleaqua*. Prone to saying "Wheee!" when paddling, and often found wearing fanny packs—sometimes attached to backrest—containing sunscreen and other accessories.

Habitat: Tranquil bays and lagoons in both freshwater and salt. Also found surfing and snorkeling in maritime locales, especially at or near trendy resorts. Occasionally migrates inland to freshwater rivers.

HOMOPADDLEAQUA SURFYAKARIA

Although it lacks the river habitat of *H. hairballensis, H. surfyakaria* retains the species' highly evolved adrenal glands and utilizes them in saline environments. Evolved from crossbreeding between inland kayakers and ocean boardsurfers. Subspecies include: *H. waveskiei* and *H. surfskiei*. Competes at annual gatherings where often more time is spent discussing the sport's politics than paddling.

Species Characteristics: Discernable from other *Homopaddleaqua* by a constant flow of saltwater from the sinuses. Identifying features include crimson cheeks, blonde-streaked hair, sodium chloride residue, and—especially in the case of *H. internationalclassicus*— occasional whining to judges.

Habitat: Beaches on the East and West coasts; any wave bigger than two feet. Those low on the food chain often found surfing sideways uncontrollably in the soup. Believed to have migrated from the United Kingdom.

HOMOPADDLEAQUA COMMERCIALCLIENTEI

A parasitic species relying on the skills of other *Homopaddleaqua* for food, gear, and general survival. *H. commercialclientei,* however, isn't entirely self-serving; it has a symbiotic relationship with other species enabling all to survive. Generally subordinate to *H. raftguidensis, H. commercialclientei* is easily herded and domesticated, but not highly responsive. Occupies bottom rung on survival ladder.

Species Characteristics: Willful giving of money to *H. raftguidensis,* especially if prompted by "tip" jokes. Frequently seen wearing cotton T-shirts and carrying non-waterproof cameras. Generally lacks the survival techniques mastered by other *Homopaddleaqua* as illustrated by ineffective paddle strokes and the asking of such questions as "How deep's the water?" and "Do we end up at the same place we started?" Displays obnoxious tendency to start waterfights and has annoying habit of yelling "Wheeee!"

Habitat: Over-crowded waterways throughout North America. Often seen congregating en masse at put-ins and inside accessory shops.

HOMOPADDLEAQUA RAFTGUIDENSIS

Most aesthetically pleasing of entire *Homopaddleaqua* genus. Capable of surviving only when in close proximity to *H. commercialclientei.* One of few *Homopaddleaqua* that fights among itself for subsistence on domesticated *H. commercialclientei.*

Species Characteristics: White teeth, bronzed arms, blonde hair, and ability to herd *H. commercialclientei.* Frequently seen with carabiners clipped to lifejacket for no apparent reason. Anatomical traits include vocal chords adapted for shouting and memory bank evolved for retaining bad jokes and local history trivia. Also known for blurting out sarcastic answers to stupid questions.

Habitat: Trailer parks, raft warehouses, campgrounds, VW vans, happy hours, and Mexican restaurants.

HOMOPADDLEAQUA PRIVATEBOATERUS

Performs annual ritual to obtain rites of passage on waterways. If successful in its permit hunt, *H. privateboaterus* displays a high degree of independence, often substituting enthusiasm for skill.

Species Characteristics: Extreme aversion to *H. raftguidensis* and *H. commercialclientei*. Often found wearing 1970's era wetsuits and Mae West lifejackets, frequently on over-loaded rafts. Subspecies exhibit highly evolved organizational and paddling skills, while others adhere to Baptism by Fire school. Displays odd behavior of transporting human excrement and campfire ashes. Usually found in a variety of high-volume kayaks, duckies, tub-floored and self-bailing rafts. Identifiable by duct tape on dry bags.

Habitat: Clustered around mailboxes waiting for permit applications. Also found at ranger stations, campgrounds, trip meetings, liquor stores, and markets.

HOMOPADDLEAQUA SHUTTLEBUNNICUS

A creature devoted—occasionally against its will—to transporting other species to their appropriate habitat. Altruistic in nature. Evolved over the years from mates of *H. hairballensis, H. rodeodica, H. creekboaterus,* and other *Homopaddleaqua.* Often gets stuck paying speeding tickets and gas bills. Respected by all *Homopaddleaqua,* especially when cold beer is provided at take-out.

Species Characteristics: Well-developed navigational instincts and ability to stay awake for long periods of time. Frequently seen reading magazines and looking at watches. Propensity for owning large-racked vehicles capable of carrying inordinate numbers of boats.

Habitat: Roadways leading to *Homopaddleaqua* habitat. May also be seen waiting in vehicles, hanging out at put-ins and take-outs, hiding behind paperbacks, consulting maps, and playing hacky sack.

HOMOPADDLEAQUA YUPPICUS

Stands out from other *Homopaddle-aqua* by brightest, newest, and most expensive plumage. Spends more time buying equipment than actually using it. Would rather purchase new wardrobe than fix something with duct tape.

Species Characteristics: Talks about paddling more than pursuing it, and purchases gear largely for sake of image. Look for lack of scruff marks on bottom of boat; also identifiable by color of boat matching that of lifejacket. Displays affinity for lattes before and after paddles. Frequently found in brand new Toyota 4-Runners and Nissan Pathfinders with equally new roofracks. Drives around with boat on top of car . . . in February.

Habitat: Espresso bars, cellular phone stores, REI, high-profile paddling events, and city-pool rolling sessions. Rarely seen on non-chlorinated water.

Kayaking with Dr. Spock

by Eugene Buchanan

Having a child is a rite of passage every bit as much as sticking one's first combat roll. Unfortunately, I was made all too aware from friends reaching this milestone that kids and kayaking don't always go hand-in-hand. So with my wife due in February, I did what any expectant father would do: I called a few buddies to go run waterfalls down in Mexico. A last hurrah of sorts, I figured, before paddling gave way to parenting.

Timing, of course, was still an issue. I would return, I told my well-endowed wife, on Jan. 10—in plenty of time should she experience a premature runoff. Hall pass granted, I pitched a few paddling friends on the last hurrah angle and booked reservations with AguaAzul Adventures in the heart of the aptly named Sierra Madre. And the trip wasn't entirely self-serving; to help justify the time away from wife and zygote, I vowed to not just run waterfalls but also to polish up on the nuances of parenthood.

To help with the latter, I enlisted the help of the renowned Dr. Spock and his timeless *Baby and Child Care* book. If anything could help prepare me for fatherhood as much as a boating trip to Mexico, this was it. Bringing it along meant exposing my jugular to my boating buddies, but I was willing to risk the jeers from my peers if it meant becoming a better father. Like my wife disguising her pregnancy with maternity clothes, I tried to hide the book on the plane, stuffing it inside an in-flight magazine to serve as a shield. Inevitably, I was discovered. "Hey! Look who brought a baby book!" said my rowmate Dave when he glimpsed the cover. "I bet you only get ten pages read the whole trip."

Soon my remaining friends joined in; the heckling had begun and we hadn't even touched ground. Vowing to prove my detractors wrong, I ignored their remarks and attempted to digest the good doctor's advice. My reading plan, I quickly learned, was ambitious—almost as ambitious as our plan to paddle six of the next seven days. It would take a few shuttle breakdowns to get through the book's 939 pages, but I resolved to put my head down and punch through it—just like powering through a hydraulic. Like negotiating a long rapid, it didn't take long to get disoriented—especially when I turned to the 14-page-long Table of Contents.

Subheads such as "The Parents' Part," "Common Behavior Problems," and "First Year Feeding" soon had my head swirling as if I was upside-down in a whirlpool. But then I saw it, the first Spockism I could relate to: "Many fathers feel they're being called on to give up all their freedom and former pleasures. Others forget their hobbies and interests. Even if they do occasionally sneak off, they feel too guilty to get full enjoyment." Is that the way I would feel at the brink of my first waterfall? Before I had time to answer, my reverie was interrupted. Sitting next to me, Dave broke out a battered copy of Tom Robey's *A Gringo's Guide to Mexican Whitewater,* dangling it like a carrot in front of a horse. I put Dr. Spock away.

After changing planes in Houston, I gave the doctor another chance. Once again his words struck home: "For too long fathers have gotten away with the clever ruse that they lacked the intelligence, manual dexterity and visual motor-skills to change a smelly diaper." What better way to enhance one's intelligence, manual dexterity, and visual motor-skills, I reasoned, than by paddling? I made a note to apply the skills I learned on this trip to my baby's bottom back home.

After taking a bus to Ciudad Valles, a few miles from our base camp on the Rio Micos, we pacified ourselves by sucking down a few Coronas while waiting for our pick-up. We used the time to meet the rest of the clients, getting to know one another like couples in the Lamaze class my wife and I had just finished back home. This, however, was a markedly rougher crowd. When I used my limited Spanish to say "I am happy,"

Jeff, a return client from Washington, saw the opening and pounced. "Yeah, well, you better enjoy it," he chided. "Your life's over." Heckle session round two had begun. Naturally, I countered. "How do you know?" I asked. "Do you have kids?" His response put an end to the subject. "Nope," he replied. "I had a vasectomy when I was 20."

At camp we settled around a fire with another pacifying round of Coronas, and I took the time to assess what I was up against. The respective kid-factors of my cohorts didn't look promising. Homer, my cousin from Salida, CO, was the only one with a child. The rest were staunch birth control boaters—John: kidless; the snipped Jeff: kidless for life; Dave: kidless, wifeless, and dogless; 21-year-old Annie: still a kid; Mike and Dion: married seven years, DINKS (double income no kids). I wasn't going to find much sympathy from this crew.

Retiring to my palapa, I sought advice from the venerable doctor, glancing through such subheads as "The Reluctant Weaner," "The Important Sucking Instinct," and "Breast Engorgement Due to Plugged Ducts." As I read, I noticed baby reminders everywhere. Outside, the lapping of the river took on the metronome of a wind-up baby swing. Above, mosquito netting hung down like a mobile. And in the cot next to me, John's raspy breathing painted a future of having to share a room with another body. The reminders continued as I awoke to parrots squawking the next morning. "Better get used to it," said John, unable to resist an early morning jab. "Soon those squawks will come from your baby."

After breakfast, we chose from a line of kayaks in a rack, pointing fingers like fathers in a nursery. The selection process evoked a not-too-flattering image of my wife. Eight months into it, she was beginning to look a lot like Perception's Mr. Clean—skinny on the ends and rather bulbous in the middle, like the snake who swallowed an elephant in *The Little Prince*. Pushing the image aside, I piled into the shuttle rig with the rest of the group and headed for the Micos, which means "monkey." "You know . . . those cute, small, cuddly things," said Dave from the backseat. "Like a baby with hair."

The water at the put-in was baby-bottle warm. "Might want to test it by slapping some on your arm," said John. Dave threw the next punch, handing me a tube of Water Babies sunscreen. My only escape lay in the river. Cinching my PFD as tight as a Snuggly, I paddled off the first drop, severing my umbilical cord from the eddy above. As soon as I landed I wished I hadn't snipped it so soon. I also yearned for some of my wife's belly—the extra forward weight might have kept me from a flat landing.

Like a toddler taking a few stove touches to learn the word "hot," we ran the drop again and again, even after experiencing less-than-perfect lines. Child psychologist Jean Piaget calls the first two years of development the "sensori-motor period, where infants learn by doing . . ." We too were learning by doing. When someone landed flat, everyone else adjusted their behavior by leaning forward. When someone landed too far forward, everyone else leaned back. It was operant conditioning at its finest, and if my newborn was capable

of learning half as quickly, she would be in fine shape.

On the paddle-out at the end of the day, we ran into another group from Colorado, here to film a video. Their ringleader quickly explained why producer Paul Tefft wasn't with them: he was saddled down with newborn twins back home. Vasectomized Jeff pounced. "Better enjoy it," he said again. "You probably won't be getting out much after this either." Another harbinger reared itself farther downstream; just before camp a large stork stood pretzeled in the middle of the river. "Might want to call your wife," said John. "It could be an omen." That night I took his advice, borrowing the camp's satellite phone. She wasn't home.

The harassing continued that night when I took off my shorts and exposed an adult version of diaper rash. Drying the offending neoprene in front of the fire, I felt like target practice for a Hecklers Anonymous meeting. "You won't be needing to keep that part of your body warm any more," said Jeff. "It can freeze up now—it's served its purpose." To escape similar barbs, I retired to my palapa and sought solace from the benevolent doctor. Tonight's lesson: How Human Beings Get Their Aspirations. "A man may react to his wife's pregnancy with various feelings. There can be a feeling of being left out, which may be expressed as . . . wanting to spend more time with his men friends." Not if they treat you like this, I thought. Then again, maybe there was something to the doctor's words after all. The passage could be loosely interpreted to mean paddling is a natural reaction to fatherhood. Intrigued, I continued. The next chapter was entitled, "What Kind of Delivery Do You Want?" For my wife, it boiled down to one word: epidural. I was simply hoping for a painless delivery off of the next day's 25-foot waterfall on the Rio Salto.

At the fall's brink the next morning, I felt a few Braxton Hicks-like contractions as my stomach tightened with nerves. Luckily, I had another Spockism to rely on: "Trust yourself . . . you know more than you think you do." Helping me gain the necessary knowledge was Dave, who missed his line, exited his boat like a c-sectioned baby, and swam at the fall's base. Armed with his miscalculation, I stroked for the left and sailed off into a perfect delivery, my bow bouncing up at the bottom like a baby in a jumpy-seat. Eventually we reached the take-out, located at the brink of an 85-foot waterfall called El Meco. On the shuttle home, I asked our driver what it meant. The answer shouldn't have been surprising: The Sperm.

The remainder of the week was filled with more rivers, more heckling, and more reminders of my impending date with parenthood. On our last night I called home again and finally got through. I wasted no time in finding out the crucial information on everyone's mind . . . the Broncos would face Miami in the playoffs. Returning to the fire, I shared the news to a loud cheer. To celebrate the playoffs, my wife not going into labor, and a successful week of waterfalls, we sang and gave toasts until we all crawled like babies to bed. The next morning, I felt better prepared for fatherhood than ever—at least for the sleep-deprivation part. I felt even more prepared when I strolled over to the campfire site, which looked like a band of toddlers had ravaged someone's living room. Chairs were overturned, clothes were strewn about, and bottles lay in disarray.

After cleaning things up and saying our good-byes, we caught a bus to Tampico and hopped on our plane. On the flight home, I again pulled out Dr. Spock, this time settling into a chapter on ear infections—an especially pertinent one, I thought, since my own were hurting from time spent upside-down. "Still reading that?" interrupted Dave from across the aisle "How far did you get?"

Not very, I replied. But if Dr. Spock was a paddler, I'm sure he would understand.

DESTINATIONS

The Mirage of Wilderness

by Richard Bangs

It's impossible not to confront the Janus nature of the island. Its rivers run clean and clear; its air spins with the breath of honeysuckle. Its forbidding interior is a land without litter. Its craggy edges and joints are lodged with deeply religious Protestants and Roman Catholics renowned for their charity and moral excellence. On a sunny day the place seems like heaven. Yet the incessant storms, the frigid waters have snuffed countless lives and a pall of violence forever hangs. The people here are children of their beloved enemy, the sea. They move with the rhythm of the natural world. Often characterized as optimistic fatalists, they are a thick and gentle people who exterminated the Beothuk Indians, hunted the great auk to extinction, and brought the pilot whale to the brink. For 450 years, the economic mainstay was a seemingly inexhaustible supply of saltfish. Now the stock has been reduced to a slim fraction of the glory days. Not long ago, livelihoods included clubbing young seals to death. Presently they include mining, damming wild rivers, and felling trees. Despite these intrusions into its wilderness, few places survive with such environmental integrity and harmony; yet urban environmentalists have painted it as a house for eco-bandits. The island is Newfoundland.

If you paddle the ripsaw coastline of what the Newfies call The Granite Planet, it's easy to fall into mindless reveries about its beauty. It's a world of whirring wings. Millions of them. Arrow-swift murres, Pillsbury doughbird puffins with clown-colored beaks, great-winged gannets flying arabesques, and an occasional, improbable, wildly fragile tiger-swallowed butterfly. It's also a world of lobster buoys, abandoned outport towns sunk into what some tourists might call "quaintness," and dead puffins drowned in cod nets.

We paddled Trinity Bay and the rugged southeast coast, and we paddled the magnificent wilderness of Gros Morne National Park, on the Gulf of St. Lawrence. And we loved it. We'd go again in a heartbeat. But as we paddled and marveled and "ooohed" and "aaahed," something was gnawing. Something was wrong here. It wasn't the people of Newfoundland, for sure, however maligned they may be by armchair environmentalists who drive fuel-efficient, $40,000 cars and live in energy-efficient $400,000 homes. And it wasn't The Granite Planet.

There was that day in the Random Islands, at the mouth of Trinity Bay, when we paddled to a small island called Ireland's Eye. Legend has it that you can look through a hole in a rock there and see the Emerald Isle on a clear day.

Suddenly, we were paddling into the 17th century. Big, chimney-potted clapboard houses with mansard roofs and curved dormers perched the on cliffs on both sides. Directly in front of us, at the end of the bay, stood a large, white, wooden, neo-Gothic Anglican church. But the windows had no eyes here; the pews gave no songs. Ireland's Eye was a ghost town now. The only living creature was a great bald eagle that swooped over us, glowering with amber eyes, signaling, it seemed, that he was now the mayor and constituency of Ireland's Eye.

The town was one of 148 communities in the Random Island area resettled in the 1960s by a purblind government in an effort to centralize population in "growth centers" where public services could more readily be provided and the island could be recast into an industrialized principality. Over 20,000 people were promised new jobs and a better life as they were coerced to move as part of this visionary program that saw Newfoundland turning its back on the ocean and becoming a neo-Detroit. By and large the jobs were made of hot air and sea foam, and the new life was one of psychic and spiritual havoc. Now the town is most famous for a drug bust. In August 1988, local fisherman, suspicious of high-speed boats zipping in and out of Ireland's Eye, called the mounties, and Canada's largest hash bust took place. Sixteen tons, with a street value of $200 million Canadian dollars, had

been stashed inside the cavernous Anglican church.

The sun shimmered as though dipped in a bowl of crystal as we packed the following day, belying the task ahead, a grueling five-hour return paddle to Lower Lance Cove. When at last we pulled our boats on shore we met two plucky white-haired women, Blanche Ivany and her cousin Martha Stone. In a burr rich as Irish cream, they told me why they were there. Blanche, a widow, was born in Ireland's Eye in a four-square, two-story house in 1931, and lived there with her fisherman husband, Lambert, until 1963. Then the government withdrew funds for the post office, the school, and the government store, and residents were inveigled to move. She and her husband were given nothing for their land or home—just $600 in expenses to reestablish within Trinity Bay. But once moved they could find no work, so Lambert used his dory to make the long trip back to his old fishing grounds at Ireland's Eye. He died, she said, in 1987 at the age of 61 of a broken heart. Now, every Sunday she and her cousin, also a victim of relocation, come down to the shale beach at Lower Lance Cove and look across the water toward their old home.

The next day we were paddling off the windswept eastern coast of the Avalon Peninsula, as far east as a paddler can get and still be in North American waters. We were in the Witless Bay Ecological Preserve, on our way to Great Island, one of the world's largest puffin rookeries. We paused in clangorous cove at Great Island to gawk at the wheeling masses of beer-bellied puffins, black-legged kittiwakes, stubby-winged guillemots, cannon murres, and yellow-headed gannets, Newfoundland's largest sea bird. I had never seen such a sight. The sky blazed with wings!

After circumnavigating Great Island, we worked our way back to the mainland, and hove to at the wharf at Bauling East, an active fishing community with a knot of confetti-colored houses that would put Nova Scotia's famed Peggy's Cove one step down the ladder in picturesque. And with the great wonders of Witless Bay and Great Island fresh in my mind, I was assaulted by a sharp stench that cut through the iodine tang of kelp. Dozens of dead puffins, their dumpy figures looking even more bloated, were floating in the tidewash. They weren't victims of oil spills, poaching, or insecticides, but of cod fisherman's dragnets, which inevitably capture a few puffins floating on the surface.

But what's the tradeoff? Stop fishing? Go on the dole in the winter, and work for minimum wage in the short summer's tourist trade? Or pack up and go to Toronto—if you can afford to. All these grim thoughts came to a head after we'd paddled the length of that imposing fjord called Moose Pond in Gros Morne National Park. We'd set aside a day to scramble up the imposing cliffs to the rim, from where one of the grandest and least-seen vistas in all Newfoundland can be savored. It was an intoxicating hike. Waterfalls materialized out of river rock; the views became grander with every step. This was July, yet patches of snow lit up the gray fans of scree in cirques. Then after a couple of hours scrambling up a recent rock slide, I found a side canyon that looked as though it offered passage to the top.

After an hour of swimming upstream in a goblin forest of birch and juniper, I emerged above the tree line onto a glacial drumlin, and surveyed the landscape. It didn't look good. The gully I had hoped to scale narrowed into a dark chimney, and the final pitch of 100 feet or so was slippery and sheer, impossible to traverse without ropes and pitons. I had successfully climbed to a dead end.

I sat down on a lichen-covered rock and pulled a Mirage chocolate bar from my pocket. As I unwrapped it I looked back down the valley for the first time in a couple of hours, and was stunned by the sight. Some blessings come from nature, unbidden and unplanned. To my left was the misty veil of the great falls, and above, a bald plateau where I could make out a small herd of barren-ground caribou cooling off on a snow patch. I could gaze all the way to the end of the Snaking Pond, and beyond to the Gulf of St. Lawrence, the waters infamous as the killing fields for millions of baby seals. When I finished the candy, I bunched up the wrapper and began to stuff it in my pocket. Then I stopped, balled the wrapper tighter, and tossed it against the cliff. Somehow it seemed the thing to do, like Ed Abbey's insistence on throwing beer cans along the highways that dissected his sacrosanct desert landscapes. But this wasn't out of anger. It was to defy the immutable morality of the environmentalists who had never visited this place, but had so heartily condemned it.

But, the small act seemed in some way to express my frustrations with the ecological invective hurled at this island and its people. There seemed a singular cohesiveness of culture and society here, and a consciousness of unity with the natural world. I deeply admired the Newfoundlanders' famous traits: self-sufficiency, adaptability, daring absolute endurance, unbounded hospitality, a rare concern for fellow man, an appreciation of wilderness, and an evergreen goodwill that triumphs over the futility in life. The history of the people here is one of foreign exploitation; of interference in the modest goals of feeding and sustaining a healthy family. For centuries they caught or killed what the biblical Great Waters offered as their currency with the world: seals, whales, and codfish. But the world turned against them, condemning the hunting of seals and whales, while foreigners employing high-tech vessels with sophisticated radar beat them in the fishing game.

In 1986, when Spain and Portugal joined the European community, they blithely ignored the voluntary fishing allocations and in years since have taken five times their quota from the shallow waters just beyond the 200-mile Canadian limits. The fall in fish stocks forced the Canadian government to cut its 1990 quotas by enough to throw 3,000 Newfoundlanders out of work, and scientists insisted quotas would have to be cut far more for stocks to revive. This in a province where, in the 1990s, the official unemployment rate was 17 percent (some told me it was closer to 30), the sales tax was an ungodly 12 percent, and incomes were only two-thirds the Canadian average. In the late 1990s, many former sealers, whalers, and fisherman turned to logging, but vocal outsiders jeered the destruction of a limited resource.

By the end of the decade, everything seemed to be running short except hard-luck stories. Nonetheless, the resourceful turned to new sources of income. I couldn't help but notice that island highways became lined with cheap motels, gas bars, waterslide parks (when there are less than 60 hot swimming days a year), and tacky tourist shops selling mock cans of Moose, ceramic Newfoundland dog decanters ("produced entirely by local craftspeople"), lobster parts glued together to look like a fisherman, "In Cod We Trust" posters, and Newfoundland-in-a-can.

In 1988, the government invested over $17 million Canadian dollars in a cucumber greenhouse scheme that quickly went bust. The Economic Recovery Commission later announced it was going to invest in an ice factory for exportation of Newfoundland ice. There is no pat answer. As components of a vulnerable living fabric, we cannot allow the destruction of any species, but it is too bad the human side of the issues are rarely adequately addressed.

Greenpeace, Brigitte Bardot (who made a well-publicized trip to an ice floe in 1977 to protest against the annual sea pup hunt), and animal rights author Farley Mowat ("Hardy Knowit" is a favorite nickname) are practically enemies in Newfoundland. They portrayed the good people of The Rock as biocidal Darth Vaders, when in fact they are decent and in many ways extraordinary folks simply trying to eke out an existence in ways deemed honorable not long ago. In order to find viable alternatives, environmental groups would do better to back off the personal censure and castigation, and work with the Newfoundlanders to build a better life—something beyond the Rod and Gun Waterslide Park.

I took one last gaze at the Mirage candy wrapper, reweighing my decision. Yes, I would leave it behind. Then a gust flew across my shoulder, picked up the wrapper, and sent it sailing into a pine tree. Soon after, another cold current funneled up the canyon, slapping my face, which had been sweating from the reflected July sun. It was a tingly combination of hot and cold, like a Baked Alaska. A storm was on its way.

I turned for a last look. The canyon was filled with blue tendrils of fog and a driving, misty rain spattered against my glasses, but for a moment the mist cleared. The sun shone through, turning the spray into a wavering spectrum of color. And the mist closed in again. A mirage of wilderness? Perhaps. Perhaps the whole week had been a mirage. I pulled up the hood of my parka, hunkered down against the wind, and began the long slog back to camp.

Kayaking and Kava

by Eugene Buchanan

I was more than a little nervous. Although I was used to wearing a sprayskirt, I wasn't accustomed to wearing a flowery one that hung down to my ankles. Having to sit cross-legged in such apparel in front of a chief while waiting for a mandatory narcotic cocktail to be passed my way didn't help matters. Fidgeting uncomfortably, I watched the coconut shell slowly work its way around the circle. On the bright side, four people separated the Chief and me, and so far none of their eyes had glazed over from ingesting the rancid liquid. When my turn came, I put my nervousness aside, clapped my hands, and drank the mud-brown concoction in four quick gulps. As was the custom, I then followed with three more claps. "Maathaa, Maathaa!" a village member yelled, "It is drained! It is drained!"

It's not uncommon to have to secure permission to go paddling. But usually it's from a spouse or landowner—not from a chief whose ancestors were cannibals. We arrived in the village of Udu only a few hours earlier, unexpected and unannounced. The chief's spokesman was the first to greet us. After offering us his house, he quickly left to set up a meeting where we would present the chief with our brown bag of kava roots to be mashed into pulp with a mortar and pestle, and turned into the narcocktail. The whole thing would be like walking into a U.S. city, knocking on the mayor's door, and handing him a bag of twigs in return for the key to the city. Only here we had come for far more than the key to the city: we had come for permission to paddle the Wailoa River.

The Kava and Cannibal Roots

The night's ceremony, called a *sevu sevu*, revolved around kava, a drink made from the pulverized root of the Yaqona plant, a member of the pepper family. Served from a large wooden bowl, the drink has been used throughout Fiji's history for everything from consummating business deals and social contracts to welcoming visitors, sending villagers on journeys, christening boats, casting magical spells, and laying foundations for houses. It is also used as a traditional gift offered by guests to a host, which is how it fit into our itinerary.

By now neither the ceremony nor the drink's numbing effect on the tongue was new to us. But its potency varies, and I still couldn't help but feel a little apprehensive.

We had arrived in Fiji five days earlier and had already done the kava routine several times while sea kayaking near an island called One. For Glenn Lewman, who put the trip together, the ceremony was even more familiar. He arrived a week earlier and suffered through five kava ceremonies in one day alone. Although he didn't look any worse for the wear, stories recounted by early explorers told a different tale. Rumors run rampant of sailors reporting back to their ships after getting caught up in nocturnal kava ceremonies. Although accounts vary, many share the following theme: the sailors passed out with their eyes open, aware of everything that was happening but unable to move a muscle in their body. Indeed, one travel writer, Gordon Gumming, who lived in Fiji from 1875 to 1880, summed up its effects this way: "Its action is peculiar, inasmuch as its drunkenness does not effect the brain, but paralyzes the muscles, so a man lies helplessly on the ground, perfectly aware of what is going on."

Although the root's chemical make-up is known, its active ingredients are not. Pharmacologists from the University of South Pacific say the root's kick comes from compounds whose nature is not unlike a stimulant such as cocaine, but not a depressant either. It has a calming effect somewhere in between. Whatever its active ingredients, local healers have used it to treat everything from tooth decay to gonorrhea. Apart from the kava, one other thing unsettled my stomach. About a hundred years ago, Fiji was home to some of the fiercest cannibals in the South Pacific. Not exactly the type of place you want to pass out with muscles frozen and your eyes open. Luckily, we

were guests. In the olden days, the islanders didn't eat their guests. Instead, they went to their enemies' camps to find someone else to sacrifice as an offering. There are also tales of victims being made to eat portions of themselves in front of everybody. These orders were given by a chief similar to the one staring at my skirt. One early observer went so far as to say, "No Eastern tyrants can rule with more absolute terror than chiefs do here."

I thought about all of this at our first kava ceremony the day after we arrived. After being met at a tiny island airstrip by Glenn and taking a two-hour boatride to an even more obscure island, we visited the headmaster of a school whose island offered enticing sea kayaking. As it turned out, I needn't have worried about Fijians' cannibal heritage. The practice is long gone, replaced with friendly smiles and warm hospitality. I got my first taste of this in line at the Los Angeles airport. "First time in Fiji?" asked Fred, a Fijian woodcarver with a warm-hearted smile that seemed out of place in L.A. "You'll love it. Fiji is paradise. It's not like here . . . No one is in a hurry there, like life should be."

The second reason I didn't have to worry about passing out from kava and finding someone nibbling on my fingers is that the root affects people differently. Effects range from general fuzzy-headedness to mild euphoria. For Glenn who at our first ceremony looked the part of an early explorer with bald head topping a ponytail, the effects were quite predictable. "It just makes me go to sleep," he said, stifling a yawn. It didn't take long to find out what effect the stuff had on me. "High-tide or low-tide?" asked the headmaster, using his fingers to indicate a full glass or half. "High," I replied. If I was going to test this stuff, I might as well go all out and drink a full coconut cup's worth. At the end of our first ceremony, I survived six full-tides. And although my mouth felt somewhat numb, that was about it. I felt relaxed sure, but who wouldn't when you know the next four days will bring nothing but sunshine, sea kayaking, and *sevu sevus*?

Sea Kayaking and *Sevu Sevus*

Our accommodations for the next four days were at a family-owned resort called Kenia just off Kadavu, the third largest of Fiji's 300 islands. Although less than 17 percent of Fijian land is privately owned—the rest is either owned by native tribes or was transferred to the government when Fiji gained its freedom in 1970 after 96 years of British rule—the resort is owned by William, or Tutu, and run by his son, Jona, and his wife, Ledua. The resort's name, Kenia, dates back to when a lawyer from Kenya came over to represent the chief in some legal matters with the state. The chief couldn't pay him, so he gave him 17 acres of the South Pacific paradise. The land eventually got passed down through the family to Tutu.

Even though they were not accustomed to visitors, our hosts were as gracious as the chief who deeded the land. They hung fresh leis around our necks as soon as we arrived, and our thatched roof huts, or *bures,* received a fresh batch of flowers daily. Even without the kava, it was hard to be anything but relaxed, with romantic huts, hammocks swinging from palm trees, and snorkeling and sea kayaking all within seconds of each other. Each day revolved around sea kayaking and eat-

ing, and both were superb. Midstream in the Equatorial current, which flows east from the trenches of Peru, the water is rich in nutrients, meaning it is also rich in fish. We paddled a new line of SOTAR inflatable sea kayaks and it didn't take long for each day's paddle to turn into a snorkel session. And while we were sea kayaking and snorkeling, Jona was spear-fishing. One lobster he caught, basted in a sweet-and-sour sauce by Ledua, fed eight people (if you don't count the native tapioca dessert).

Like all good things, the four days went quickly and we were soon faced with a going-away dinner that brought members of neighboring villages over in kayaks and pongas. Covered in banana leaves and placed in a large pit, a pig was roasted to complement the day's catch, and the ensuing farewell *sevu sevu*—filled with guitar playing, drum beating, and dancing—lasted longer than I did. Karen, a river guide from California, lasted the longest of those from the Northern Hemisphere, and it showed in her eyes when she showed up the next morning late for breakfast. "Eighteen high tides," she said.

On to the River

Tears filled the eyes of Ledua and the two other women tending the resort when we boarded the ponga to take us back to our flight to the main island. I've never felt that touched leaving an island, and my eyes watered even before the boat's speed created a headwind. During the two-hour ride, I stared north where, after being set adrift in an open boat with 18 others by the crew of the Bounty in 1789, Captain Bligh became the first white man to float into Fijian waters. Luckily he didn't get too close;

as if dehydration and hunger weren't enough, cannibal-filled war canoes quickly chased off his crew. This, of course, might well have helped them get to the Dutch settlement of Timar after 41 days at sea.

Bligh wasn't the first foreigner to sight the islands. Dutchman Abel Tasman spotted them in 1643 and Captain Cook sighted them in 1774. Although exploration of them began in earnest in the 1800s with a flourishing sandalwood and sea cucumber market, the islands' biggest transformation came in the mid-1800s during Chief Cakobau's 50-year reign, which ended when he ceded Fiji to Britain in 1874. That's when the Indians started arriving as indentured servants. By 1916, more than 60,000 had arrived, most of whom remained to live in a casteless society. The country's population is now evenly split between native Fijians and Indians.

Riding the motorboat also made it easy to see that 97 percent of Fiji's 709,000 square kilometers is nothing but water. The rest is made up of 300 islands, 100 of which are inhabited. Viti Levu, the main island where we were headed for our river trip, is the largest at 10,000 square kilometers, and contains 70 percent of the population. All of the islands are located between the Equator and the Tropic of Capricorn, and one island, located on the 180th meridian, even causes the International Date Line to make an eastward bend so the country can be in the same time zone.

At the airport we bade adieu to Jona and flew back over the type of islands and atolls you'd expect in a James Bond movie. Reefs surrounded all of them, and all boasted calm, turquoise waters.

Fiji and River Running

John Grier, who came to Fiji with the Peace Corps in the early 1980s and never left, met us at the Suva airport. Rain poured heavily, a sign that we were now on the island's windward side which gets more than 300 centimeters of rain a year. It was this rain that formed the island's five major drainages and would give us our first taste of Fijian whitewater. Wearing khaki shorts, a flowered shirt, and an island tan, Grier was responsible for founding the Nausori Kayak Club, one of three paddling clubs in the country. The two others are an army club and an international club. The focus of all three is kayak polo. The teams play each other regularly, and both travel and host games with other nearby countries.

To help with our expedition, Grier had rounded up members of two of the clubs to help with language barriers and assist us on the river. Two of them, Mala and Ratoe from the army club, are members of Fiji's military elite who have served in peace-keeping missions in Lebanon and the Middle East. Meeting them outside the airport was intimidating; Mala looked like a native version of Cool Hand Luke, complete with mirrored sunglasses, black boots, a camouflage pack, and a stern look. After a few seconds, though, he broke into a beaming ear-to-ear grin, exposing a white set of teeth and a friendly Fijian demeanor. Three members of the Nausori club also joined us: Mala, Mambo, and Iona, each of whom had been playing kayak polo for about three years.

Piling into the back of an open-walled truck, we drove to a boat trailer in a dirt parking lot where we picked up our equipment. The inside was stacked to the brim with fiberglass downriver boats, canoes, and a shipment of brand new plastic water polo boats from New Zealand. They carried the Perception logo, the Acrobat name, and a flat stern and bow that made me wince about taking them in whitewater.

Rafting in Fiji isn't new. In Air Pacific's in-flight magazine, an ad for an outfitter showed rafters happily making their way down the Ba River, one of the island's five main drainages. Of course, the industry is still primitive; in the far upper corner of the picture was the guide, standing waist-deep in water and pushing. Two outfitters offer trips on this river, but neither has run one for a few years. A smaller inset photo showed another "navigable" river, where a smiling couple sat aboard a homemade bamboo *mbilibili* raft being poled by another guide. That was the extent of Fiji's river-running industry.

Glenn had targeted another river, the Wailoa, deep inside the island's interior. A New Zealander named Barry Anderson, whom Grier brought over to teach clubs how to play water polo, ran it first. Locals told him of the river and he wasted no time in exploring it. Since then, it has been run in kayaks twice by members of the Nausori club. We would be the fourth group to kayak it and the first-ever to raft it.

The ride to the village took about five hours, all of it on winding, mountainous, jungle roads with potholes deeper than the cockpits of our boats. When we rounded one corner, a sparkling green river came into view, a welcome sight save for the fact that it didn't have a bridge. Instead, it had a large bamboo raft that would ferry us across. Fiji got its name from Tongans,

who visited the islands to have their huge seagoing canoes crafted. I doubt the builders of the truck-ferrying raft would have gotten much work from the Tongans. Tied together with vines, the raft was barely bigger than our truck and looked ramshackle even for an island job.

With visions of our truck suffering the fate of the Titanic, we climbed out and let the driver do his thing. Barely stopping in time before the front wheels fell over the edge, the Indian driver did a commendable job of getting the truck onto the raft. Now it was the polers' and liners' turn. Using a long bamboo pole to help push the behemoth upstream, a villager peeled the truck and raft out of the eddy, and soon our gear was on its way downstream to an eddy on the opposite bank. The current wasn't fast, but it was current; if the truck missed the eddy, both our gear and hopes of paddling Fijian whitewater would be forever washed away.

With water washing over the raft's bamboo beams, truck and raft made the eddy-turn, which instantly turned the craft upstream. Still marveling the successful peel-out and eddy-turn of our shuttle vehicle, we followed in a homemade, freeboardless canoe that the Tongans would have returned for a refund. Safe on the other side, we continued our trek to the village and rolled in just as darkness enveloped the jungle.

A Meeting with the Chief

When we arrived at the village, Glenn and Jona made their way to the spokesman's house to set up a meeting with the chief. When they returned, they instructed us to unload our gear into the spokesman's living room, our quarters for the next few days. From an early age, Fijians are taught that friends and family are the most important things on earth, and as a general rule, Fijians never forget the people they meet. This tradition was readily evident in the spokesman's hospitality. While we turned his living room into a mini-base-camp, he and his family moved outside to live in the kitchen.

The meeting was held in the chief's house a short walk down a narrow path from the Hotel Spokesman. At first it was hard to tell who the chief was—at least until the kava was doled out. As was customary, he was the first one served. But he didn't resemble the type of chief Dr. Livingston might have encountered during his treks across Africa. Wearing a Timex watch, and clad in a yellow skirt, orange button-down shirt, and an Afro you'd expect on a young Michael Jackson—with tinges of gray flanking the temples—he raised the coconut shell to his lips and started the ceremony. When the chief finished drinking, Jona, sitting cross-legged in front of him, began to plead our case about wanting to paddle the river that lay in the chief's domain. I couldn't understand anything, but I knew the conversation had turned to rivers when Jona's arms started waving to signify waves. Throughout it all, the chief sat silently, occasionally picking at his bare-foot toes.

After Jona finished, the drinking resumed, with the coconut shell making its way around the circle. Clapping once, I grabbed it with both hands and downed the murky liquid quickly before its taste caught up. Clapping three more times, I then handed it back to the server so he could re-dip it into the bowl of plenty. The kava pot negotiations lasted another three hours before an opening presented itself for us to take our leave. When it did, Jona's politeness and pleading paid off: we were given permission to run the river the following day.

Paddling with the Jamaican Bobsled Team

After a dinner prepared by the spokesman's family, we settled into our newfound rooms, taking our skirts off to use as sheets. At 11:00 p.m., the village lights turned off from an automatic timer on the village generator. Since many of the local children had what looked to be Lice-Be-Gone sprayed onto the dark curls of their hair, we wrapped our pillows with towels before drifting into a night of kava-fueled dreams.

A village crier woke the townsfolk at 5:00 a.m. to tend the fields. I got up shortly thereafter to go on a dawn patrol kayak session with Jona just downstream of the village. "There is big rapid around corner," he said as we snuggled ourselves into our cramped cockpits. In the flats near the village, his paddling skills shone brightly. To help wake up, he cranked out ten hand rolls in a row, a tribute to his water polo background, followed by a series of stern pivots that turned his boat on a dime. It didn't take long to figure out that while he was well-versed in water polo, whitewater was a different matter. The "big" rapid he had referred to was no more than Class II and he was over and swimming at the first wave. "Coach made us learn how to hand roll," he said, emptying the water out of his boat, "but we don't get to river much." Although he had been in countless water polo matches, he had been to a river with actual current only three times in three years.

On the walk back to the village, I learned that during the previous night's kava ceremony most of the talk centered on our being here to search for rivers. Jona explained to the Chief that Glenn was here looking for rivers to take people on in the future. The Chief didn't like that, Jona said. Most Fijian sports are related to the government (the Nausori Kayak Club's old kayaks, Combats, were now being used by the government's kayak club), and the government doesn't give any money to the villages. Jona then had to convince the Chief that our journey wasn't related to the government at all, and that Glenn promised to help the village however he could. "My body got numb from so much talk, not from the kava," Jona said.

We returned late for breakfast where everyone was comparing bug bite wounds from the night before. Jim won, and after watching him douse the winning entries with hydrogen peroxide, we hatched a plan for the day. Since there were rumors of a Class V rapid somewhere along the line, Glenn, myself, and the five Fijian kayakers would scout the river today in kayaks and plan for the first raft descent the next day. We piled into the back of the truck and made our way upstream to the put-in where once again I was exposed to a mind-numbing array of hand rolls and stern pivots by the Fijians. "We are the best whitewater kayakers in the military," Mala (a.k.a. Cool Hand Luke) told me in the eddy. Of course, he and Ratoe were also the only whitewater kayakers in the military.

Although they all hand-bombproof hand rolls, the Fijians' unfamiliarity with whitewater reared its head in the first rapid. When Jona tipped over, he discarded his paddle and hand rolled up. That's what they all did. The only problem was that this wasn't a water polo pool, and their paddles quickly got away

from them. And their boats weren't whitewater boats. They didn't have flotation, beams or grabloops, and their sprayskirts came off anytime you sneezed. When the boats swamped, they dove faster than Jona did when he caught the lobster sea kayaking. It was a lot like padding with the Jamaican Bobsled Team. Despite an abundance of enthusiasm and certain applicable skills, they were clearly out of their element, calling holes "eddy lines" and tossing their paddles away at the first sign of trouble. When I stopped to surf a wave, they looked on incredulously. "You very smart kayaker," Jona said when I returned to the eddy. "Very smart." By the end of the day, after 27 flips by the Fijians and half as many hand rolls and swims, the tally read two lost sandals, two broken paddles, one broken footpeg, and five broken egos. "What are we going to tell John Grier?" asked Jona, holding up one of the two broken but brand-new paddles. But the mission was successful: even though three of the Fijians swam it, the Class V turned out to be no more than Class IV and the entire run looked perfectly suited for a raft descent the next day.

After taking out at the village later that afternoon, I threw one of the kayaks over my shoulder and hiked upstream with the spokesman. "You ever try this?" I asked. He shook his head. "Old man," he replied.

He watched from shore as I ferried out into the rapid and surfed a hole adjacent to the village. While stationed on the wave, I looked downstream and saw a group of children bathing on the bank. Farther on was another group washing their clothes. Even though they had a great river running through their village, they had yet to learn it offered recreation as well. I was about to give them a jump start. Walking back to the spokesman's house, I grabbed an inflatable kayak and headed back to the hole. Mala and Mambo saw me and followed suit. They quickly realized the inflatables were more forgiving than their polo kayaks, and soon, to the delight of children lining the banks, they were surfing for the first time ever. Even the spokesman got into the action, going so far as to twirl his paddle in the hole. The village priest also gave it a try. Although the hole had been here longer than the village, in one afternoon the villagers had learned the basics of rodeo.

The next day we piled back in the truck for our raft descent. After the bumps and bruises suffered the day before, none of the Fijians wanted back in the hardshells. Instead, they opted for the inflatable kayaks. Somehow realizing he held the key to the whole operation, the spokesman, with a smug look of importance, cradled the pump between his legs throughout the ride. His only change of expression—a slight smile— came when he dropped his machete-wielding wife off to work in the fields. This kept with early Fijian customs: women performed drudgery tasks like weeding and washing, while men took on the more glorified duties like warfare, building, and carrying pumps.

Without the flips, broken paddles, and last-ditch handrolls, today's trip went smoothly. Waterfalls trickled out of lush foliage and flowers bloomed everywhere, a split fraction of which found their way onto the women's helmets as hairpieces. The water was emerald-clear, and birds, 70 percent of which are found nowhere else in the world, fluttered and chirped incessantly.

Before we left that afternoon, we paid our respects to the local chief again, meaning another game of gastronomical roulette with a kava ceremony. Jona accompanied us, and after we assumed our cross-legged positions in a circle on the floor, he told the chief that we enjoyed his river very much and that we hoped to be back soon. While Jona thanked the chief, I glanced out the front door and saw a group of kids playing on a bamboo raft on the far side of the river. They had lived here all their lives and had never seen the portion we discovered upstream.

After Jona finished, the chief took his turn. Jona turned to us and translated. "He said he's glad you like the river," he said. "And hopefully when you come back you can help him fix his roof." The chief saw me glance up toward the rain-stained ceiling and smiled the warm Fijian smile I had grown so accustomed to. Even if I was wearing a skirt and drinking a muscle-paralyzing concoction with a man whose ancestors were cannibals, nervousness was the furthest thing from my mind.

Sea Kayaking Sweden

by Jamie Spencer

From my vantage point at the terrace cafe on the tiny island of
Helgeandsholmen in the heart of Stockholm, the city seems made more of water
than solid earth. Directly across the inner harbor, the ornate facades of 17th- and
18th-century buildings seem to float behind a scattering of sailboats and leisurely
passenger ferries. Narrower stretches of water separate me from the busy plaza of
the Opera House on one side and the Royal Palace set high on the island of Gamla
Stan—the old town—on the other. This is a city of islands, 14 in all. But these 14
are just the beginning. The Stockholm Archipelago, which starts here in the center
of town, has some 24,000 islands, stretching 125 miles north-to-south and almost 40
miles out into the Baltic Sea. It's a kayaker's paradise.

The urban waterways of the innermost part of the archipelago offer a certain
charm for paddling: calm, clean waters and spectacular city views. But it's the outer
archipelago that draws me. The islands in the inner chain are densely populated and
share the verdant character of the mainland, but the outer ones, smooth granite
slabs called skerries, lie exposed to the Baltic's fury. On a map, the land seems to
unravel as it moves out from the coast: the ragged border of an orderly world.

Conceivably, I could start paddling a kayak at the foot of the palace walls and
just keep going until nothing but waves stood between me and Estoria. That would
certainly provide me with the full spectrum the archipelago has to offer. But as a
tourist unfamiliar with the islands' changeable climate and currents, and as a single
woman traveling alone, I decide that a tour with an experienced guide is probably
more practical. I sign on for a three-day trip with a local adventure travel company,
Aventyrsresor.

The journey to the launch point requires successively more primitive forms of
locomotion: first the T-bana, Stockholm's subway, to Slussen in the southern part of
the city; then a bus to Stavnas harbor, about 45 minutes away; and finally a taxiboat
to the island of Runmaro. On the bus, I study the other passengers to figure out
which might be fellow kayakers. The only possibility, I decide, is a thirtyish couple
carrying fishing gear. But on closer look, they seem to have too much luggage.
We're restricted to a small duffel of clothing, a sleeping bag, and a few personal

items: a camera or something to imbibe around the fire at night. The other riders all seem to be locals heading out of the city on a Friday afternoon. They carry briefcases or plastic bags from stylish Stockholm shops.

As the bus moves away from the city, suburbs become small towns, then tiny villages. The four-lane highway narrows to a winding country road that skips across bridges until the gaps between islands become too great. The bus arrives late in Stavnas, but the taxiboat captain, burly and dark-bearded, is waiting. I hold up the instruction sheet I've been given, printed in Swedish, and repeat the name of the tour company to confirm that I'm in the right place. Laughing, he waves me aboard.

Once on the taxiboat, the atmosphere feels like a neighborhood coffee shop; everyone seems to know each other. Over the drone of the engine, I hear festive chattering in Swedish as, island by island, dock by tiny dock, the locals drift off to their summer cottages for the weekend, provisioned with sacks of groceries, bottles of wine, and gloriously blossoming geraniums—purchases from the mainland.

Only 150 of the archipelago's 24,000 islands are inhabited year-round, but many more are occupied during the warmer months. After the long, dark nights of the northern winter, Swedes thrill to be outdoors in the summertime. And the sheltered waters of the archipelago's inner islands are a perfect place to enjoy the seemingly endless summer days. This time of year, close to the solstice, those days are almost 20 hours long.

I meet the rest of the group at the base camp at Runmaro. As it turns out, I've signed on to an unusual trip: I'm the only woman, and the only one who doesn't speak Swedish. Fortunately for me, our guide Thomas speaks English reasonably well and can translate essential instructions. He apologizes that there aren't other non-Swedes along. Because the others in the group are not fluent in English, he says they'll converse mostly in Swedish. Usually the trips include at least a few other Europeans or Americans, with English the common language. The groups typically include more women as well—on average more women than men, Thomas says. But I decide I've come for an adventure—I'll just have to learn a little Swedish along the way.

My companions include guides Thomas and his younger brother Jan, both in their twenties; Bengt, a fruit and vegetable dealer celebrating his 60th birthday, and his son Thomas, in his mid-thirties; and Karl-Erik, a middle-aged Stockholm policeman. (The age of the group is also unusual, I find out later. Most trips draw a somewhat younger crowd.) After the introductions, Bengt gives each of us a lighter printed with the name of his company. "AB Lenells Parti," each one reads in capital letters, and under that, "Frukt and Gront." The gesture feels festive, like a man handing out cigars in a delivery room.

Although it's nearly evening by the clock, the light feels more like early afternoon. We eat a meal of soup, fruit, cheese, and Swedish crispbread to tide us over until we reach our first night's destination and pack up the kayaks. We'll paddle about an hour before settling in for the night. Though the sun still hangs high in a bright sky as we push away from the dock, a few strokes from shore I get a different perspective: the sky behind us glowers with a storm darker than any night I've yet experienced in Sweden. A squall moves in quickly, whipping up waves in the sheltered cove, and driving us into our rain gear. We paddle toward a reedy, narrow passage between two small islands just ahead. On one of them I can make out a small yellow cottage with a dock out in front. As we get closer, a woman runs to the edge of the island, yelling something at me in Swedish and waving her arms. Jan, paddling next to me, gestures that he can't hear what she is saying, and I shrug back—he can't hear, and I can't understand. I hope it isn't anything important.

Once safely into the relative calm of the protected channel, I look back to see a sailboat pull roughly up to the dock just behind us, sails slapping as the skipper struggles to bring them down in the now-driving rain and wind. Suddenly the scene makes sense—the woman wasn't waving us away from her property; she was trying to warn us. Water drips into my eyes from the hood of my slicker; it runs down my paddle and into my sleeves; it pools on the cockpit's nylon skirt. Once into open water on the other side of the little islands, waves splash over the bow, but our Swedish-made Caribou boats feel stable, even in the rough seas.

Then, as quickly as it came, the storm moves on. Behind it, two startlingly perfect rainbows, one over the other, stand out vividly against the retreating clouds. By the time we reach our destination, the water has turned glassy. A dozen swans float just offshore. The little island curls around a leeward cove, where we pull our kayaks up onto flat granite slabs for the night. One small stand of gnarled pines will serve as our shelter from the elements. Based on what I've seen in the

short time we've been traveling, I feel thankful for their existence.

The islands of the middle archipelago are more open than those of the inner part of the chain. The most prominent plants are low-growing heather and juniper. The dense foliage we've been seeing until now gives way to granite, its smooth surfaces exposed by an ice age glacier that started to retreat some 10,000 years ago. As the ice melted, the earth's crust, released from the enormous weight of the glaciers, rose, pushing these islands up from the sea. The archipelago is still rising, at a rate of about 20 inches every 100 years.

In the slanted light of late evening, we gather to prepare dinner. The meal is almost elegant by most camping standards, but far from elaborate: a hearty reindeer stew for those who eat meat and smoked salmon for those who prefer fish, along with salad, rice, and wonderfully heavy bread. Thomas asks me for some kind of *gradde* for the reindeer stew. He doesn't know the word in English, but I have several different boxes marked something-or-other *gradde* in my kayak, part of the common food stores, so I decide to get them all out and let him choose. When he pours in the one he wants, I realize it's cream. By the *fett* content on the boxes, I figure out that two of the three kinds are half-and-half and whipping cream; the other turns out to be some kind of traditional Swedish sauce for herring.

Our equipment list for the trip mentioned wine under the optional items, and around the campfire after dinner, the other guests pour around what they've brought. Though I don't speak the language, they make an effort to include me, with Thomas translating some of the details for my benefit. Mostly I just let the conversation wash over me, my limited knowledge of German clueing me in now and then to the topic at hand. Bengt passes a flask of whiskey and shrugs at me when I signal that I'll stick with my wine. "To each his own," he seems to be saying. The others laugh. I realize that I might be misinterpreting my half-translations and educated guesses, but I decide I like it that way. I laugh with them.

In the morning we take a leisurely scouting trip around the island, collecting garlicky wild herbs to use for that night's dinner, before departing for the outermost skerries. The waters of this section of the archipelago are bustling already with sailboats taking advantage of a rising wind and clear skies. North of us just a few miles lies Sandhamn, the archipelago's most renowned sailing port. We plot a course away from the busier islands, heading south and east across open water toward the more remote parts of the chain. As we approach the outer edge of the archipelago, the islands shrink to rocky outcrops, many of them covered with seabirds. Cormorants sun themselves with wings spread to absorb maximum warmth. Eider ducks, prized for their downy feathers, float on the easy swells. Terns and gulls screech overhead. I keep my eyes open for the white-tailed eagle, Sweden's largest bird, with a wing-span greater than six feet across. About 60 pairs live in the outer archipelago, most on protected reserves. But they stay well hidden.

In late winter, the shallow, brackish water between the islands often freezes solid, drawing Swedes out to the archipelago for inter-island skating expeditions. As I paddle, I try to picture the granite

domes of the skerries rising out of the white surface, skaters bundled against the northern wind darting from point to point—something to try another time, perhaps. For now, the extended summer days allow us plenty of time for exploring on our way to our destination for the second night. To keep clear of the roughest currents and cross-winds, we zig-zag our way from island to island, outcrop to outcrop. The pace is steady, but not strenuous. We pull into a protected cove on one of the smaller islands for lunch, where we spot another small group of kayakers—the first we've seen—just heading out. Out of the mild wind, the sun and the warm rocks lure a few of us into a quick cat nap.

Thomas' weather radio promises more rain that evening, so we soon pack up and move on. Our destination is a tiny island on the far eastern side of the archipelago. It isn't until we come ashore for the night that I can see we've finally reached the edge. I clamber over the few rocks separating me from the Baltic and stand where the waves just lap onto the shore. Swans float on the calm water of a small cove behind me; ahead stretches nothing but open sea. An object bobbing against the rocks catches my eye: a clear plastic bottle, worn by the tides. The printing on it is still clear—it's Cryllic. But I find no message inside. We set up our tents in the shelter of a few hardy trees, but decide to have dinner on the rocks overlooking the cove. We manage to finish eating before the wind picks up again, presaging the coming storm. The chill chases us back to our camp under the pines, where we set up candles on a slab of granite and pour around the last of the wine. No fires are allowed on the ecologically fragile outer islands. Though the candles supply little warmth, they lend the scene a comforting glow. With the first raindrops, we crawl into our tents.

In the morning, I wake to shouting above the roar of wind and surf. I open the tent-flap an inch, but can't see anybody. I pull on my shoes and slicker, thinking something must have happened to the boats, and run down to the cove. Bengt and Thomas are there, covered head to toe in their rainsuits, pulling gear out of their kayaks and talking over the wind. Nothing appears to be wrong. "Is there a problem?" I say in English to Thomas. Bengt waves and smiles. Thomas just shrugs. I stare at the waves crashing against the rocks from out in the Baltic. Thomas says something in Swedish; I gesture that I don't understand. "The old sea," he says, enunciating carefully—a show of power left behind by the retreating storm.

We dawdle a bit over breakfast, giving ourselves a chance to dry out, and the old sea to dissipate. By the time we pack up and launch our boats, the storm itself has moved well on its way. But the old sea stays with us for much of the day. We make a detour to a nature preserve on the island of Bulleron, a short hop from where we spent the night. A small museum provided a history of some of the early settlers of the archipelago—fisherman and hardy farmers—as well as information about its natural features. Bulleron was at one time home to one of Sweden's most well-known artists, Bruno Lillefors, and some of his paintings of birds and other wildlife are on display. A photograph of the white-tailed eagle provides me with my only glimpse of this endangered bird.

As we head north again from Bulleron, the swells cause us to struggle against the sea as the waves push westward across our bows. Again, we try to stay in the lee of rocks and small islands, keeping out of open water as much as possible. Toward the inner islands, the evidence of the storm finally begins to wane. Just a few ripples disturb the surface of the cove where we stop for lunch and a chilly but refreshing swim to cap off our adventure. Thomas has saved the most traditionally Swedish meal for last: herring, herring, and more herring. The morning's paddling has made us hungry, and I dig in with the rest, gorging on pickled herring, herring in garlic sauce, mustard herring, Swedish crispbread, lingonberry jam, and a pale beer. We sprawl on a blue-checked cloth laid over the ever-present granite and let the sun warm us. In just a few hours, I'll be back in the urban bustle of Stockholm, but for now this shore-side picnic seems a perfect way to end my trip to a place where water dominates land.

Sea Kayaking Ireland

by Denise Dowling

Ever since my cousin raised eyebrows and tempers by eloping with a local fisherman during a semester abroad in County Clare, I've wanted to visit Ireland. Several of my relatives live there, and I recall their whiskey-stale breath whispering of the mystical land during a Christmas reunion. So when I finally get the chance to go sea kayaking for a week off Connemara coast in the midwest of Ireland, I barely blink before boarding a flight to Shannon. It's the first time I'll travel without instantly being identified as a foreigner, since I'm camouflaged by freckles, red-laced hair, and ruddy skin.

When I step outside the airport, a boy is muttering to his mother, "It was raining when I left Ireland and it's raining when I come back." I soon learn that Irish weather does vary. Some days it's misty, other times it rains, and on occasion it pours. But the rain is what has glazed the country green. As the bus rumbles into the countryside, I see how Ireland gave birth to a nation of poets. Black-faced sheep nurse grass fences by climbing blackberry bushes as thick clouds suddenly part, leaving valleys to bask in a halo of sun. Like the Inuit Eskimos with their 16 words for snow, the Irish have even more words for green. Lore claims at least 40 words to describe the various shades.

When we reach Killary, someone from the Adventure Center retrieves three of us from the bus to drive us to the Center. My tongue is rusty from not speaking, muted by the landscape and a dose of jet lag. I roll down the window to sniff for salt. The ocean stretches below, framed by marbled cliffs, child-like red and blue fishing boats straining at their lines. The rest of the group sits around a table at the Center, steam rising from mugs of Irish tea, the evidence of dinner on the table. The other six paddlers are British, except for one Irish woman. Our trip leader "Spike" is British, but settled in Ireland because of its slower pace of life. Everyone has done some paddling, either whitewater or flatwater or both. It's a nice group: it doesn't appear there will be any egos to throw overboard. Spike introduces us to the maps and tide charts we'll be using, and points out the islands we'll visit. He explains that we'll be ferrying to the island where the boats are after practicing rescues the next morning.

The next day we walk to the water and try on the boats. Fishermen in vessels like tugboats lift lines heavy with mussels, which have attached themselves to the ropes. We paddle and practice strokes in the harbor until Spike wants us to do rescues. I ask Spike if I really have to flip since I have no plans of capsizing during the trip since the water is so cold. Spike smiles and says nothing, which is a lot for him. Of course I made myself flip many times when I was learning to roll, but that moment when I'm just about to go under feels like the time we had to prick our own finger in the 7th grade science class to test our blood type—I wimped out and smeared a friend's blood on my slide. I can't cheat this time, so I decide to just get it over with. The Atlantic stings for a moment and then it fades. My partner and I successfully complete the mission, though I notice her looking around for someone else to call on if she *really* gets into trouble.

As we ride the ferry to Inishbofin, I recall the words of one whitewater paddler who declared, "Flatwater is for sissies." She must not have seen Ireland's version of flatwater. The Atlantic possessed an Irish temper that day, seething and spitting foamy swells. After we reach the boats, we paddle out and surf the waves, whooping like cowboys. A seal pokes its nose up, watching the crazy foreigners at the zoo. We head back to set up camp on the beach. I spy a pair of islanders and walk over to their trailer. The two ten-year-old boys are burning hay so that new grass can grow for sheep. They're trying to ignite it the traditional way, by hovering magnifying glasses over tissues. It's an ambitious endeavor, considering there's no sun. They fill me in on local lore while their father tinkers with

machinery. We discuss the merits of sharing one classroom with students of all ages and what they do for fun on this island of 250 people. They like to practice driving on the beach. There are no police to pull them over and demand to see a license, or at least a library card. The boys say crime is rare on Inishbofin, but if something is stolen, everyone knows a tourist did it. "There are a lot of losses, though," one boy says. "Ya' know, people falling overboard and disappearing. One man was eaten by eels!" As legend claims, the Irish may not be the world's biggest liars, but they are the best. The losses are enough excitement for the duo, who say they'd rather live on the island than the mainland because it's quieter. Americans tend to think the grass is always greener somewhere else, but the Irish think the green grass under their feet is verdant enough.

I wish the budding pyros luck and wander back to help with dinner. We cook pasta *Connemara,* spaghetti with a milk sauce instead of cream, and nibble fresh crab for an appetizer. We sit by the fire after dusk, breathing the smoky incense of peat, which islanders burn to keep warm. The only light is the yellow window of a house on the hill. Thirsty for some nightlife, several of us trek a dirt road blooming with rock roses to the local pub, where Spike passes around some tourist information about the island. "The monks dominated Inishbofin for centuries," the literature begins. "Crops were stored in the monastery for safekeeping and all grain was brought there to be ground. It was forbidden on pain of death for anyone else to own a grindstone, a custom that provoked resentment among locals, who hired assassins to kill six of the monks.

The blood of the murdered men is said to bubble out of the ground on the anniversary of the deed each year." With blood bubbling out of the soil and men being devoured by eels, perhaps life on Inishbofin isn't so sedate. Though I wonder if it's possible to date someone who doesn't share your last name.

I get an oblivious night's sleep when we return, sheltered from the wind inside my tent, and lulled by two pints of bitter. It's a good thing I've slept well, for I need my strength and wits the next morning to pack the kayak. How do you fit a tent, sleeping bag, clothing, cooking gear, camera, and food into two small holes without enlisting an engineer? Trial and error seems to work best, and each day we whittled time off the previous morning's packing record. The sea has slept off its rage and remains calm for the rest of the trip. We stop in the village for water and tour the remains of a Spanish fort occupied in the 16th century. The castle was used as fortified barracks during Cromwellian times, when it housed monks and priests. We're still able to discern a floor plan and argue about where the Irish noblewoman and her Spanish lover had their trysts.

We then paddle four miles to Inishark, an island last populated in the 1950s. The younger residents migrated off the island, leaving only elders who weren't strong enough to plow the fields and haul boats. The islanders still lived without electricity and running water in 1959 and they finally asked to be taken away. The headline of a newspaper account detailing their rescue shouts, "Get us off here!" A German family later bought property on Inishark and demanded that the sheep be removed and no visitors allowed. Neither request was well-received. The family came home one night and discovered that someone other than the Welcome Wagon had stopped by. With their house in shambles, they fled the island like their predecessors.

The island is a skeleton of stone cottages littered with sheep's bleached bones. I want to take one back with me as a Georgia O'Keeffe–esque addition to my apartment, but the kayak can't hold any souvenirs. We explore the cottages, unearthing symbols of ancient Christianity (figurines) and primitive footwear (cheap black shoes). Everyone is silent as we walk on a trail that winds through ribs of "lazy beds," the furrows that buried potatoes during the famine that killed more than one million Irish in the 1840s. Nearly all of the Irish Catholics refused to bow to the British and denounce their religion in exchange for food.

The path leads to cliffs sculpted by the sea. Spike wanders off alone, dreaming of the day he'll climb the stags, while a flock of seagulls chase each other in circles. It's like stumbling into a wilderness church, a scene that could make an atheist believe in God. Ireland's beauty is primordial and melancholy, a gorgeous child with haunting eyes. If the light is right, the sea can be a shade of indigo. But usually it is muddy blue, full of secrets. Ireland is beautiful the way a scar can be, a design that hints at a troubled past and the wisdom that follows.

Yeats characterized the inhabitants of Connemara as "passionate and simple," but that stereotype is not completely accurate. There is nothing simple or easy about their lives. The islanders know the raw drama of a life dependent on the land and the ocean. The fisherman fight 15-foot swells to pull nets from the belly of the sea. Long past dusk, men are still scything in the fields and unloading bales of hay from a ship. Each day I feel more awake, as if this were reality and I was sleepwalking in New York. When I've paddled five miles into a nine-mile stretch, it feels like paddling through porridge. But my muscles grow stronger with each stroke, while the rhythm induces a Zen-state.

When we reach Inishturk, it's the first day of a burning sun, though it hasn't really rained since we left. A couple of paddlers want to rinse off in the Atlantic. After a few days in a wetsuit without bathing, we've acquired a ripe aura that keeps even the sheep at bay. I decide to brave the 58-degree sea, and once the numbness kicks in, I'm feeling no pain. Spike returns from hiking to town with news that there's a food shortage on the island. I begin to fear another famine, but in Ireland there's one supermarket that's always stocked. The owner of the local pub hurries her husband out to fish the ocean so she can cook us fresh mackerel that night. While we eat, the family is crowded in the kitchen telling stories punctuated by laughter, their tongues loosened by sips of Scotch.

Turk is an island of 80 people. The mailboat arrives once a week, and there was one applicant for the island's only teaching post. If we had odds like that back in the States, even I might be able to get a real job. The next morning we paddle to Caher, an island formerly used by monks. The island is cloaked in heather and Celtic stone crosses from the seventh and eighth centuries that still stand, barnacled by moss. We explore a roofless church where a priest's stone offering bowl holds rusted 50-pence coins left on pilgrimages to

the island. It's the last island we'll visit, and that night we visit together until the fire is just embers, sipping tea and swapping stories.

The next day we paddle nine miles back to Killary, where there's a sauna for our salt-licked skin. The nine miles feel like four and I backpaddle when we near the harbor, aching for a hot shower but not wanting the journey to end. The return is complete with a sighting of a pair of porpoise diving and surfacing as if guiding us back. Two of us stop to talk with a fisherman who speaks with a thick Gaelic accent. My friend translates. The fisherman's boat is a *currach*, framed with wooden slats and covered in canvas, then coated in several layers of black tar. The Germans are starting to build fiberglass *currachs* in recognition of their sturdiness.

After dinner back at the Center, we sit around playing Pictionary and drinking beer, our sketches of animals looking more like roadkill with every sip. I break away from the group for a while to scribble in my journal, reflecting on the distance we've traveled. Friends in the States will ask if I saw Dublin, if I went to the shops painted like doll-houses, and visited the former home of James Joyce. "No," I will tell them, "we didn't see that Ireland." But I think we saw Ireland the way it's meant to be viewed; traveling in ancient-styled vessels, sleeping on the shores, and bathing in the sea.

When I return to New York, I hear that Guinness is sponsoring an essay contest and the prize is your own cottage in Ireland for ten years. I grab pencil and paper, dreaming of the day I can return to its savage shores. Maybe the company will even toss in a ten-year supply of its stout to fatten the deal.

Canoeing Alaska's Iniakuk

by Eugene Buchanan

"What's that?" asked our pilot, Gus, as we glided to a halt on Lake Ernie deep in the heart of Alaska's Brooks Range. "It looks like an eaten canoe." As the prop wound down until we could see its blades, the plane's floats carried us to shore, touching with a precision born from years of flying in the bush. Jumping to shore, I walked over to the object of Gus' attention. An old aluminum Grumman canoe, left the summer before, lay in scraps. Chris picked up a piece and examined it. "Yep . . . looks like a griz' got it," he said nonchalantly. "You can tell by the hair." I leaned closer and saw a matted wad of fur clinging to one of the rivets. "Welcome to the Brooks Range," I thought, "where bears dine on canoes." But what else did I expect when I signed on to paddle the Iniakuk, a river only two people had ever run?

Even with several seasons raft guiding in Alaska under my belt, the Brooks Range, named in 1925 after geologist Dr. Alfred Hulsz Brooks, had always been an elusive goal. The problem is accessibility. Running east-west for 700 miles at 70 degrees latitude, getting there requires two commercial flights from Anchorage just to reach the bush flight. The only firsthand information I could round up—apart from a "To-Bring" letter from Chris which listed such things as a headnet—came from climber Rod Hancock, owner of the Moose's Tooth pizza parlor in Anchorage. "It's pretty awesome," he said the night before I departed. "It's about as out there as you can get anymore." He then asked me the river's name, and his crunched eyebrows told me it wasn't run-of-the-mill. "It flows into the Malamute Fork and then into the Alatna," I said, repeating what little I knew. "Only two people have ever done it." That, of course, is exactly why Chris White, owner of Arctic Divide Expeditions, wanted me along.

Each flight got progressively bushier as I worked my way north. After taking a 737 to Anchorage, a 40-person jet whisked me to Fairbanks, where I transferred to an 8-person twin-prop that took me two hours north to Bettles. The flight soared over a sea of clouds broken by vast tracts of tundra stretching as far as the eye could see. Waking from a nap, I spotted an expanse of mountains as vast as the tundra: the Brooks Range, the largest dedicated wilderness area in the world.

Chris, 33, met the plane as it coasted to a halt on a gravel runway. His large, toothy grin told me instantly we would get along fine. A collared flannel shirt with missing buttons was tucked into white cotton pants showing stains from previous trips. A hole in the crotch indicated he spent a fair amount of time crouched around a fire, and wet legs caused the pants to sag around his waist. By the end of the trip he would remedy this by making a pair of suspenders out of a 12-foot NRS camstrap. By all accounts, he fit the part of a dyed-in-the-wool Alaskan guide, one more concerned with exploring new waterways than purchasing apparel from Patagonia. He looked like he must have when he first came to Alaska when he was 19, hoboing in on a train from Minneapolis to Wenatchee, WA, and then hitchhiking for two weeks north to Alaska. He has come up every summer since, 14 in all, and has been guiding in the Brooks for 11 years. During that time he has run 27 rivers in the Brooks, including five first descents.

Standing behind him were Dave and Nancy, whitewater kayakers from Pennsylvania celebrating their honeymoon, with Chris as a chaperone. After brief introductions, we went to the lodge where, over coffee, Chris outlined our tentative itinerary. "My specialty is running rivers no one else wants to do," he said matter-of-factly. "There are a lot of outfitters who guide the classics up here. I like doing the ones that are a pain in the ass to get to." After breakfast, Chris led me to the gates of the Arctic National Park ranger office, a mobile home serving as the communications headquarters for the park. On a one-inch-equals-25-miles map covering the

wall, he pointed out the Iniakuk, located along an index finger's length northwest of Bettles. It started in the park and flowed south until joining the Alatna and Koyakuk. I also saw countless other threads of blue cutting through tight topo lines. Some names, like the Nahtuk, Wolverine, Mettonpherg, Malamute, and Tinayguk reeked of Jack London. Others, like the Helpmejack, seemed less native. Still, the whole place evoked the Great North—from the river names to the giant caribou rack mounted on the wall— and I still had one more flight to go.

Of all the rivers Chris has run in the Brooks, the Iniakuk is his favorite. "It's so much different than all the other rivers here," he said as we walked to the hangar to sort gear. "A lot of others are just as beautiful, but they're not the same. On most of them swift current takes you through large, glaciated valleys. The Iniakuk is a lot more technical." Chris first noticed the Iniakuk when he was flying north to guide on the Noatak. After several trips he convinced his pilot to swing in for a closer look. What he saw wasn't encouraging. The river disappeared in places into a sheer-walled canyon no more than 12-feet wide. He then sought out information from a trapper who confirmed what he saw; the area was littered with impassable waterfalls. He kept digging, and next found a 1970s government document entitled "Exploration of the Iniakuk River Valley by Foot," which also spoke of great waterfalls and an inaccessible canyon. He then studied topo maps, finding the crux: a 4-mile canyon where the contour lines appeared solid. He also had to deal with the problem of access; the nearest lake a floatplane could land on was a three-mile bushwhack away. With all these strikes against him, he decided to give it a go anyway and recorded the first descent in 1996. A year later he took a sole client down. We were party number three.

After piling our gear into a beat-up Ford truck, we drove 100 yards to the Koyakuk River where Gus was waiting with Whiskey, his 1958 single-prop DeHavilland Beaver, by far the bushiest plane yet. As was the custom with 40-year-old bush planes, he let it warm up by idling upstream for 20 minutes before turning an abrupt 180, throwing the throttle down, and taking off for the Brooks. Twenty minutes of bog-covered tundra later, we soared up the Mettonpherg valley and entered the mountains. Far below, a lone moose strolled upstream on a cobblestone bank. Side creeks spilled out of nowhere and gray clouds highlighted varying shades of green. A few minutes later, a silver shine indicated the abandoned homestead of Ernie Johnson, a Swede who spent more than 40 years trapping and mining in the area during the early 1900s. Gus coaxed Whiskey into a turn and landed on Ernie's namesake lake, our floats sending ripples toward the rises of trout and grayling.

We unloaded our gear, including four Austrian-made Grabner inflatable canoes, and loaded the bear-eaten canoe in the plane. Waving Gus, and our only tie to civilization, good-bye, I scanned the terrain. Dense alders circled the lake, with high, tundra-clad mountains soaring overhead. Wolf prints and moose droppings lay a paddle-length from our gear. Shouldering our loads, we began the portage to an unnamed creek that would deliver us in a day and a half to the Iniakuk. It was an appropriate time for Chris to give us his bear talk.

They were all around, he said, and they were wild. "They're not like the ones you see in Denali and Katmai," he said, mopping sweat off his brow. "Here they're unpredictable . . . many of them have never seen humans."

To a degree, the bears' wildness played in our favor—they hadn't yet learned to associate people with food. On the downside, said Chris, they treat you as either a squirrel or a moose depending how you present yourself. As in bear country everywhere, your best bet is to talk gently, wave your arms, and slowly back away. If a bear charges, your last resort—save for Chris' 12-guage shotgun—is to curl up in a fetal position and cross your hands behind your head. "We'll definitely see some," continued Chris, "especially on the lower portion. Out of all the rivers I've done here, this one is by far the beariest." He then launched into a story about his first trip down the Iniakuk when he got charged twice. He had to hop out of his boat into thigh-deep water, tie the canoe to his leg and gain control of his nerves enough to raise his gun to his shoulder. "I just stood there shaking," he said. "I was as scared as I've ever been up here."

I stayed behind at the lake on the return portage to take advantage of the raindrop-like fish rises. I soon had a string of six grayling, but paid for it in lost blood. If the area's bears have never seen people before, neither have its mosquitoes. Their maliciousness, of course, is nothing new. When Sir John Franklin sailed across the Arctic Coast in 1826 and became the first white man to see the Brooks, he wrote: "We had the discomfort of being tormented the whole way by a myriad of mosquitoes." Lieutenant J.C. Cantwell, the first person to explore the Kobuk and Noatak rivers, didn't fare any better: "We would have called it Utopia," he wrote, "had not the mosquitoes nearly driven us wild." Then there's *Four Seasons North* author Billie Wright, who lived in the Brooks for 20 years and once killed 21 mosquitoes in one swat to her arm.

Chris wasn't as bothered by the mosquitoes as we were, and I felt a masochistic sense of glee when I finally saw him give in and swat a few. "You get used to them after a while," he said, swatting his head with a filet knife in hand. "Either that or they drive you crazy." Humans aren't the only ones they drive bonkers. Caribou can lose up to a pint of blood a day to mosquitoes. They also base their breeding patterns around them—and other predators—by migrating to the North Slope every summer to calve where it's open, cold, and breezy.

With drybags fastened in the bow and stern—and Chris' gun propped up within easy reach—we put in on the tiny, unnamed creek that would deliver us to the Iniakuk. It didn't take long to feel inept. Chris, well-versed in low-water rock-dodging, quickly pulled ahead while the rest of us lumbered behind. Float a few feet, get hung up like the Exxon Valdez, get out and pull the canoe through the water—all while playing host to the local mosquito population which seemed to wait until we got stuck before making a move.

A light drizzle fell and we pulled the boats high up a rock ledge to camp. The creek would rise quickly if it kept up; everything two to three feet down is either rock or permafrost, leaving no room for absorption. In a way I hoped the rain continued, as higher water would make the next day's paddle easier.

For now, however, I was content to set up a tarp, swat mosquitoes, and cook my catch over a fire. Campfire talk turned to canoes being the vehicle of choice in the Brooks. "People who run rivers here are in it for the wilderness," said Chris, poking the embers. "It's a canoe thing. People don't come up here to play in rapids, they come for the tranquility." Getting boats into the area, however, is a tough hurdle. Park law prohibits using helicopters in the wilderness, meaning access is restricted to where planes can land—on either large bodies of water or gravel bars. And planes have a hard time carrying boats that don't break down; on trips like the Noatak, outfitters leave their canoes at the river year-round. For the rivers Chris likes to run, inflatables are indispensable. They can fit inside floatplanes, withstand the bumps of whitewater, and carry gear for a two-week trip. When we thought we were tired, we crawled into our tents—even though darkness wasn't there to remind us how tired we really were. At midnight, the sky looked as if it could have been noon.

It didn't take long to start cursing again the next day, both because of the mosquitoes and round two of pinball-your-way-down-a-creek. Once again, we lapsed into a familiar routine: paddle a few strokes, swat mosquitoes, get out and push. But it beat bushwhacking through the alders, our only alternative. Eventually we made it to the confluence, where a large snowfield separated the Iniakuk from the creek. We were thankful for the extra water, as it made maneuvering easier and allowed time to take in the grandeur of the broad, glaciated valley; upstream rose layers of mountains and untamed wilderness.

Mild Class II–III soon delivered us to the gorge. Eddying out on river left, we tied up our boats and climbed a ramp leading to the top of the chasm. The spongy slope was littered with fresh scat and bear-hiding alders, as well as a forest of stunted spruce trying to survive in the harsh environment. By counting rings, environmentalist Bob Marshall, deemed the father of the Arctic conservation movement, once found a three-inch diameter spruce to be 346 years old. In his field journals, he also noted 20-year-old saplings barely more than a foot tall. We, of course, had our own survival to think about. Bear signs were all around, and our only way out was the river far below. The top part of the gorge was runnable, but the river ended at a colander of rocks forming a mandatory portage.

We ran one by one to the brink of the portage where we began lining our boats through the sieve. On his first trip, it took Chris a couple of days to get through the gorge. Although the rapid had changed somewhat, this time it was easier. "This is why I love it up here," said Chris as we scrambled along the dark basalt cliffs, lining and carrying the boats. "None of the other rivers up here let you do this kind of thing." When we couldn't line any more, we pushed the boats overhead through a triangle-shaped opening and dropped them to a pool far below. Another rainstorm kicked in as soon as we began paddling, but we were too protected by the chasm's sheer walls to pay it much mind. While everyone else continued downstream to camp, I stayed behind to pull dinner out of the gorge's deep green waters. "If you catch anything, make sure to string it in the water," Chris advised as they paddled

away. "We don't want any bears ripping up our boats out here."

I paddled upstream to where a Class III drop emptied into a pool and turned my boat sideways until the bow and stern wedged on the gorge's walls, holding me in place against the current. Sitting alone in the bowels of the Brooks, casting to fish that had never seen lures, I became entranced with a surreal sense of aloneness. Only two other people had ever been here. That, of course, helped explain why I caught an 18-inch grayling on my first cast. Against Chris' wishes, it flopped, bleeding, in the boat longer than it should have, and I washed the bear-attracting blood off my gear as best I could. When my spell ended, I had a string of six, which I tied to the boat and threw over the side.

Paddling to camp, I felt like Ernie the Bachelor surviving alone in the wilderness. Only I wasn't quite as confident. Chris said camp would probably be in another 20 minutes, and after a half-hour of solo paddling, self-doubt crept in. Had I somehow missed them and floated by? Chris had the tent, but at least I had matches and a string of grayling. Like Ernie, I could survive. Just as my second-guessings began to control my thoughts, I picked up the scent of a campfire wafting upstream. Before I had time to give it much thought, I rounded a corner and saw camp on a large cobblestone beach. The area's wildness was evident immediately: at one end of a small sandbar were fresh grizzly tracks; in the middle were wolf tracks; and on the other end were tracks from a bull caribou who opted not to follow his herd north. High overhead the drone of a bushplane broke the silence. It was probably headed to the Noatak, said

Chris, dropping off people or provisions. In earlier times, the only way natives could get outside provisions was by trading. And canoes played an important role. Eskimos would canoe down the Noatak to trade at its mouth with Indians who paddled down the Kobuk.

Morning dawned gray and raining, with a thick fog engulfing distant peaks. Today was a layover, which meant gearing up for a major hike. When I saw Chris putting on bug dope, I realized I had better do the same. After bear-proofing camp, we ferried across the river and took part in the Alaskan sport of alder-bashing, picking our way through a tangled web of ankle-grabbing undergrowth. At the top of a ridge, we rested in a cool breeze and looked downstream at the start of the second gorge. Next to my water bottle was a wolf print the size of my hand.

We gained a peak, most likely never climbed before, and dropped over the other side to a creek that led us to an unnamed tributary we passed the day before. It didn't take long to spot our first bear, a grizzly sauntering down a hill and intersecting our path at the creek. We waited as he stood up, caught a whiff, and continued down to the creek and up the other side. We waited another 20 minutes before moving. Our bear encounters weren't over. At the unnamed tributary the creek fed into, two more bears, a sow, and two-year-old cub surprised us by flouncing out of the bush. This one was a close call. While the sow seemed content to let us be— pacing nervously back and forth less than 20 yards away—the cub was curious and made several false charges. The mother's instincts warned her to leave well enough alone, but not the cub's.

"You go your way and we'll go ours," said Chris, as we backed up and waved our arms. Chris was calm, but rattled. It was a tough situation. If the cub charged, the sow would follow, and one of them likely would get us. Chris raised the gun to his shoulder as the cub made another fake charge. The gun's first round contained buckshot, whose wider pattern helps ensure a hit. The next three rounds were slugs. He used to carry all slugs, but another guide convinced him to first go with buckshot. Not that Chris wanted to shoot. It would seem a sacrilege to kill such a majestic animal in such a pristine setting. Park rules also mandate that you're supposed to carry out the head, hide, and claws if you do, and none of us relished the idea of canoeing six days with the remains.

Luckily, the sow convinced her cub to move on. With hearts pounding we did the same. As we continued down the tributary's cobblestone banks, Chris said he has only had two other close bear encounters in 11 years of guiding. Both were on the Iniakuk. "This is the richest bear valley in the Brooks I've seen," he said. "And we haven't even gotten to the beary part of the river yet." He then explained the pros and cons of carrying guns. "Bears can sense your attitude," he added. "They're complicated creatures. Even if you never use it—which hopefully you won't have to— a gun gives you that much more confidence, which bears can sense." He related a story of a 20-year Brooks guide who had achieved that same sense of confidence without having to carry a gun. It's a tough bluff to carry through. "I believe him," said Chris, "but I don't think I could do it—not with the experiences I've had."

Before reaching the Iniakuk, we traversed around a narrow Class V gorge that would have been a whitewater kayaker's dream. Although I ran the drops in my mind, it didn't seem right to risk one's life for recreation in an area where everything else, from spruce to grizzlies, struggles to survive. This survival instinct showed itself at the top of the gorge where a lone pile of scat rested inches away from the cliff. "Wolf," said Chris. "They hang out at the tops of cliffs to scout for prey."

We shoved off early the next morning and soon approached the second gorge, where once again the water was walled in by tight, curving cliffs. This time the paddling was Class III and everyone's runs, as if we had taken survival lessons from the flora and fauna, were flawless. At the bottom, the ravine dumped into an emerald-green pool where a quick cast brought in the first grayling of the day. Whereas yesterday's wilderness experience brought bears, today's took on a different tone. At the next deep pool, Chris landed a 28-inch lake trout that had worked its way upstream during a recent flood. Farther on, Nancy found a huge caribou rack, the result of a wolf kill. After holding it over our heads and posing for photos, we tied it to her bow and continued downstream. At camp, we cut open the trout's stomach and found a small grayling and half-decomposed mouse—complete with tail, head and appendages—encased in a black paté of mosquito corpses. Despite their annoyances, it was obvious mosquitoes fill an important role and that the food chain might collapse without them. "Yeah it might," said Chris, waving the filet knife dangerously close to his head to

ward them off, "but I'd be willing to find out."

I tried to get my directional bearings after dinner and failed miserably. At 8:30 p.m., I stared north straight into the sun, disorienting any sense of direction I might have had. In mid-July, the sun doesn't set; it traverses behind jagged ridges, casting peaks on the opposite side of the valley in alternating bands of light. A mountain might be shaded one moment, banded with light another, and banded in a different place an hour later. When the moon appeared, we tried to figure its path by using rocks as props from the heavens. Soon we were so discombobulated thinking about rotations, latitudes, orbits, and axes that sleep came easily.

We laid over again the next day for another hike, this time up a grotto-filled creek to the top of another unnamed peak that had also likely never been climbed. Coming from Colorado, the thought of scaling two unclimbed peaks was as hard for us to digest as an aluminum canoe was for a bear. In the distance we could make out the Arrigetch, a string of towering granite walls dubbed the Patagonia of the North for its 20-pitch, weather-prone climbs. Far below ran the Iniakuk. Anywhere else in the world, this river would be reason enough for traveling halfway around the globe. Here it is one of hundreds, most of which are unnamed. Glancing from the peaks and rivers to the map, I saw that the entire quadrangle had only one named feature: the Iniakuk, way down in the bottom right.

The pitter-patter of rain matched the pitter-patter of my heart the next morning. Today was bear day, and we would travel 15 miles through the meandering section of alder-lined rivers where Chris was charged twice. After yesterday's hike, it was nice to get back on the river and let the scenery pass us by, but I harbored a growing apprehension about the "beary" part of the trip. I slept uneasily the night before, as if I were facing a day of Class V. On his first trip, after getting charged twice, Chris spent two hours paddling through willow-lined narrows, singing at the top of his lungs. Then, instead of continuing down to the Alatna, he hiked through the willows to a lake where a pilot could pick him up. When he arrived, he stumbled upon the half-buried carcass of a caribou, meaning the bear was still nearby. He quickly pumped up his boat and paddled to the other side of the lake. "That was pretty spooky," he said. "I didn't sleep all night." I was spooked as well, and made plenty of noise as we paddled around blind corners. Our singing must have worked; when we got to bear corner, all we saw were tracks paralleling shore in dark glacial silt. I laid my baseball cap next to one and saw that it easily extended beyond the brim. An afternoon thunderstorm struck just in time to hatch the next batch of mosquitoes before it headed north to the Arrigetch, whose spires were now visible up a broad valley. While Chris made a goal to go a whole day without bug dope, I applied it like aftershave. We saw several beaches suitable for camping, but discarded them—bear tracks covered them from river to bush.

The next day the Malamute Fork delivered us to the Alatna, and the emerald water of the Iniakuk was replaced by muddy brown. I caught a large northern pike on the way to camp—by now we had given up trying

to find a camp without prints—where we de-rigged the boats for the next day's airplane pickup. The fish was a blessing, since it allowed us to conserve dwindling rations. Twenty-seven groups were once stranded for four days on the Noatak because of weather, Chris said, and he once had to wait six days for a plane. In 1994, a group was stranded without food for seven days—they made do by paddling out and killing a caribou they found swimming across the river.

That night, a Swiss woman paddled up to camp in a breakdown canoe. It was our first human contact in eight days. We offered her some tea and learned she had been out in the bush for two weeks. More pressing to her, however, was relating the previous day's bear encounter. At the confluence of the Alatna and the Malamute Fork, which we had passed a few hours earlier, a bear charged and swam after her. Armed only with pepper spray, she escaped by paddling away as fast as she could.

A light rain fell, and once our chores were complete we sat under a tarp and warmed ourselves by the fire. Chris already had his eyes set on another first descent the following summer: the Upper Kobuk, requiring a five-day hike over the Arrigetch and a parachute drop from a bushplane to deliver boats. And he is not worried about anyone else beating him to the punch. "No one else up here is pursuing first descents," he said, blowing steam off his tea. "If there were I'd know about it because they would have to pass through Bettles."

The next day, thick fog blanketed the river and we huddled under the tarp for eight hours until Whiskey's drone pierced the silence. Craning my neck on the flight back, I looked out to the

Iniakuk Valley, still shrouded in clouds. Somewhere beneath lay the gorges, mountains, bears, fish, and campsites we had called home. Somewhere below was the wilderness that keeps Chris coming back year after year.

PROFILES

Paddlers of the Century

by Eugene Buchanan and Tom Bie

As we celebrate the end of a spectacular century of paddling, certain individuals stand out from the crowd. Some are well known as visionaries, innovators, Olympic athletes, or legendary explorers, while others have gone quietly about the business of paddling for its own sake, logging thousands of miles for nothing more than the experience itself and some entries in an obscure river journal. Many of you will have heard of these people. One of them may have discovered your favorite river or designed the boat you're sitting in. One of them may have taught you to roll. Some you've likely never heard of at all. But this group shares something in common, something more important than fame: a love of paddling and water, with a lifetime spent discovering both.

Did we miss anyone? Perhaps. And we're sure you'll let us know who it was. But like the rivers themselves, this list will always be changing; growing and evolving and shifting shapes like so many sandy beaches. What we share here is a sampling of those who've made a difference, 100 paddlers from the United States alone, whose head, heart, and bow were always pointed the right direction and who, without even knowing it, took us along for the ride. The heroes of the next century are already being created. Here's to those who paved the way.

Richard Bangs

The Awash, Omo, Baro, Blue Nile, Euphrates, Indus, Bio Bio, Zambezi, Yangtze, Tatshenshini. The list goes on and on. Perhaps no other paddler has more big name first descents throughout the world than Sobek founder Richard Bangs. Where Powell, Holmstrom, and other pioneers are known for one or two first descents, Bangs has more than 40, in lands as exotic as Ethiopia, New Guinea, and Tasmania. And he's managed to make a career of it. Bangs grew up in Bethesda, MD, taking canoe trips down the Potomac before guiding on the Grand. The international bug bit in 1973 when he went to Ethiopia to notch a first descent of the

Awash, a trip that inspired him to co-found Sobek Expeditions. As prolific a writer as he is a paddler, Bangs has authored several books, including *Riding the Dragon's Back,* an account of the race to run China's Yangtze. But perhaps no river trip meant as much to him as his 1996 journey down Ethiopia's Tekeze, documented in his most recent book, *The Lost River.* "That trip really closed a loop for me," says Bangs, of finally paddling the river that eluded him in the '70s. "It was very emotional to return after 23 years."

Gordon Black

It seems like Gordon Black has been teaching paddling in canoes and kayaks since the invention of water. Long-time head of instruction at Nantahala Outdoor Center, Black serves on the American Canoe Association's Instruction Council and Board of Directors. Anyone who has ever worked with him has fond memories of his sense of humor, sparse but clean verbalizations, and quick competence. A feared competitor in slalom and down-river, Black, while maintaining his position as one of the most effective instructors on the planet, is also mastering the mysteries of the ten-inch chef's knife, fast becoming one of paddlesport's greatest gourmets.

Walt Blackadar

Until Walt Blackadar, the public's perception of kayaking was the exciting but genteel sport of slalom. Blackadar was anything but genteel. In 1971, at the age of 49, he made an astonishing solo journey down Turnback Canyon on Alaska's Alsek River, a feat often compared to the first ascent of Everest. When his Alsek story appeared in *Sports Illustrated,* it caused a stir that grew to a clamor. Over the next several years, the flamboyant doctor took on North America's biggest whitewater, seen by millions on ABC's American Sportsman and even in a feature length movie. Old films of Blackadar battling the mammoth waves towering and crashing over his fragile fiberglass kayak still take one's breath away. Blackadar died in 1978 on the South Fork of the Payette River in Idaho.

David Brower

"I never ran a boat," says David Brower. " I was always a passenger." But most rafting passengers don't change the course of river conservation, as Brower did in 1953. At the time, the Bureau of Reclamation was threatening to build two dams on the Green River in Dinosaur National Monument. As executive director of the Sierra Club, Brower mounted a fierce campaign, using rafting trips, films, magazine articles, and a book *(This is Dinosaur)* that he sent to every member of Congress. In 1956, Congress voted the dams down. In 1967, Brower used the same strategy to help prevent the damming of the Colorado in the Grand Canyon. He's also helped defeat dams in Alaska and Quebec and at age 87 he remains a passionate champion of free-flowing water.

Jim Cassady

Though well known as the author of several popular river guidebooks, including *California Whitewater, Western Whitewater,* and, most recently, *World Whitewater,* Cassady's biggest contribution to paddling may have come in 1983, when he invented the self-bailing raft for SOTAR. These rafts changed the sport, opening up new possibilities for legions of river runners. One of few river rats to progress from kayaking to rafting, Cassady started taking rafts to "kayak only" northern California rivers in the late '70s. In 1980, he went to work for outfitter Bill McGinnis and found himself testing many California rivers for commercial viability. "I had every river runner's dream job," Cassady says. "I was put in charge of river exploration and got paid to do it."

Marge Cline

Known as every paddler's River Mom, Marge Cline started paddling in 1949 in a dugout canoe and has been teaching kayaking and canoeing ever since. Cline has started tens of thousands of paddlers on their way to a lifetime of fun through a program offered by the Chicago Whitewater Association and still finds time to organize "Paddle in the Park" in suburban Chicago, judge film festivals, and teach throughout the country. Cline's love of paddling was illustrated this spring when, after suffering chest pains, and driving herself to the hospital where she underwent angioplastic surgery, she rested a day and was paddling the next afternoon.

Harold Deal

If an award was ever given for unsung paddling heros, it could well go to the modest Harold Deal, 51, of Riverton, PA. An 18-time Open Canoe National Champion, Deal is largely credited with inventing "freestyle" canoeing, where participants paddle choreographed routines to music. The discipline named a stroke after him, the Hiding Harold. He is also an accomplished designer, inventing such canoes as the Crossfire (before Dagger used the name for a kayak), and the Dragonfly and Shaman. He also designed a race paddle for Sawyer Paddles and Oars. Instruction takes up a good chunk of his resume, with many of his techniques employed by such canoe icons as Tom Foster and Bob Foote. In a canoeing instructional video, producer Kent Ford even thanks Deal for his contributions with an end credit. "He's very unassuming," says friend John Rako. "Most people don't even know about him."

Frank Dodge

Frank Dodge was a boatman for the U.S. Geological Surveys in Utah and Arizona the 1930s and later worked as a freelance boatman for just about everyone doing work in the area. He had a reputation as a very salty character, as evidenced by a letter of apology he wrote to Norm Nevills in the late '30s. Nevills had come to visit Dodge at Lee's Ferry: "Sorry I set the dogs on you when you stopped by, Norm, but I was drinking homemade fig wine and that always makes me mean."

John Dowd

John Dowd had already earned himself a reputation as an extraordinary paddler before founding *Sea Kayaker* magazine in 1984. He paddled from Singapore to Java in 1970, hit 1,100 miles of South American coastline for *National Geographic* in 1973, and paddled across the Caribbean twice, most recently in 1977 when he led a group of four on a 2,000-mile trip from Venezuela to Florida. "That was quite an epic," he says. "It was very physically demanding, with lots of close calls." A former instructor for Outward Bound, Dowd also founded the Trade Association of Sea Kayaking and once worked as a commercial scuba diver for oil rigs in the North Sea.

Ann Dwyer

As she celebrates the tenth anniversary of Kiwi Kayaks, company founder Ann Dwyer must be rather flattered. "At first people just thought my boats were little toys, not real kayaks," she says. "But many competitors have since copied the design so I must have been on to something." Dwyer, now 74, has always prided herself in being an innovator. She is generally credited with conceiving the idea of short, semi-decked, open-cockpit kayaks—an industry that has grown to over 350,000 users. "My boats are so user-friendly," she says. "They allow you to begin at kindergarten and continue through grad school."

Jib Ellison

The concept of rafting with Russians seemed a pretty outrageous idea in 1987, a time when relations between the two nations weren't exactly chummy. But Jib Ellison had a vision, one that placed Americans and Russians together in boats at Siberia's Chuya Raft Rally in an attempt to work toward peace. "It was the little piece I could contribute to prevent the holocaust," says Ellison of founding Project RAFT (Russians and Americans for Teamwork). Taking place at a different country every two years (including Russia, Costa Rica, the U.S., and Turkey), the project soon grew to bridge barriers between other nations as well, with more than 700 paddlers participating from countries all over the world. As well as fostering environmental awareness, participants notched more than ten first descents in the culture-sharing process.

Bill Endicott

As coach of the U.S. slalom team from 1977–92, Bethesda, MD's Bill Endicott, 54, has had more influence on the U.S. slalom scene than any other person in the world. A successful competitor in his own right, with C-2 appearances in the 1971 and '73 World Championships and a ninth-place showing in the '71 C-2 Wildwater Championships, it is his coaching that remains his legacy. In his 15 years at the helm of the U.S. Canoe & Kayak Team, Endicott coached athletes who won 57 medals in World Cup, World Championship, and Olympic competitions, 27 of them gold. Never one to steal the limelight, he naturally downplays his contributions: "We just started getting athletes who started at a really young age and who could train year-round," he says.

Cully Erdman

While founding Slickrock Adventures in 1977, Moab, Utah's Cully Erdman, 48, was also busy opening up Mexico to paddling by exploring and kayaking more than a dozen runs throughout the country, including the postcard-perfect Agua Azul and Jatate. A veteran river explorer who has participated in films for National Geographic Explorer and American Sportsman, one of Erdman's crowning moments came in 1979 with a first descent of Nepal's Arun River, again for American Sportsman. "Although the sport's changed entirely, there are still people doing exploratory river runs," he says. "That's my favorite part of the sport."

Bob Foote

Most paddlers met Bob Foote in 1981 when he became one of the first people to run the Grand Canyon in an open canoe. His articles on rolling and other paddling techniques also helped him earn a name in the sport, as did his design skills (the Dagger Genesis and two Loon models from Navaro Canoe Company are his creations). He's designed whitewater and flatwater canoes, paddles, and accessories, and continues to teach, write, and lead Central and South American adventures while maintaining his position as one of the world's premier paddlers. His videos, including *Open Canoeing the Grand Canyon,* are legendary among the big water canoe crowd.

Kent Ford

Kent Ford's paddling career began from his home in Washington, D.C., as a C-1 Slalom racer. He won his first National Championship title and placed seventh in his first World Championships in 1977. For the next ten years he would call Bryson City, NC, home, allowing him to compete while working as Head of Instruction at the Nantahala Outdoor Center. It was this transition from competitor to instructor that solidified Ford's place in the history of paddlesports. Ford's company, Durango, CO–based Performance Video, is now one of the world's top producers of instructional books and videos. "I've been able to gather expertise from across the industry," he says, "looking for the positives in different people's viewpoints."

Tom Foster

Tom Foster, a former outdoor recreation instructor at Greenfield College, left academia to found a technical paddling school called the Outdoor Center of New England. Long-time chair of the American Canoe Association's National Instruction Committee, Foster developed the theory-based presentation of paddling, with an emphasis on biomechanics that helped reshape modern paddling. Foster's insistence on high standards with in-service training honed instructor corps throughout the country. Co-author of *Catch Every Eddy, Surf Every Wave,* Foster designs OC1s and leads whitewater trips in Costa Rica.

Ralph Frese

A blacksmith who loves paddling, Ralph Frese operates a smithy and a specialty canoe shop in Chicago, just a few hundred yards from where Joliet must have passed on his way down the Mississippi in 1673. Frese also manufactures composite re-creations of Voyageur canoes and has designed a series of modern tripping canoes. He is a serious historian of his sport, with 4,000 book titles and a collection of over 100 canoes. His ambition is to live long enough to read all his books. Frese says he will donate his accumulations to the Chicago Maritime Museum to initiate a national canoe and kayak collection. Frese ushered in the new canoeing millennium leading a New Year's Day paddle on the upper Chicago River.

Nathaniel Galloway

Next time you row backwards and ferry upstream above a big rapid, you can thank Nathaniel Galloway. It was Galloway who first applied the principle of facing the danger, and he was the first to run rapids confidently instead of paddling them with fear. Contrary to the accepted practice of the time, he faced his boat downstream, using his oars to position himself for the best run. Galloway also designed his own boats—light skiffs about 14 feet long, flat-bottomed, with a pronounced curve fore and aft. The Galloway boat became the standard river craft until the advent of inflatable rafts at the end of World War II. A friend once remarked that all Galloway needed to successfully run a boat was "a heavy dew."

Stewart Gardiner

On Oct. 23, 1938, Stewart Gardiner took a folding kayak bought from a catalog and put in at Hideout Flat on the Green River. He had no problems with Ashley Falls, but just below Red Creek Rapid he lost his spare paddle, which would come back to haunt him. In Whirlpool Canyon, Gardiner capsized on a sleeper rock, lost his paddle, and came close to drowning when he discovered that his lifejacket was defective and wouldn't keep him afloat. He carved a new paddle out of driftwood and made his way out of the canyons without further trouble. The next year, Gardiner made a folding boat trip down the Middle Fork of the Salmon.

Ed Gillet

Long-distance sea kayaker Ed Gillet has no concept of starting slow. "The first time I paddled a kayak I went 600 miles from San Felipe to La Paz," he says. A year later Gillet paddled solo from Glacier Bay, Alaska to Seattle, Washington following that jaunt with a tour from San Diego to Cabo San Lucas and that one with a 4,500-mile journey along the South American coastline. An experienced sailor, Gillet credits his knowledge of open-water navigation skills for helping him complete a 1987 63-day journey from Monterey, CA, to Hawaii, during which he ran out of food and subsisted on toothpaste. Why the long trips? "I was never trying to make a mark," Gillet says from his San Diego home. "I just have a high tolerance for boredom and suffering."

Alexander "Zee" Grant

In 1941, Alexander "Zee" Grant, joined Norm Nevills' expedition and became the first person to paddle a kayak through the Grand Canyon. Grant's Escalante boat was a larger version of the standard folding kayak available at the time. For flotation, he stuffed the inside of the kayak with brightly colored beachballs. Grant miscalculated in Badger, the first major rapid in the Grand Canyon, and was thrown from his kayak. But he caught up, climbed aboard, and paddled through the tailwaves sitting backwards on top of the overturned boat. Grant later went on to help found the American Whitewater Affiliation and run early descents on many other American rivers.

Sheri Griffith

During high school in the late '60s, Sheri Griffith and her brother started a rafting business in Steamboat Springs, CO, exploring such now-famous waterways as Gore Canyon and the Arkansas. In 1971, she moved to Moab, Utah, and founded Sheri Griffith River Expeditions, where she has spent the past 29 years. "The one-day trips weren't doing it for me," Griffith says. "I wanted to make a difference in the world—to take people out and enhance their lives." In the mid '80s Griffith was elected the first woman president of the Western River Guides Association, where she helped create America Outdoors, giving the guiding community from East and West a common voice in Washington.

Bus, Ted, & Don Hatch

Bus Hatch and Frank Swain, cousins in Vernal, Utah, got the idea of running rivers from the great river runner Nathaniel Galloway's son Parley, whom the sheriff had locked in the county jail. Swain sprung Galloway from jail to take them river running, only to have him skip town. No matter. Hatch and Swain built boats anyway and, with brothers Ted and Don as well as other family members and friends, learned to run rivers throughout the West. When the Sierra Club went looking for someone to take groups through dam-endangered Echo Park in the 1950s, they found Bus Hatch. The resulting trips formed the basis of Hatch River Expeditions and fueled the country's fledgling river rafting business.

Dave & Judy Harrison

As founders of *Canoe and Kayak* magazine, Dave and Judy Harrison had the vision for an industry publication before there was even an industry. Both had years of paddling experience before buying *Canoe* in 1973 and moving from Boston to Seattle to follow their dreams. In addition to publishing the oldest magazine in the business before selling it in 1998, the Harrisons gave graciously of their time and knowledge to help the industry grow as a whole. They were involved in numerous projects and influenced almost every aspect of paddlesports, from conservation efforts to promotional projects, in order to help the sport grow into what it has become today.

Bart Hauthaway

Bart Hauthaway was a world-class slalom competitor in the '60s and such a student of the sport he later became the U.S. Olympic Coach in the same event. He won several national championships in canoe sailing, and convinced Old Town Canoe to manufacture variations of the Adirondack pack canoe he developed. Short, open-topped, and paddled with a double paddle, Hauthaway's pack canoes started the movement towards the open-cockpit recreational kayaks growing in today's industry.

Jim Henry

Jim Henry's Mad River Malecite won prizes as an art object. Thirty years later, as part of Confluence's Mad River Canoe line, it's on everyone's list of top ten canoes of all time. Henry won races, took trips to far northern rivers, wrote about them, and took compelling photographs. He designed and molded the first Royalex touring canoes and was the first laminator to use Kevlar. Racer, tripper, designer, photographer, and engineer, Henry started Mad River Canoe in a garage in '72 and was the country's second largest canoe builder within a decade.

Bill Hoffman & John Achilich

Bill Hoffman, on vacation from building fighter aircraft during World War II, took a canoe trip in the Adirondacks in the summer of 1944. Finding wood and canvas canoes fragile and heavy, and knowing how to stretch form shapes into aluminum, he founded Grumman Canoe. Designed by engineer John Achilich, Grumman placed six models into production by the end of the war. Two mergers and 600,000 canoes later, employee-owned Marathon Canoes is still the staple of the outfitting trade. Hoffman and Achilich influenced canoeing in the last half of the 20th century like few others by introducing light, rugged boats at an easily affordable price.

Lars Holbek

With as many as 70 first descents in the Sierras, Chile, British Columbia, Mexico and Costa Rica, California's Lars Holbek, 41, has pioneered more waterways than perhaps any other kayaker.

Starting his exploits in 1978 with Richard Montgomery and Chuck Stanley, and continuing full swing until 1986, he has paddled enough new rivers to write a book, which he has with the third edition of *Whitewater Guide to California* and a recent guidebook on Chile. And he is still at it. This year alone he notched two more first descents within two hours of his home in Coloma, CA "I've dabbled in the sport's other disciplines," he says, "but the first-descent, cutting-edge scene is what I like most."

Buzz Holmstrom

In November of 1937, Buzz Holmstrom, an unknown service station attendant from the tiny logging town of Coquille, OR, made headlines across the country by navigating over a thousand miles of the rapid-strewn Green and Colorado Rivers in a boat he designed and built himself. He spent the previous three years designing and building whitewater boats in which he soloed the Rogue and Salmon rivers. How he came to have the boatbuilding or river-running skills, or even the desire to do such things, remains unclear. His unexplainable death at 37 intensifies his mystery.

Skip Horner

After a few seasons in the Grand Canyon in the early '70s, Skip Horner set out to see the world's rivers and mountains. He joined Sobek for the first complete descent of the Bio Bio in 1979, and followed that with first descents of the Zambezi, Coruh, Yangtze, Yarkand, and Gilgit-Indus, plus others in New Guinea, Madagascar, Nepal, India, and elsewhere. "Rich Bangs and John Yost always inspired me with their energy and creativity," Horner says, "but they always left the serious rowing to us." When Horner moved on to mountaineering, he became the first person to guide the "Seven Summits"—the highest peak on each continent.

Cliff Jacobson

With 16 books in print and hundreds of articles, Cliff Jacobson is the most published paddling author of the twentieth century. He is also an accomplished wilderness canoe guide, leading trips to northern rivers for the Science Museum of Minnesota. Jacobson's interest and persistence were major factors in the re-development of the solo open canoe. Jacobson teaches environmental science to middle school students and has developed programs on water quality, wilderness meals, and wilderness

experience for challenged youth. All are used in middle schools nationally. A popular speaker at paddling events around the world, Jacobson puts on stellar shows while gently promoting "Leave No Trace" camping.

Gene Jensen

Gene Jensen is largely responsible for a revolution in the way recreational canoes are designed. What Jensen did was take the skills he'd learned designing marathon racers and apply them to the average family touring canoe, making paddling easier for everyone. "Nobody wants to take two strokes to go someplace they can go in one," he says. "Experimentation is the key when it comes to design. You have to keep an open mind." Jensen not only brought a new sophistication to recreational canoes, he's also the inventor of the bent-shaft paddle.

Bunny Johns

Long-time competitor Bunny Johns has won her share of medals and races over the years, including the 1981 mixed doubles competition at the Wildwater World Championships with partner Mike Hipshire. But she still feels her strongest asset is teaching. "It was a career highlight for me when I became good enough to teach and it is still a thrill for me to help others achieve their paddling goals," she says. As a long-time leader and current president of North Carolina's Nantahala Outdoor Center, Johns has had a strong influence on thousands of paddlers and was one of the lead consultants for the '96 Olympics on the Ocoee.

Tom Johnson

The year was 1938—Orson Wells was scaring the country with his martian invasion radio dramatization and Tom Johnson was building canoes. Johnson went on to make the first fiberglass canoe in 1942, and design the first roto-molded plastic kayak—the "River Chaser"—for Hollowform in 1974. The next year he started whitewater racing and went on to win national champi-onships in K-1, OC-2, and C-2 Masters slalom. Despite his success as a designer and racer, Johnson lists his coaching accomplishments as some of his greatest achievements. Now 81, Johnson still paddles and instructs on a regular basis. "Had a lesson this morning," he said in October. "It was great being out there."

John Kazimierczyk

Called the "Jon Lugbill" of open canoeing, John "Kaz" Kazimierczyk came on the open canoe slalom racing scene in 1981. By 1989, he was Open Canoe National Champion and other than 1991 (when it went to friendly rival Kent Ford), he has dominated the event, winning it ten times. In addition to slalom, he is a three-time Downriver National Champion and has won a whopping 68 national titles. Now living in Weare, NH with his wife Linda (a well known instructor in her own right), he owns Millbrook Boats and is respon-sible for designing and building the majority of the hottest slalom open canoes in today's market.

Payson Kennedy

Playing the stunt double for Burt Reynolds in *Deliverance* would garner anyone inclusion in a listing of Paddlers of the Century. But Nantahala Outdoor Center founder Payson Kennedy has laurels that go far beyond Deliverance. Kennedy began his paddling career about as far away from his current base as he could be without leaving the coun-try. He was stationed in Washington state in the 1950s where he bought a folding kayak and began hitting count-less waterways in the Northwest. He founded NOC at its present site in North Carolina in 1972 with Horace Holden, at which time it was a combina-tion motel, restaurant, store, and outfitting business. A couple of years later Kennedy started racing, eventually winning the national championship in C-2 six times between '74 and '84. NOC now employees more than 400 people, but Kennedy still gets out on occasion to guide a trip.

Peter Kennedy

A former freestyle skier and rock band drummer, Peter Kennedy has dedicated his life to teaching kids to achieve top international levels in slalom, rodeo, and extreme kayaking. Developing the "Quadrant Theory" of teaching kayaking to kids, Kennedy founded Woodstock, VT's Adventure Quest, a top residential summer, primary, and secondary school emphasizing outdoor adventure. Kennedy also is a junior Olympic Coach for USACK and serves on the American Canoe Association Instruction Council.

Walter Kirschbaum

As a teenager with a fondness for paddling, Walter Kirschbaum was drafted into the German military at age 15, only to be captured by the Russian army and released six years later in 1950. He quickly started paddling again, winning the slalom World Championships in K-1 in 1955. Moving to the U.S. in 1957 and teaching kayaking for the Colorado Rocky Mountain School in Carbondale, CO, he turned his attention to the region's first descents, most of which he ran in homemade boats. "His goal was to run every significant piece of whitewater in the Colorado drainage," says guidebook author Fletcher Anderson. He did a good job. In 1959, he became the first person to run the Colorado's Cataract Canyon without portaging, and in 1960 he accomplished the same feat on the Grand Canyon. Modern day paddlers witness his namesake on the Kirschbaum rapid of the Colorado's Gore Canyon, of which he notched the first descent in 1965. He came to a tragic end when he drowned in his bathtub in New Mexico in 1969.

Emery & Ellsworth Kolb

In 1911, Emery and Ellsworth Kolb, photographers based on the South Rim of the Grand Canyon, embarked on a novel, some would say hairball, adventure. They bought two boats and began retracing John Wesley Powell's trip down the Green and Colorado, taking photographs and making movies as they went. Although neither knew a thing about whitewater when they began, their fortitude, quickness, and adaptability molded them into skilled river runners by voyage end. Emery showed their movie at the South Rim four times a day until he died at the age of 96—the longest running movie of all time.

Verlen Kruger

Verlen Kruger is the world record holder for long distance paddling, with an excess of 88,000 miles and more than 40 million paddle strokes under his belt. That, of course, includes his 21,000-mile, three-year, top-to-bottom world canoe paddle at the age of 64, and a 28,000-mile paddle across North America. With those kinds of numbers you might expect a paddling prodigy, but Kruger didn't even set foot in a canoe until he was 41. "It was a 17-foot Grumman," says Kruger, on-pace to log 100,000 miles in a canoe by the time he turns 80. "And it just grabbed me. From that point on my lifelong passion was canoeing." Today, the Lansing, MI–based paddling legend spends most of his time building custom canoes and taking shorter trips—including a recent 400-mile paddle in Alaska.

Howie LaBrant

By 1964 Howie LaBrant was a regular on the Chicago paddling circuit, winning every leg of the 10-day, 450-mile race from Lake Itasca to Minneapolis in a plywood canoe—high-kneeling the whole way. The same year he helped found the United States Canoe Association. His essay "The Principles of Canoe Design," published in the 1962 *Whitewater Journal,* was the beginning of modern performance canoeing. LaBrant designed the Canadian for Chicagoland Canoe Base and the legendary Viper and Venom for Moore Canoe. A great athlete and visionary designer who influenced Lynn Tuttle, Ralph Frese, Pat Moore, and David Yost, he carried his passion with him to the bitter end, dying of a heart attack while delivering canoes.

Rob Lesser

One of the finest expeditionary paddlers in the country, Rob Lesser is also known as an outstanding ambassador of the sport and a tireless advocate of free-flowing rivers. Lesser organized the first descent of Canada's Grand Canyon of the Stikine in 1981, a year after helping organize the Payette Rodeo—generally considered, along with the Stanley, Idaho rodeo in the late '70s—to be the genesis of the modern freestyle circuit. Lesser worked for years as a sales rep for Perception kayaks, helping create the modern retail trade of paddlesports. "My time in Alaska really defined the type of river-runner I became," Lesser says. "My work with

Perception certainly had a larger impact on the sport, but the Stikine trip, from a mental standpoint, is probably my biggest accomplishment."

Martin Litton

Martin Litton rowed his first wooden boat through the Grand Canyon in 1955. It was Litton who adapted the Oregon Drift Boat to big water, enlarging it, decking it over, and creating the commodious Grand Canyon Dory. Litton has been a tireless crusader for the canyons, mountains, rivers, and forests of the West. As a director of the Sierra Club, it was Litton's fiery speech that helped prevent two planned dams in the Grand Canyon. In 1999, Litton once again broke his own record as the oldest person to ever navigate the Grand. At 82 he's still rowing his dory and planning his next trip. Asked why he prefers the rigid boat, he replies: "If you have to ask, you'll never understand."

Tom Long

One of the foremost innovators of instruction for kids, Tom Long has been teaching children to kayak for more than 20 years. He starting kayaking in Southern California and paddled throughout the West before settling in Idaho and founding Cascade Raft and Kayak School. A talented guide and businessman, Long is known for what he brought to instruction, especially for kids. "I combined river running skills and my desire to teach with early childhood education and slalom technique," Long says. "When my kids were young (Long has three boys, Kenneth, Chad, and Tren, all excellent paddlers), people used to say, 'You can't teach kids to kayak, it's impossible.' Now there's kids' boats, kids' life jackets, kids' everything."

Yurek Majcherczyk

In the early 1980s, just before martial law was declared in his native Poland, Yurek Majcherczyk spent over a year and a half on a personal river-running odyssey with friends that took him to more than 30 rivers in Central and South America. His epic journey included over 15 first descents, including Peru's infamous Colca Canyon and Ecuador's Rio Qiujos, and involved a stop in Honduras when a military faction thought their kayaks were torpedoes. Now residing in New Jersey, Majcherczyk began his paddling career when he took up kayaking as a 20-year-old engineering student in Krakow, Poland. His adventures eventually led to the founding of CanoAndes Expeditions, a company specializing in adventure travel to Latin America.

Bill Masters

Ask anyone who started kayaking in the 1970s or '80s what their first boat was, and Perception will invariably come up in the answer followed by such boat names as the Mirage and Dancer. Founding his company in 1976 in a garage, company president Bill Masters is indirectly responsible for getting more people involved in the sport than anyone else in the world. In keeping with his track record, he can't resist an analogy to paddling as he moves on to other ventures after selling the company in 1998. "Paddlesports helped mold who I am," he says. "It's been a good ride and I've enjoyed it . . . now I'm just going out to run another river."

Tom McEwan

Known for his pioneering first descent of the Potomac River's Great Falls in 1975, as well as several first descents in the Himalayas, former U.S. Kayak team member Tom McEwan is as hard core as paddlers come. "He knows no other life," says Todd Balf, a writer for *Men's Journal* who covered McEwan's ill-fated first descent down Tibet's TsangPo Gorge in 1998. A paddling instructor in the Washington, D.C., area since 1972—most recently with the Calleva School of Paddling—McEwan, the national wildwater champion of 1973, has influenced such modern day paddlers as Andy Bridge, John Weld, Joe Jacobi, Norm Bellingham, and Elliot Weintraub. And paddling runs in the family. His younger brother, Jamie, won the bronze at the 1972 Olympics in C-1, and son Andrew is the number-one ranked wildwater paddler in the country.

Bill McGinnis

When Bill McGinnis wrote *Whitewater Rafting* in 1975—the same year he founded his rafting company, Whitewater Voyages—the sport as a commercial endeavor was still in its infancy. When his second book, *The Guide's Guide,* was published in 1981, it helped shape the way boatmen look at a trip and a lifestyle. McGinnis learned to guide in 1965 at the age of 16, and though he has a number of first descents and pioneering raft runs in California to his credit, McGinnis says he is most proud of his influence on guiding. "I helped foster a style of guiding that got everyone involved," he says. "It made everyone a component of the overall trip."

Norm Nevills

Norm Nevills got his start river running when he rowed his bride down the San Juan River in a modified horse trough. In the years that followed, he designed and built plywood punts and ran hundreds of commercial trips down the San Juan and through Glen Canyon on the Colorado. What he is best known for, however, are his Grand Canyon trips. From his first trip in 1938 until his untimely death in 1949, Nevills was the unquestioned king of commercial river running. His effervescent personality and hunger for publicity brought him renown in the West, yet it was that same charisma that finally repelled some of his most ardent admirers. To this day, few have a neutral opinion of Norm Nevills.

Tim Niemier

Sick of getting pounded by the Malibu coast on his surfboard, Tim Niemier came up with an invention that changed the sport. By putting depressions in a surfboard and developing perhaps the world's first sit-on-top kayak in the early 1970s, Niemier, founder of Ocean Kayak, helped introduce kayaking to the recreational masses. "There wasn't a lightbulb that clicked on or anything," he says. "I was just sick of getting hit over the head with waves." By 1986, he had built more than 1,200 such boats out of fiberglass before coming up with a roto-molded version. Ever the tinkerer, he operated his first oven with his garage door opener.

Tim Palmer

Nobody has put pen to paper more eloquently to protect our waterways than Tim Palmer. Author of ten books on river conservation, Palmer first fell in love with rivers as a 12-year-old on the Youghiogheny and since then has spent most of his life fighting for their protection. His first big battle was against a proposed dam on California's Stanislaus in the early 1980s. The fight was lost and Palmer says, "I came out with a resolve not to let it happen again." Winner of the Lifetime Achievement Award from American Rivers in 1988, Palmer sits on the Board of Trustees for the Portland, OR–based River Network.

Roger Paris

One of few paddlers to move from canoeing to kayaking and remain competitive, Roger Paris (pronounced "Rogét Pear-ree") placed second in C-2 with partner Claude Neveu at the 1949 World Championships and took first in 1951 and '55 paddling for France. After moving to the U.S. and settling down in Carbondale, CO, in the early '60s, Paris (admitting he's now over 60) switched to kayaking, competing for the U.S. at the World Championships in 1965, and winning three U.S. Nationals. Perhaps his biggest contribution to the sport, however, is in helping others as a long-time instructor for the Colorado Rocky Mountain School. "He's famous for teaching by the school of hard knocks," says friend Kent Ford. "He influenced quite a few people who then moved on to share their knowledge in other parts of the country."

Joe Pulliam & Steve Scarborough

When Dagger was founded in 1988, Joe Pulliam was working at Perception and Steve Scarborough was designing paddles for his own company, Dagger Paddles. Together the two led a resurgence in innovation that still defines Dagger today. Placing an emphasis on research, development, and new design technology has helped the two innovators build Dagger into one of the fastest-growing companies in the paddlesports industry. "We used to play hooky to go paddling," says Pulliam, who bought his first canoe at age 14. Pulliam went on to build his first canoe at age 17, which someone stole from his backyard. "It was the ugliest boat we ever made," he says. "Everyone joked about why someone would want to steal it."

Royal Robbins

When Royal Robbins was diagnosed with arthritis in the mid-1970s, he took up kayaking and attacked it with the same vengeance that earned him fame as a climber. At an age when many are looking to retire, Robbins switched from rocks to rivers, eventually completing over 30 first descents in California and Chile. From 1980 to 1984, Robbins scored first descents on several major Sierra Nevada waterways, including the San Joaquin, South Fork and Upper Kern, Middle Fork of the Kings, and Yosemite's Grand Canyon of the Tuolumne. In 1988, Robbins was also one of the first Americans to raft and kayak Siberia's Bashkaus River.

Harry Roberts

In between stints as editor of *Wilderness Camping, Canoe Sport Journal* and *Paddler,* Harry Roberts served as marketing head for Hyperform and Sawyer. He held his editorships as a community trust, nurturing many new writers, including Cliff Jacobson. Roberts was a Renaissance man in a time of specialists: an athlete, a man of letters, a builder and salesman, a family man, and a community man. A spellbinding speaker and fixture at paddlesports events nationwide, he promoted a marathon-based paddling style he termed "Touring Technique." The industry lost a leader with his untimely death in 1992.

Ralph Sawyer

Ralph Sawyer dominated early marathon racing. He was so unbeatable in the Ausable Marathon in upper Michigan, it was assumed he had secret portages on the oxbows. Sawyer Canoe, started in 1957, was one of the first manufacturers of cloth-laminated, high performance canoes. He designed and built successful recreational and race canoes before moving to Oregon's Rogue River in 1967. Sawyer crafted fiberglass-reinforced wooden canoe paddles and later developed laminated rowing oars for rafts that were more appropriate to the Rogue. An innovator in competition and in canoe, paddle, and oar building, Sawyer now lives on a sailboat in Anacortes, WA.

Jim Slade

Jim Slade has probably logged more exploratory miles than any human alive, and he's still going. In the early 1970s, he rafted Mexico's Rio Grande de Santiago, and found himself shot at by bandits. It was the beginning of a lifetime of exotic rafting adventures. Soon afterwards he joined Sobek and the ill-fated Baro expedition in Ethiopia. While most other team members abandoned the trip after a drowning, Slade showed his mettle and kept going. He emerged a leader in a field of independent souls, and has led scores of expeditions since. His knack for detailed planning and logistics, quick thinking, and unbridled passion for wild rivers has made him a legend in whitewater rafting.

Jeff & Jim Snyder

Those fancy, new-school rodeo moves you see practiced in local play spots are due to the antics of Maryland's Jim and Jeff Snyder, affectionately dubbed the Fathers of Squirt Boating. Although neither can remember when they started paddling ("All I remember is having to sit on a telephone book to see over the cockpit," says Jeff), both are responsible for revolutionizing paddling with their antics on the squirt scene: Jim as a designer of countless boats and author of *The Squirt Book;* and Jeff as his primary test pilot. "I think I helped influence the sport by pushing the limits," says Jeff, who has about ten first descents to his credit. "Some runs I did people thought were crazy . . . some were fun and some even I'm left scratching my head at."

Chris Spelius

Chris "Spe" Spelius has a 25-year river resume that includes stints as a rodeo competitor, kayak designer, Olympian, and ten-year instructor for the Nantahala Outdoor Center. He also holds the prestigious, although illegal, first descent of the Niagara Gorge in 1976. Perhaps his biggest claim to fame, however, is as an all-around ambassador for the sport, which he accomplishes through his kayak outfitting company on Chile's Rio Futaleufu and by guest appearances through sponsor Dagger at paddling events throughout the country.

Jim Stohlquist

As founder of Stohlquist Water Ware, Jim Stohlquist sounds like just another success story in the paddlesports industry. But factor in that he built his first folding boat at the age of 15, his first fiberglass kayak at the age of 17, and that he founded Colorado Kayak Supply to help pay his way through college. Also factor in that he continued to build boats throughout the early 1970s, fueling Colorado's early whitewater craze, and that he notched several first descents that are now considered classics, and you start to see that he isn't just your regular businessman. Stohlquist

is also the author of *Colorado Rivers and Creeks,* a book he wrote in the '70s after gathering years of hands-on experience.

Audrey Sutherland

When Hawaii's Audrey Sutherland flew over the coastline of Molokai in 1967, she decided she wanted to see the rugged 3,400-ft. cliffs of the island up close. After a couple of exploratory swimming trips, she bought an inflatable six-foot canoe and began her paddling career. Over 8,000 paddling miles later Sutherland is still at it and considers any trip less than 300 miles to be short. Author of *Paddling Hawaii,* Sutherland has also put in many of her miles in Alaska, usually solo. "I'm like the whales," she says. "I spend the winter in Hawaii and the summer in Alaska."

Joy Ungritch

Joy Ungritch was a preeminent female river explorer, who participated in such Sobek first descents as Pakistan's Indus and Africa's Zambezi rivers. Her fortitude, as remembered by Sobek founder Richard Bangs, showed itself on the Indus when the raft they were in got stuck in a huge hydraulic. "Though she was a tiny woman, she put so much energy and heft into the effort to get us out that I think she saved our lives," he says. Utah's Ungritch went on to run her own expeditions, including a first all-woman descent of the Luangua River in Zambia, before passing away in the late 1990s. "She was an extraordinary spirit and loved rivers to her core," says Bangs.

Charlie Walbridge

Before selling the company in 1994, Charlie Walbridge operated Wildwater Design in suburban Philadelphia, an industry leader in outfitting design. During that time, he also served on the Board of American Whitewater (AW) and the American Canoe Association (ACA), and was integral to each organization's instructional programs. A renowned safety expert, Walbridge co-authored *Whitewater Rescue: The River Safety Anthology,* helped develop the ACA's Swiftwater Rescue Program, and continues to compile AW's annual *Accident Overview Report,* and the *ACA's River Safety Report,* helping people learn from other's mistakes. If you trust your paddling partners to help when needed, thank Walbridge.

Ken Warren

With a burning desire to be the first to run China's Yangtze River, Ken Warren made two trips to the famed Asian waterway. The last one, in 1986, ended in mutiny after the controversial death of the expedition photographer. Warren took criticism from many for his leadership tactics and his ego, but there's no discounting his accomplishments. "Ken was an incredibly strong and incredibly determined boatman," says Oregon's Andy Griffith, who joined Warren on the first descent of India's Ganges River in 1977, which was filmed for American Sportsman. "And he was as good as anyone in the world when he was running

rivers." Warren died of a heart attack in 1989 while mowing his lawn.

John Wasson

When Hollywood needs a paddling scene, or when organizations like the X Games need rigging advice, the first phone calls placed are to Idaho's John Wasson. The main safety and rigging expert for such films as *A River Runs Through It* and *The River Wild,* Wasson got his start rafting in Colorado in 1969. After switching to kayaking and running the classics of Colorado and Idaho, he got invited on a 32-day self-support trip in 1977 down Peru's Maraòon. "That's what got me hooked on paddling in wild, exotic places," he says. A year later, he joined such expedition paddlers as Matt Gaines, Cully Erdman, and Rob Lesser for a film project with American Sportsman on the Yampa River's Cross Mountain Canyon, which cemented his love affair with films and floating.

George Wendt

A former Los Angeles schoolteacher, George Wendt spent summers on the Grand Canyon and secured one of the Grand's early commercial permits. After hearing about a river up north called the Stanislaus, he and his wife moved to Angels Camp, CA, and founded Outdoor Adventure River Specialists (O.A.R.S.). The company ran more than 3,000 people down the "Stan" each summer until it was buried under New Melones Reservoir in the early 1980s. Wendt was convinced the dam went in because not enough people had seen the beauty of the river, so he swore he'd show people other important rivers, opening up commercial rafting in many places he felt were important to protect.

Georgie White

The Grand Canyon's most famous raft guide, Georgie White—also known as Georgie Clark—began running the Grand in 1944, eventually making more than 200 trips down the Big Ditch. Georgie was founder of the "wave-buster," a 35-person raft she often guided in her famous leopard-skin bikini. "Georgie was a tough bird," says Ted Hatch, owner of the Grand Canyon division of Hatch Expeditions. "She was one-of-a-kind." Hatch recalls one time in the early 1960s when he stole one of Georgie's favorite campsites, only to get mooned by all 35 of her passengers. Georgie swam more than 80 miles through the Grand Canyon in 1945, wearing little more than a life jacket. She sold her rafting company just six months before her death on May 12, 1992, ending a career that spanned three-and-a-half decades.

Nolan Whitesell

"I don't know when I started paddling, but it was before I was ten years old," says canoe builder and open-boat pioneer Nolan Whitesell. Whitesell lives on North Carolina's Nantahala River where he builds paddles and whitewater canoes and gives private instruction. Besides claiming some of the hairiest open-boat first descents in the country, Whitesell has contributed in other ways to the paddling world. "I believe I'm known for having opened up design ideas in canoes and making them play-boats," he says. "Before that, canoes were used only for transportation and racing."

Jesse Whittemore

If Jimmy Snyder is the father of squirtboating, then Jesse Whittemore is the grandfather. Whittemore brought about a revolution in boat design and technique that inspired not only squirt boats, but also playboating in general. He is also a pioneer in the construction and use of laminates such as Kevlar in fiberglass boats. "He's an amazing crafts-man," says Mountain Surf founder and long-time friend John Mason. "Jesse is the link between the racing and recreation worlds of boating. You just learn so much every time you paddle with him."

Alfred Wickett

Alfred who? Though long forgotten in contemporary paddling circles, Alfred Wickett is largely responsible for the first commercially produced canvas-covered canoe. As the first designer, chief builder, and operations manager for Old Town Canoe from 1900 to 1914, Wickett helped build both a company and an industry. After leaving Old Town, Wickett founded the Penobscot Canoe Company and in 1922 moved to St. Louis to open the St. Louis Boat and Canoe Company. Using his 35 years of canoe-building experience, Wickett invented the Arrowhead Canoe, one of the most popular models of the time. Wickett died in 1943 and his gravestone in Kirkwood, MO, bears a carving of a canoe.

David Yost

Known to paddlers everywhere as "DY," David Yost designed his first racing canoe, the Minuteman, in 1973, and was soon designing for Sawyer. Deals with Tubbs, Curtis, Loon Works, Perception, Swift, and Bell Canoe followed. Fifty-six hulls reaching production by seven manufacturers make Yost the century's most prolific designer of human-powered watercraft. A student of historical boats and the effect of materials on design, Yost continues to design for construction in wood strip, wood-and-fabric, laminated plastic, vacuum forming, and roto-molding. Yost's designs emphasize seakindlyness and user-comfort over speed. He describes his work as an out-of-hand hobby of designing hulls for friends.

John Yost

John Yost was involved in most of the great first descents of the 1970s and '80s, including the Zambezi, the Indus, the Euphrates, and the Yangtze, yet he has maintained the lowest of profiles. He never carried a camera or a notebook, always believing the purest way to run a river was to be completely there with it, not to see it through a lens, or interpret it with a journal. He was never motivated by money (well, there was that time on the Zambezi he was offered $500 by the ABC executive to flip a boat, and he did, but no one ever knew if it was on purpose). Yost has carried clarity of purpose in his drybag for 30 years.

Olympic Paddlers of the Century

Greg Barton

What can we say about sprint kayaker Greg Barton, the most successful Olympic paddler in U.S. history? We'll let his accomplishments do the talking. A member of four consecutive Olympic teams, Barton won the bronze in K-1 1,000 in 1984 and 1992. It was at the 1988 Games, however, that he stole the show, winning the gold in K-1 1,000 and then coming back 90 minutes later to team with Norm Bellingham to win the gold in K-2 1,000. No other athlete has won both 1,000-meter titles in a single Olympics, and no American paddler has won two Olympic golds in an Olympic Games at all. "Greg Barton's the best paddler in the world," maintains long-time adversary Lee McGregor of South Africa.

Norm Bellingham

The highlight of sprint paddler Norm Bellingham's career occurred at the 1988 Olympics in Seoul when, teaming with Greg Barton, he won the gold in men's K-2 1,000. The three-time Olympian (1984, '88, and '92) closed out his sprint stint with a fourth-place finish in K-1 500 at the '92 Olympics in Barcelona. A double gold medalist at the 1987 Pan American Games, the Fairfax, VA, native enjoyed his best World Championships performance with a third-place finish in 1988 in Germany.

Dana Chladek

After her first run at the 1996 Olympics on Tennessee's Ocoee River, kayaker Dana Chladek was in a dismal second-to-last place. What followed is nothing short of miraculous. Putting it all on the line on her second run, she tied the winner to the nearest hundredth of a second. Although she had to settle for the silver, her time was good enough for the gold. Combined with a bronze medal at the '92 Olympics in Barcelona, she is the top slalom Olympic medal winner in U.S. history. Add two silver-medal finishes at World Championships and it's easy to see why she is now happily retired from competition, raising a family, and running her Rapidstyle paddling apparel business in Kensington, MD.

Fritz & Lecky Haller

Although they've rotated partners throughout the years, achieving varying results in World Cup, Olympic, and World Championship competition, C-2ers Fritz and Lecky Haller remain perhaps the best-known brothers in paddling. The duo's heyday came in 1983, when they shocked the world with a gold-medal performance at the World Championships in Italy. They regained their form in 1994–95, when, after winning the final 1994 World Cup for a bronze overall, they won the first race of the '95 season. They also won the national championships that year, a title they also held in 1984. When not paired with his brother, Lecky teamed with Jamie McEwan to win the silver at the 1987 World Championships in France; the next year Lecky and McEwan were the overall champions in the inaugural World Cup and placed second in '89.

Mike Harbold

By winning the 1993 Finlandia Clean Water Challenge, a 1,000-mile stage race from Chicago to New York City, Hawaii's Mike Harbold proved himself a member of sprint paddling's elite. The fact that he has also appeared in three Olympic Games (1988, '92 and '96) further cements his place among the sport's finest.

Frank & Bill Havens

Never have two American paddling brothers dominated the sprint scene as much as Frank and Bill Havens did in the 1940s and '50s. To this day, Frank remains the only American ever to capture the Olympic Gold in men's C-1, a feat he accomplished at the 1952 Games in Helsinki. He also competed in three other Olympics ('48, '56, and '60), winning the C-1 silver in London in '48. He also earned five of six possible national championships, winning events in K-1, K-2, K-4, C-2, and C-4. It was in K-2 that Frank and older brother Bill (a.k.a. "Junior") broke the world record by more than five minutes. The two were slated to compete together in K-2 in '52, but Bill—who made the Olympic team in 1936, '40, and '44 (with the latter two cancelled because of World War II) and 1948—got injured and had to bow out. The two were also ringleaders in the then-popular sport of canoe tilting, with Bill holding the national crown from 1935 to 1960. "That was quite a reign," said Frank of his brother upon accepting the duo's 1999 Legend of Paddling Award from the American Canoe Association. Neither brother has hung up his paddle. Frank celebrated his 75th birthday by paddling 150 miles from Chesapeake Bay to the Washington Canoe Club in Washington, DC.

Davey Hearn

A member of the U.S. team since 1977, Bethesda, MD's Davey Hearn enjoys one of the longest-running canoe- and kayak-team tenures of any paddler, alive or dead. Highlights include Olympic C-1 appearances in 1992, '96, and 2000, as well as gold medal C-1 performances at the World Championships in 1985 and 1995. He was also named in 1995's "Top Ten Sportsmen of the Year" by the U.S. Olympic Committee. He is showing no signs of letting up, and plans to continue his Olympic participation. "I'm going to keep doing this as long as I'm still having fun," he says.

Cathy Hearn

As with her brother Davey, slalom kayaker Cathy Hearn has put in more than 20 years on the U.S. kayak team, with Olympic appearances in 1992 and '96. Far from lying in the slalom shadow of her brothers (brother Bill is also an accomplished slalom paddler), one of her crowning moments came in 1979 when she won the gold at the World Championships, and won three of four possible golds in every event she entered. One of the most diligent female kayakers on the slalom scene, she has her sights set on future Olympic competitions.

Eric Jackson

Perhaps best known for his exploits on the current rodeo scene—winning a gold medal at the 1993 World Championships in Tennessee, breaking his ribs in the '95 finals in Munich, and placing second in '97 in Ontario—Washington, DC.'s (when he's not traveling in his motor home) Eric Jackson, also an accomplished C-1 paddler, is one of the most versatile kayakers on the planet. A member of the U.S. slalom team since 1989, he was the top-placing U.S. kayaker in the 1992 Olympics in Spain, taking 13th, and he won the U.S. Slalom National Championships in 1995. "Slalom and rodeo are similar in that they both take a lot of focus and commitment," he says.

Joe Jacobi & Scott Strausbaugh

In a move that would have qualified him for the national limbo team, Joe Jacobi leaned back just far enough at gate 24 of the 1992 Olympic slalom course in Barcelona to avoid a five-second penalty and secure him and C-2 partner Scott Strausbaugh the United States' first and only Olympic gold medal in whitewater. Jacobi, who runs a bed and breakfast in Copperhill, TN, still competes, now in C-1. With medal in hand, Strausbaugh has retired from competition, content to give motivational speeches throughout the country.

Harry & Karl Knight, Charles Havens, John Larcombe

When kayaking was first brought to the Olympic Games as a demonstration sport in the 1924 Paris Olympiad, the U.S. was more than adequately represented. Not only did sprint paddlers Harry Knight, Karl Knight, Charles Havens, and John Larcombe win every single kayaking event, but they finished second behind Canada in the sport's four canoeing events. As an interesting twist, Charles (a.k.a. Bud)—who could have competed in either wrestling or paddling—went only at the last minute in place of his brother, Bill Sr., whose wife was pregnant with son Frank. Serendipity had Frank return in 1952 to win the gold his father couldn't.

Jon Lugbill

Jon Lugbill is generally recognized as the best paddler ever to compete in whitewater canoeing. He's a five-time world champion in C-1, a one-time silver medalist, a seven-time member of a gold-medal-winning team, and is the only athlete in history to have won 12 golds in the Whitewater World Championships. "He was the group leader," says his former coach, Bill Endicott. "He was surprisingly selfless and was always thinking about the team. Yet he always wanted to be the best." Lugbill is also the only paddler ever to have his picture on a Wheaties Box. It hangs on the wall in his office at Richmond Sports Backers in Richmond, VA.

Steve Lysek

Steve Lysek was the lead paddler on the first-place U.S. Olympic C-2 10,000-meter team of Lysek and Steve Macknowski in 1948. He designed and built the boat—controlling warping by book-matching the wood—and developed a shorter, more efficient stroke using torso rotation. Asked to protest another contestant's incursion into his lane in the 1,000-meter race, he refused—stating the paddler had not impeded his progress.

Jamie McEwan

When the International Olympic Committee debuted Whitewater Slalom in the 1972 Munich Olympic Games, no one gave the U.S. much hope. All that changed when a 19-year-old named Jamie McEwan stormed to win the bronze in C-1, legitimizing the sport for a long line of followers. "That was a milestone for U.S. paddling," says Bill Endicott, former coach of the U.S. team. "Americans didn't believe in themselves until that moment." McEwan accomplished just as remarkable a feat when, coming out of retirement 20 years later, he placed fourth in C-2 with Lecky Haller at the 1992 Olympics in Spain.

Scott Shipley

If it weren't for tough twists of fate, Scott Shipley could well have six World Cup K-1 titles under his sprayskirt. As it is, he'll have to settle for three—in 1993, '95, and '97—with seconds in '98 and '99 and a third-place finish in '94. Even without his missed victories, he is by far the most successful slalom kayaker in U.S. history, if not the world. Apart from coaches and fellow competitors, the first people to recognize this are the townsfolk from his home in Poulsbo, WA, where a sign leading into town reads, "Welcome to Poulsbo . . . Home of Scott Shipley, 1993–1995–1997 World Cup Kayak Champion."

Jim Terrell

Not many athletes have appeared in the Olympics four times in a row. Then again, not many athletes, no matter how gifted, have the stamina of sprint canoeist Jim Terrell, 34, who competed in the Games in 1984, '88, '92, and '96. A woodsman by trade who makes custom paddles for elite canoeists, Terrell also holds the prestige of tallying 27 U.S. Olympic Festival (USOF) medals, including 17 golds, ranking him second in USOF history.

Rich Weiss

Although he might not have gained the notoriety of fellow U.S. teammate Scott Shipley, to this date two-time Olympian Rich Weiss enjoys the country's highest Olympic K-1 slalom placing with a sixth-place showing in the 1996 Games on the Ocoee. He also became the first American to medal in men's kayak at the World Championships in 1993. A long-time member of the U.S. kayak team, Weiss came to a tragic end in 1997 when he died kayaking Washington State's Upper White Salmon River.

Compiled by Eugene Buchanan, Tom Bie, Richard Bangs, Aaron Bible, Jodie Deignan, Brad Dimock, David Gonzalez, Peter Kennedy, Ron Watters, Charlie Wilson, and Roy Webb

Into the 21st Century

We can hardly pay tribute to Paddlers of the Century without taking a look at those who will be carrying the torch into the 21st Century. Following is a sampling of paddlers, aged 21 or younger, to keep an eye on in the new millennium.

Adam Boyd

Woodstock, VT's Adam Boyd started paddling at age nine. Career highlights include gold and silver C-1 medals at the 1995 U.S. Olympic Festival, and the C-1 bronze at the pre-World Rodeo Championships in 1996 and Rodeo World Championships in 1997. Now in his early 20s, Boyd has his sights set on the Olympics.

Greg Chinn

In 1999, at age 19, Greg Chinn finished fourth in the Junior World Championships (Zagreb, Croatia) in the C-1 1,000-meter event, bringing home the best Junior World result in U.S. history. In the same event, he finished sixth in the 500-meter competition. He is a bright hope for the USA in sprint C-1 for the 2004 Olympics.

Casey Eichfeld

Casey Eichfeld's first canoe trip was at 18 months. He started paddling on his own at age five and competing at age six. Since age eight, he has been a member of the Cadet National Slalom Team. In 1999, at age nine, he became an Open Canoe National Champion with partner John Kazimierczyk. His paddling goal is to match Jon Lugbill's record in competitive slalom and compete in the Olympic Games.

Gwen Greeley

In 1999, though only a cadet competitor (age 14 and under), Gwen Greeley topped the entire K-1 junior women's field at every major slalom competition including Junior U.S. team trials and Junior Nationals. Her primary training ground is the East Race Waterway in South Bend, Indiana. She has been a member of the Cadet National Slalom Team since 1996, and been featured in *Sports Illustrated for Kids.*

Brett Heyl

Brett Heyl's paddling career began in 1990 at the age nine. Since that time, he has been at the forefront of cadet, junior, and senior slalom competition, including a fifth place finish at the U.S. Nationals at age 15, two Junior Olympic titles, and a Junior National Slalom title. In 1999, he became the first U.S. Junior Slalom Kayaker to win an individual medal (bronze) in World or pre-World competition since Scott Shipley in 1988. He has been a member of the U.S. Junior Team since 1995.

Tamara Jenkins

Tamara Jenkins won the silver medal in the K-2, 500-meter event for the U.S. at age 21 in the 1999 Pan Am Games in Winnipeg, Canada. At the Linz, Austria International Regatta she won the gold in the K-2, 500- and 1,000-meter events, and won the 1999 Nationals in all K-2 events with her partner, Kathy Collin.

Hannah Larsen

Hannah Larsen honed her technique in New Hampshire with David and Peggy Mitchell. A member of the Junior U.S. Team in 1995, 1997, and 1998, she completed her junior career with a bronze medal at the 1998 Junior World Championships in the K-1W team event with Aleta Miller and Anna Jorgensen. In 1999, Larsen stepped from the Junior U.S. Slalom Team right onto the U.S. "B" Team. A student at Emory University, she paddles with the Emory Eagles.

Tren Long

Tren Long is the younger brother of U.S. Team athletes Chad and Kenneth Long. Formerly a slalom kayaker, Tren switched to C-1 several years back, and in 1999 took second at the Ocoee Doubleheader in the men's C-1 Class. He was the number-one C-1 on the 1999 Junior U.S. Slalom team and is a bright hope for a medal at the Junior World Championships. When not racing, he often spends time in Idaho safety boating for his family's raft company.

Brad Ludden

Montana's Brad Ludden won the bronze medal at the World Rodeo Championships in Canada in 1997. He has also traveled extensively throughout the world to compete in places like Japan (where he topped the men's expert kayak field in 1998) and film extreme sports videos throughout Europe. In 1999 he was the top junior rodeo paddler in the U.S. and competed in the World Freestyle Championships in New Zealand.

Scott Mann

Scott Mann began his career at age ten, and within four years won the Cadet National Slalom Championships. He is the youngest paddler ever to tackle the Batoka Gorge on Africa's mighty Zambezi, and in 1999 he was a member of the Junior U.S. Slalom Team, competing in Europe and the pre-World Championships. Despite being mainly a slalom competitor, Mann placed eighth at the 1999 U.S. Rodeo East Team Trials and finished fourth in expert junior freestyle at the Ottawa Rodeo.

Nathan McDade

Nathan McDade, a graduate of The Academy at Adventure Quest, was the NOWR junior points leader in 1998. As with teammate Brad Ludden, his name could be found at or near the top of most junior, expert classes in freestyle competitions. The number two junior kayak on the 1999 U.S. Team, he competed in New Zealand at the 1999 World Championships.

Aleta Miller

One of the top young women kayakers today, Aleta Miller represented the U.S. at the 1999 Surf Kayak World Championships in Brazil. In 1998, she was a top finisher on the U.S. rodeo circuit and a member of the Junior Slalom team. At the Junior World Championships in Austria, she won a bronze in K-1 for the women's team. When not competing, she can be found trashing herself on the Ocoee or bombing down some obscure Appalachian creek.

Jesse Murphy

Though probably the youngest paddler on the 1999 tour, Jesse Murphy proved his stuff against the big boys with a bronze-medal finish at the Maupin Daze Rodeo. He studied at the Adventure Quest Academy in New Zealand, and is a bright hope for the future of rodeo.

Scott Parsons

Scott Parsons was a member of the Junior U.S. Slalom Team from 1994 to 1997. He became the first U.S. junior to win a Junior World Cup (Poland), and won team medals (silver with Josh Russell and Kyle Elliott, and bronze with Louis Geltman and Brett Heyl) in the 1994 World and 1997 pre-World Championships, respectively. A member of the U.S. Slalom Team, he competed in the finals of the 1999 World Championships.

Becca Red

Tennessee's Becca Red has already won three national championships and six gold medals while still in her early teens. She finished first in the Junior Women class at the Ocoee Rodeo and took two firsts in the C-2 at the Junior Olympics. Red is certainly one of the youngest designers in the country, playing a critical role in the creation of Dagger's Dynamo, designed specifically for kids. She is also a straight-A student and winner of a President's Award for Academic Excellence.

Rusty Sage

In 1998, Rusty Sage topped the field in Men's Kayak at the pre-World Rodeo Championships in Taupo, New Zealand. A former slalom paddler turned rodeo star, Sage has been at or near the top of the freestyle circuit for several years. He also competed at the 1999 World Freestyle Championships.

Ethan Winger

Ethan Winger has already logged river miles in more than 20 countries. In 1995, he won the Cadet National Championships, and the next year he competed at the World Surf Kayak Championships (at age 15) in Costa Rica. In 1998, he was the number one U.S. junior slalom kayaker in international competition and is the only U.S. athlete to compete on both the 1999 Junior Slalom and 1999 Freestyle (Rodeo) Teams.

Bartosz Wolski

Bartosz Wolski finished 7th in the Junior Worlds in K-1 500-meter in 1997. In 1998, he won the bronze in K-1 500 in the Junior World Cup. At the 1999 Sprint Nationals in Lake Placid, N.Y., Wolski won the 200-meter race and placed second in the 500-meter.

Compiled with help from Peter Kennedy

Canadian Paddlers

Not to ignore our neighbors to the north, who actually have a longer, richer paddling history than we do in the U.S., the following is a sampling of those who have made Canada's Paddling Hall of Fame. Understanding that this is a country easily capable of producing its own Top 100, we'll simply whet your appetite with 10.

Serge Corbin

Perhaps no other canoeist has commanded his or her discipline as well as Quebec marathon racer Serge Corbin, who has won the famed Triple Crown of North American Canoe Racing—consisting of the 70-mile General Clinton Canoe Race, 120-mile Ausable Marathon, and Canada's La Classique de Canots de la Maurice—every year since its inception in 1992. Included in these results are victories in 20 of 22 races since the Triple Crown was formed. With 55 major victories in 23 years of racing events comprising the Triple Crown, he is clearly one of Canada's preeminent paddlers. "For more than 20 years he has dominated marathon canoe racing to an extent unmatched by any competitor in any other sport," says Triple Crown spokesman Phil Weiler. "His record is comparable to a single athlete winning 50 major PGA golf tournaments or 50 Grand Slam tennis tournaments over 20 years."

Claudia Kerckhoff-van Wijk

With parents Hermann and Christa Kerckhoff founding Canada's Madawaska Canoe Center in 1972 after Hermann's appearance in the 1972 Olympics, Claudia Kerckhoff-van Wijk has an established pedigree among Canada's paddling elite. But as a former world medalist, she has blossomed in her own right. Now retired from competition, she has served as the director of Madawaska since 1989. "My parents started small," she says. "Their attitude was, 'If this doesn't work, we can always use it as a family cottage.'" Thousands of paddlers who have attended the school—one of the finest in the world—are glad the school has succeeded.

Bill Mason

Known as the Father of Canadian Paddling, the late Bill Mason distinguished himself among Canadian paddlers not just as a skilled canoeist and whitewater boater (most often in his cherished 16-foot Chestnut Prospector), but also as an author, artist, photographer, speaker, environmentalist, and filmmaker. One of his most famous works was the acclaimed *Path of the Paddle,* a film celebrating the sport and Canada's wilderness. His spirit lives on in the Water-Walker Film and Video Festival, held every two years. "He had a passion and a respect for the resource," says Joseph Agnew, of the Canadian Recreational Canoeing Association. "And he did an incredible job of communicating that."

Eric Morse

As one of Canada's more modern-day explorers, Eric Morse mapped much of the northern waterways of Canada. A prolific author, he paddled and explored throughout the 1930s, '40s, and '50s, and though he didn't discover the waters he mapped, he popularized and documented their existence for much of the world. He is also well known for taking trips with such dignitaries as former Prime Minister Pierre Trudeau.

Mark Scriver

One of the most talented open boaters in North America, Mark Scriver, an instructor at Black Feather Wilderness Adventures on Ontario's Ottawa River, has been instrumental in developing freestyle and rodeo canoeing in Canada. Co-author with Paul Mason of the acclaimed instruction manual *Thrill of the Paddle,* Scriver took first in open canoe at the 1996 Rodeo Pre-Worlds, first at the 1997 Rodeo Worlds (the same year he made the first open canoe descent of the Firth River), and first again at the 1998 Pre-Worlds in New Zealand.

Don Starkell

From 1980–82, Don Starkell set an unheard-of world record by paddling 12,181 miles from Winnipeg, Manitoba, to Belem, Brazil. Although his record was later broken by Verlen Kruger and most recently by Britain's Neil Armstrong and Chris Maguire, Starkell's feat stands out as a milestone for expedition canoeists across the world. He

was also the first to solo kayak through the Arctic Passage.

Omer Stringer

An accomplished instructor, wilderness guide, and author, Omer Stringer is credited with developing the Canadian style of solo canoeing in the 1960s and '70s. As a guide, Stringer became known around the globe as the legend of Ontario's Algonquin Park, one of the world's most famous wilderness-tripping areas.

Ken Whiting

Showing the world that Canada isn't just a land of canoeists, Ken Whiting took the freestyle kayaking world by storm by winning the 1997 World Rodeo Championships on his hometown river, the Ottawa. The unassuming ambassador of freestyle kayaking is also an accomplished instructor, video producer, and author of *The Play Boaters Handbook,* detailing the moves that got him to the top.

Hap Wilson

A longtime guide and former outfitter, Hap Wilson has spent much of his life mapping, studying, and fighting for the preservation of the beautiful Temagami Region in northwest Ontario. His guidebooks are renowned for their detail and offer much more than just directions—describing not only paddling routes but also history, people, and necessary conservation plans. Wilson led the charge on many Canadian environmental issues.

Kirk Wipper

One of the last of the living canoe legends in Canada, Kirk Wipper, a former Outdoor Education professor at the University of Toronto, was instrumental in developing Canada's National Canoe School. Wipper had a love affair with the heritage of the canoe, believing that every canoe had a story to tell. True to his beliefs, he donated an enormous collection of canoes to the Canadian Canoe Museum. As a further testament to his canoeing fame, he was knighted by Canada's Governor General.

Of Geezers and Goals: Paddling San Francisco's Race for Treasure

by Paul McHugh

Much of this sea kayak race seems well-organized. So when that starting horn blows too early, the shock nearly blows me out of my sprayskirt.

I emerge from my hiding place behind a mothballed Navy freighter on the west side of the Oakland Estuary in response to the three-minute warning blast. I'd just filled my ears with the tiny headphones of my waterproof Walkman and turned it on. Yet I must clear that looming gray wall of maritime steel before I can tune it to a radio station with the right sound track for my movie: "Geezer Paddler From Hell."

As I half-drift around the freighter's stern with ears jam-full of headphone static, my scope of vision suddenly dilates to reveal a wide stretch of estuary surface whipped into a white froth. About a hundred paddlers windmill away from the starting line before me. Some of those guys on surf skis have already surged 75 feet out in front.

Damn! That start horn went off less than two minutes after the warning horn! And with my headphones crackling, I hadn't even heard it.

Adrenaline now ripples voltage up my spine, adding urgency to a dense buzz from that cafe mocha I'd swilled, plus the two chunks of ginseng root I'd chewed— in a careful dose of amateur pharmacology—an hour before the start.

But this combo of ingested stimuli now seems to overwhelm more than invigorate. I find myself breathing frantically and flailing at the water while I charge after the pack. OK, OK! that rational observer that responds at the core of everyone's mind yips to the rest of my consciousness. Chill out, old boy, settle down . . . Remember your original, strategic reasons for coming over to lurk behind the Navy freighter. Make all those tactics happen.

First off, that west-side start spot actually gives me a straighter shot out through the curve of this channel to the bay. Two, there's always the chance a sailboat, powerboat, or (most precious!) a tug with a steep wake might ride down the center of the channel, heading out to the broad reaches of San Francisco Bay. Any of these could net me a lovely, jet assisted boost. You see, under "Race for Treasure" rules, surfing a boat's wake or drafting same have been acceptable ways to jump ahead. Such maneuvers might steam a purist, but—for me and a few others— the prospect of a sneaky push adds nicely to the tactical possibilities.

In fact, I'd hidden behind the Navy freighter once I'd reached the west end of the starting line mainly to keep from alerting everyone as to how much I might try to gain some early boosts from wake-surfing. But, now, after my late start, I have to paddle furiously just to catch the pack! So-o-o brilliant, you lobotomized genius you, I remark kindly to myself.

Out of curiosity, I glance back over my shoulder. Ah, beauty! A sailboat is in fact showing up to drive down-channel after me. She's a fat sloop, motoring on auxiliary power against a light breeze ascending from the Bay. As she overtakes me, I surf briefly on her port wake, cross over, and draft in the white stream of prop bubbles just behind her upraised rump, then move on to surf the star-board wake for twenty seconds or so.

Great! Although hotshot paddle stars like John Weed and Alyx Oppedyk are still pulling away further out in the lead, my little ploy brings me up even with the main body of the fleet. Weed and Oppedyk and other major paddle-swinging stallions such as Dan Crandall are on the 13.5-mile course that goes through the Oakland Estuary and into the open waters of San Francisco Bay. It then swings around under both wings of the soaring Bay Bridge to circumnavi-gate the naval base of Treasure Island.

But the main body of paddlers are mostly on a ten-mile course that goes out to a beach on Treasure Island, in the shadow of a buttress of that bridge span,

then spins around for a quick return. This will be the group I hope to beat.

OK. First goal achieved! I'm even with them, although still out in the cen-ter of the channel. I expend one valuable second to drop a thumb onto the dial of the sport Walkman jammed down my life vest. A station comes in tune. I've just got time to dial one. Potluck! Destiny will make it my sound-track . . . God is good! It's classical FM, mid-way through a symphony dominat-ed by imperious French horns. Dah-dah-da-DAHH-HH! I pour emotional pulses from that music into my arms, crank my slim Necky Arluk 1.9 after the leaders, and finish my ferry across the canal.

I look back over my other shoulder. Another sailboat! Heh-heh. This time, I only surf the right wake for a few sec-onds, but it boosts me after the top twen-ty boats. They all hug the eastern, rip-rap bank of the channel, trying to avoid buf-fets of a head current from a rising tide as it ascends the estuary against us.

My strategic assessment: a good wake surf or two would far outweigh any disadvantage involved in crossing the channel against the current. So far, so good. I've even made up for my awful start.

Now I pick out a white sea kayak, slightly ahead and far to the right, that I want to fall in behind. I try to smooth out my stroke and find a good, aerobic rhythm for my paddling. Doesn't work. Still feel far too hyper. Due to the gin-seng? Pure adrenaline? Perhaps a more problematic substance: ambition.

You see, I've been whitewater kayaking for 20 years. Before that, in college in Tallahassee, it was canoes— big old battered, echoing Grummans that I bashed down the tannin-stained rivers of the Florida Panhandle. So, self-propulsion in small boats I have always found a seductive form of fun.

I've lived near San Francisco Bay now for most of the past decade. I'd joined a sea kayak race or two in the early 1990s, almost by default, as a way to visit with fellow paddlers. But my lackadaisical attitude toward kayak racing itself underwent a seachange in 1994, when I found myself taking third in the inaugural "Race for the Treasure" (ten-mile course, traditional men's single sea kayaks, open division), at age 43. I actually won a gol-dang medal.

A strong lust to compete and to excel began to rear its head. It was not stimulated by this brass trinket, per se. A far bigger stimulus was a born-again pride in physicality, something I hadn't felt for a while. I, a geezer in my 40s, had somehow found the stuff to actually do well. This experience gave me hope for the future . . . in every conceivable way.

So, here I was, whipping waters of the Oakland Estuary once again, enacting a further phase of that hope. Having done so serendipitously before, this time I'd grown determined early on to devote physical effort—as well as some strategic thought—to doing better.

Keith and Tammy Miller, droll proprietors of California Canoe & Kayak (a Jack London Square–based string of shops in Oakland which sponsors this race) are my pals, so they made contributions to the war effort. First, they helped me get my mitts on the slim, fast Arluk 1.9, a demo boat borrowed from a Necky rep. Second, Keith and I went on a number of training runs up and down the Oakland Estuary in the weeks prior to the race.

The rest was up to me. I had my ideal boat, and I had my paddle—a long (240cm.) and ancient Perception blade. It's a patched-up artifact from an obsolete stroking philosophy, especially compared to my ultra sleek, ultra modern boat, but it still did me just fine. I also had my strategy: part dealt with that starting line maneuver; part dealt with swiping momentum pushed from the wakes of passing boats; some involved my analysis of Bay tidal currents and vectors. The ultimate aspect meant using knowledge of my own body and the best way to pace my physical effort.

Beyond that stuff, considerable consideration now goes into picking the rest of my gear. For racing, from the head down, I wear: a Sequel visored cap with neck cape (this hat was invented by a former Mount Rainier ranger, and it's the world's best for dealing with wind and harsh sunlight); I sport a new pair of Ray-Ban Wayfarers (these sunglasses feel quite comfortable on me, and nothing cuts water glare like their dark, polarizing lenses. Besides, ever since Don Johnson re-popularized them on the old TV show "Miami Vice," Wayfarer glasses have radiated a tad of bad coolth, a kind of retro, Art Deco sang-froid). Beneath both of these, I wear a thick scum of AloeGator SPF 40 sungel, to keep my paleface Celtic hide from blistering in case I need to shed the hat at some point.

On my back, I wear a fluid pod from Mark Pack, with a drinking tube poised right next to a corner of my mouth, so I wouldn't even need to break paddling cadence to bend my head and slurp a sip. People can have different reactions to the array of sports energy drinks on the market. In my case,

Cytomax (a favorite of most bicycle racers) seems to work best, so my pod is brimfull of this liquid rocket fuel (Hawaiian Punch flavor, if you really want to know.)

Under my life vest, I wear a beat-up, sleeveless T-shirt with a logo from the Tlingit tribe of Haines, Alaska, on it: a leaping salmon with the words "Lkoot Kwaan" ("The People of the Salmon"). On a trip to Alaska, I'd swapped a Tlingit woman a walking stick for this shirt. By wearing it now, I intended to invoke the energy of the Tatshenshini, one of the wildest river canyons of which I know.

Under the T-shirt, I wear thick gobs of Vaseline smeared in my armpits to relieve friction from the paddling motion, and small strips of adhesive over my nipples to keep the life vest movement from rubbing them raw. (Is this a sexy sport, or what?)

So, as you can see, my ducks are in a row, my loins girded, my spell cast. Now, it's showtime, racetime, put-up-or-shut-up hour.

The fluster and flurry of the start are over. Even though the lead paddlers have not yet left the channel, our match-up already enters its next phase. Racers now stretch out into a ragged string, with segments or clusters of boats along its length. Within these loose groupings, individuals focus on gaining on the boat just ahead and losing those behind.

As I vector across the channel, I lower my theoretical crosshairs on particular bearded gent who paddles a Wilderness Systems Sealution. I fall behind and begin drafting him, to save my muscle energy in the trip out the channel. I figure I'll bust out on my own once I reach the rough waters of the open Bay. Drafting will be more difficult out there anyway.

The nose of my Arluk hovers scant inches away from his rudder post. I can feel an ease imparted from his cleaving of the surface for me, as well as a certain amount of glide granted by the surge-swell that rises directly in his wake and right under my hull. I enjoy the sensation, the feel that the level of energy needed to maintain speed is reduced.

But this paddler leading me—later, I learn his name is Larry Froley—evidently hates being drafted. He surges ahead then slows down, glances over his shoulder to glare at me with one baleful eye, then kicks his rudder from side to side, trying to shake me off his path.

Amusing. Of course, were our positions reversed, I might hate it too. Even though I am not harming his performance directly by parasitizing it, he seems to object to me using anything of his to make my own race easier. By this very reaction—spurting ahead then slowing and altering course—I feel that he is harming himself far more than me.

For awhile, I tag along anyway, trying to mimic his shifty tactics. But Froley spurts far harder than I, so I eventually drop off and attach myself like a remora to another paddler who apparently could care less about being drafted.

Doesn't last long anyway. The channel spoon pours itself into the wide sparkling waters of the San Francisco Bay. Those waters sparkle, of course, because of waves, lots of waves, shifting in the sunlight. The Bay is rarely calm. Rather, it is a melange of shifting tidal currents, as a half a trillion gallons of sea water slosh in and out under the GoldenGate bridge four times each day. Just to give you an idea of the scale of what's involved, at mean low tide the Bay's surface area sprawls out to 260 square miles. Jets of tidal current can hit between three and five knots.

As California's great Central Valley heats up, winds pour in from the sea too, swirling and bounding over the waters, and sometimes drawing great gouts of fog, thick banks that pour through the city and around Angel Island and Alcatraz like dry ice vapors steaming off Neptune's vasty stein.

Today is sunny, but breezy, and those fabled currents are doing their thing. My tidelog (a beautifully crafted journal put out by Pacific Publishers of Bolinas) shows a 0.8-knot incoming current that will increase to a 1.9-knot current over the period of the race. My plans are laid accordingly. Instead of darting straight for the Treasure Island beach that is our turnaround point, I intend to take a more southerly route, going past two buoys in order to gain fresh information about the force and direction of these specific tidal streams. Then I'll approach the beach from a more southerly direction, somewhat in the island's current shadow.

I'm out on my own now, far from any possibility of drafting. Except for one last, large sailboat motoring out past me from the estuary to play with breezes on the Bay. Wake-surfing does not work on this choppy surface, but I give it a go and manage to gain a few spurts when bay wave and boat wake synchronize their undulation.

The guys on the boat, including one round Dennis Connor look-alike, who stands swathed in spotless yachting whites, holler something at me.

"Can't hear you!" I yell back. "I've got headphones on, and I'm swinging this paddle to Flamenco guitar right now!" And it's true. My lucky radio station is hosing my brain down with muchissimo Machismo classico, and as that wild guitar spurts and strums, I stomp my paddle blades down into the brine and forge on.

Now that I am not seeking to catch or closely match any other paddler, I finally get my own rhythm. The heartbeats, the lung intakes, the shoulder swing, the bite and pull of the paddle, all fit themselves as a counterpoint to the strum of the strings of the radio guitar. No matter what happens from here on out, hitting that harmony for maximal physical output is a sweet if sweaty sensation, and I smile and think that the race will have been worth it for this experience alone.

The first buoy is tilted on its anchor chain. The second one, out farther in the channel between the island and Oakland, is really heeled over by the force of the tidal current. Its angle of lean helps me plot a course for my eventual return trip. I think a moon-arc course. However, theirs could belly far to the south. They may lose control of their final angle of re-entry to the estuary, and thus could wind up fighting back into this current much more than they gain any boost from it.

This thought alone gives me confidence as I finally near the floating marker of the turn-around off the Treasure Island beach. Otherwise, my situation lacks charm. Froley in his Sealution and another guy on a long "surf ski" have actually gained some lengths on me, perhaps as many as 20, by going straight for the beach instead of past the mid-channel buoys.

They round the course marker at Treasure Island and pass me heading back in the opposite direction. They feel so secure with their lead, both these guys even deign to offer me some encouragement as they blow by. Grrr! I think. Thanks for the help, but I actually would like it better if you feared more that I might catch up to you!

So I swing around the marker myself and strike out for the north. This is my big gamble. If it works, I've got a fighting chance. If it doesn't, ah well, they had me beat anyway.

There's a part in a long race that is intensely private and solitary. It deals with how well you relate to your own body when you push it to extremes, how much you listen to the resistance of the muscles and the small aches and pains . . . how much do you drive yourself past them toward a zone of your own personal best.

In this case, my energy is up. I am slurping the Cytomax from my back pack's sip tube now, and feel like I have plenty of gas. The ultra-long paddle seems to swing well and my form with it is good as long as I remember to snap the blade out of the water soon enough to avoid drag from that inefficient, last part of the stroke. My shoulder muscles and forearms don't cramp up, as they did a bit last year in my race for Treasure.

Only problem is that my T-shirt has ridden up, baring the skin at my waist, and the edge of the kayak backrest is chafing me, chafing with every stroke. Well, I can stop, lose a few precious strokes of momentum, fiddle with it, and make it comfy, or I can ignore all the pain and press on. My nose is fastened like a questing hound on the scent of Froley's stern. I wanna blow that guy

away! Big, aggressive, stupid ape instinct, sure, yet very enjoyable. So I press on.

Now I ride in the main thrust of the tidal current, and I let my bow swing with it. As this arc completes, I sweep down with the tide toward the mouth of the estuary. Hallelujah! This part of the plan works. I gain 15 boatlengths on Froley with this single maneuver. I can see that his course got bellied out to the south, and he's fighting a sideways push from the current much more than I.

Knowledge that I am gaining inspires more power for my stroke. The classical music on my headphones breaks up into static, but now I don't mind losing it. A visceral harmony resonates out of my spine, nerves, and muscles.

Passing Froley now. For some reason, as we re-enter the estuary, he rudders back over the rip-rap along the rocky east bank. Doesn't he know the strongest push from the tidal current will be found out here plumb in the center of the channel!?!? Ah well, not my problem! Ta-ta!

There! Past the huge gantry cranes for Oakland cargo ships that look like spectral, skeletal, Trojan horses reared against the sky. There, in the distance, the American flag floats and wrinkles atop the big flagpole in Jack London Square. Right underneath is the finish line. The old Stars 'n Stripes never looked so good.

Wham, wham, wham. That big old paddle takes every bit of strength I can bend onto the shaft, and then the dock comes into sight. I take a half second to whip my hat off and ram it down the front of my life vest. Light bounces from my bald head like a beacon as I drive for the line and I make out friends bouncing and yelling on the sideline as I cut the blades deep for one last lunge, then scoot across the finish to let that long, lean 1.9 coast for the first time in a long time.

I kick the rudder over hard to starboard so she circles to give me a good view of the rest of the racers as they come on in. My time is one hour, fifty-three minutes, seven seconds.

Here comes Froley. His time is 1:55:37. Immediately, as he drifts to a stop, I seek him out. Not to bask in my triumph of beating him in the second half—although in some wormy, ego-addled part of my psyche that motivation probably slithers around—but because I want to remove any sting I may have caused by trying to draft him in the first half.

Froley is quite friendly and congratulatory.

"I couldn't believe it when I saw you pass me back there," he says. "I thought, he CAN'T have that much energy left!"

"I didn't," I say.

He regards me with silent inquiry.

"Tidal current," I say. "Down the center of the channel. Helped. A lot."

Wry comprehension dawns on his face. "I didn't take time to study the tide charts," he admits.

"Ah," says I.

Something in our encounter makes me think of that classic T-shirt slogan: Age and Treachery Will Beat Youth and Skill Every Time. Not that that's true, mind you. But it's an entertaining notion. Particularly today.

Yet Froley has scored his own triumph. He entered himself in the Open Division for traditional, single sea kayaks, whereas I had signed up in the Masters. In his division, Larry takes first, whereas I was up against the other geezers who were far leaner, meaner, and better schemers than I (also guys who had been racing years longer). And in that grizzled, geezer Masters Division, my time didn't even place. Our Masters winner was Mike Riordan, in an Eddyline Sea Star, with a time of 1:36:30.

So the only medal I take home from this race is a round spot where chafing from that backrest wore completely through my hide. (This wound will take three weeks to heal and leave a round pink scar.)

I vow that from now on I'm only going to enter the Open Division, to beat up on the young guys. Those old birds in Masters, many of whom have been racing for decades, are just too tough 'n smart.

In my mind, I lay a course toward the next two races in our area, the Sea Trek Regatta in Sausalito in the fall, and the Tsunami Rangers' Sea Gypsy open-ocean race out of Half Moon Bay that comes in late spring. More training runs are called for, perhaps many more. Out to Tomales Bay, Drake's Estero, Elkhorn Slough— perhaps any of Northern California's sweet paddling venues.

How interesting, I think, that the sea kayak, a sublime yet simple watercraft dating back at least six millennia, should become the sort of conveyance for humanity it is nowadays. In bygone times, the kayak transported bold Greenland hunters in search of the walrus and Aleut near-slaves to grab sea otter hides for their Russkie overlords.

Now it takes over-urbanized men out on a voyage to discover wild marine excitement and physical health as they paddle on in their middle years. We are like Tennyson's Ulysses setting sail from Ithaca again. The boon of leathery, tough, and risible old age shall be our ultimate trophy.

When not calculating devious ways to stay ahead of the pack in local sea kayak races, Paul McHugh can be found behind his desk at the San Francisco Chronicle, *where he works as an outdoors writer.*

Huck Finn-style on the Potomac

by Richard Bangs

It's a singularly American rite of passage, reading Mark Twain's master-piece, *The Adventures of Huckleberry Finn.* I was a junior at Walt Whitman High School in Bethesda, MD, and the story of Huck and Jim and their raft trip down the Mississippi affected me in a way that Jay Gatsby and his silk shirts, or John Marcher and his figurative beast, or George Babbit's conformity, or even Natty Bumppo's "noble savage" never would. Huck discovered adventure, beauty, self-reliance, peace, and true human values by rafting down the river. "It's lovely to live on a raft," Huck said, and I believed him. I wanted to raft a river.

I lived just a few miles from the Potomac, the "River of the Traders," as the 17th-century Indians who bartered tobacco and catfish near my house called it. One Sunday my family took a hike on the towpath of the Chesapeake and Ohio (C&O) canal near Great Falls, 15 miles above Washington, D.C., where the river is squeezed through an obstacle course of massive boulders and in just a half a mile roars down-ward some 75 feet. Juno, our golden retriever, saw a squirrel and made a beeline down a tight, overgrown path. I followed, and found myself on the edge of a 200-foot-high cliff overlooking the Potomac as she swirled through Mather Gorge, a granite defile described at the turn of the century as "The Grand Canyon of the East." The sight was dazzling, the fast currents spinning the reflecting light as thousands of silver pinwheels were washing downstream. I was hypnotized, drawn towards the shimmering water, and I knew I had to get on that river.

Monday morning I announced to Miss Hammonad, my English teacher, I want-ed to build a raft and journey down the Potomac just like Huckleberry Finn. She said fine, as long as I didn't miss any school. The three-day Memorial Day weekend was coming up, so I thought that would be the chance. I recruited my camping friends John Yost, Ricky Vierbuchen, Dave Nurney, Fred Higgins, and Steve Hatlegerg, and together we started gathering the equipment we'd need to build our raft and float the Potomac. We picked out an eight-mile run through Mather Gorge, one that expert kayakers had been running for years. Though, as we talked to the experts, including a Scuba rescue team who would routinely retrieve drowned bodies from the river, the prognosis was that we wouldn't make it through on a log raft; the rapids were too treacherous. The word of our expedition spread through the student body, and the editor of the school newspaper, Dan Reifsnyder, approached me for the exclusive story. At 17, Dan was already hardboiled and he smelled disaster in my little plan. He made no pretense of his looking for blood, or a spectacular failure, to fill column space in an upcoming issue. I said I was happy to give him the story but I was certain he'd be disappointed: we planned to make it down the river on time and intact.

On Friday afternoon we all set up camp not far below Great Falls, and with axes and saws started cutting the timber we needed. We rolled the logs to our assembly spot down by the river and began binding them with cross pieces and eight-inch gutter nails. Our raft was about half-finished when a stentorian voice echoed across the canyon. "Have you ever messed with a German Shepherd?" It was a park ranger, calling from atop a palisade of gneiss on the Virginia side, a huge dog at his side. "You're on National Park land. You can't cut down trees, you can't build a raft, and you can't camp. Now get outta' there before I come get ya'." It was the end of our dream trip. We slowly packed up and trudged back to the parking lot. On the drive out we passed a ranger vehicle coming in and guessed it was our friend with the German Shepherd.

We still had two days of vacation left and couldn't go back home—not with everyone expecting us to have at least attempted our raft expedition. So we headed for Bear Island, a popular camping spot below Mather Gorge, and

holed up there for the rest of the long weekend, swimming, fishing, and trying to forget our failure.

Monday night we were back at my house cleaning the camping gear when the phone range. It was Dan Reifsnyder, pompous editor of the *Black and White,* our school rag, and he wanted the scoop on our expedition. I put my hand over the receiver, and talked to our team. "Let's tell him we did it," I proposed with a grin. "We can't," Steve Hatleberg countered. "It's not the Christian thing to do." In *The Adventures of Huckleberry Finn,* Huck has to battle with his conscience continuously because according to the morality of society and the church he should have reported runaway slave Jim, whom he had come to love as a brother. His final decision in Jim's favor was concluded with his famous reflection, "All right then, I'll go to hell!" I put the receiver to my mouth and started to tell Dan about our raft trip.

On June 9, the article appeared, entitled "Rapids Capsize Craft; Raftsman Score First." It went on to say, "The raft had to be scrapped in the middle of Yellow Rapids. 'We scrambled for the inner tubes and kept going,' boasted junior Richard Bangs . . . 'You wondered if you were going to live,' . . . 'Man, was I scared,' . . . 'It was out of sight, like an LSD trip.' These were just a few of the emotions described by the group, all of whom made the entire passage alive."

The article gave us some notoriety and inspired us to form "The Raft Club," which would later become SOBEK. Steve Hatleberg couldn't live with our secret though, and one day told Dan the full and true story. To Dan's credit, he never pursued it in print, but whenever I passed him in the hall he gave me that drop-dead stare that editors around the world have mastered. And it made me want to make good on the Potomac.

It was still early summer when I saw an ad on the bulletin board at the grocery store. It told of a 17.5-foot fiberglass Old Town canoe for sale, for $150. I called all the members of The Raft Club and asked if anyone would go in with me on halves. Ricky Vierbuchen had the $75, so we bought the canoe, painted R&R on the stern (we flipped a coin for top billing), and toted our new toy down to Bear Island. We launched and headed upstream towards the crystalline mouth of Mather Gorge.

We were awkward paddlers, and the canoe cranked through the water as though drunk. We bobbed and weaved upstream and slowly picked up some proficiency as we angled towards Difficult Run Rapids, marking the end of the gorge. The white-breasted water got faster as we got closer, and my blood accelerated correspondingly. This was exciting. Then we were in the roostertails of the rapid, being flung up and down on a dizzy aquatic seesaw, paddling with all of our strength. "Let's go higher," I screamed over the rapid's roar, and we sunk our blades deeper and lunged forward. Then the bow snapped to its side, abruptly capsizing the canoe and precipitating us into the spume. We'd been christened as river runners.

Rick and I spent all our free time that summer in our blue canoe, exploring new routes, refining techniques, scoring the bottom of our boat with a matrix of scratches and dents. We made many of the classic runs, including the coup de grace run of the Potomac beginning at the base of Great Falls, where the Potomac spectacularly drops over the edge of the continental bedrock onto the sedimentary soil of the coastal plain. Above Great Falls the river stretches to a half-mile in width; below, it pinches into the 60-foot-wide Mather Gorge, where we would negotiate through S-Turn Rapids, Rocky Island Rapids, Wet Bottom Chute, and past the ancient rocks that formed the exit gate to the canyon. We would continue downstream on a wider, but no less magnificent, river through Yellow Rapids and Stubblefield Falls, underneath the Cabin John Bridge carrying the Capital Beltway (I-495) past the Carderock Picnic Area where climbers crawl like flies on impossible faces, down to Sycamore Island and the Brookmont Dam. Constructed in the 1950s for the city water supply with no thought for the safety of boaters, the deceptively innocuous weir is a death-trap for upset paddlers, with a perpetual hydraulic that, like a black hole with stray light, sucks in boats and bodies, never to let them go. A sign adjacent to the pumping station states that an average of seven people a year drown in this area. Its nickname is "The Drowning Machine."

Below Brookmont is the most exciting single mile of navigable whitewater along the entire 383-mile course of the Potomac, culminating in the explosive Little Falls, in which the entire river is funneled from parking lot width to a Grand Prix raceway, then spectacularly split in two by a sharp granite-slab island. It was here Captain John Smith, in his search for the elusive Northwest Passage, was stopped in his upriver journey in 1608. Little Falls is the last whitewater, or the first, depending on which way you're traveling. In the massive flood of 1936, the velocity of the water was recorded as the fastest ever in nature. Just below is Chain Bridge. A short way beyond the river this becomes tidewater and the nation's capital begins to spread its concrete tentacles along the banks.

Rick and I never canoed the Little Falls section; it was beyond our abilities. But that didn't mean we couldn't run it. With the money I'd saved working as a car hop at the local Kentucky Fried Chicken outlet, I purchased a yellow Taiwanese-made, four-man raft from Sunny's Surplus. And with it we paddled out to Snake Island across from Brookmont pumping station, and slipped over the killer weir where we thought the one clear passage down a fish ladder was supposed to be. But we missed and were suddenly in the backwashing hydraulic, capsized, bouncing about in the aerated water along with beach balls, chunks of cooler Styrofoam, rubber sandals, branches, and other debris stuck in the eternal washing machine. I remembered reading that the only way to escape a strong recirculating hydraulic was to abandon one's lifejacket and dive beneath the surface where the water makes its deep-water exit. But I couldn't bring myself to take off my flotation, which was propping my mouth just above the terrible soapy froth. I looked over to Ricky, who was choking with water splashed into his throat. "Let's swim toward the island," I yelled above the weir's gargling. And though it was slow going, we found it possible to dog paddle perpendicular to the current, along the hydraulic line, back toward Snake Island. I towed our little yellow raft, and after several scary minutes we reached the edge of the island, where the water accelerated as the river narrowed and the waves grew thicker with each stroke. Then the final pitch

presented itself, with the river piling up onto the anvil-shaped island, spilling off either side into huge, complex rapids. We blasted straight down the middle, plowed into the saber-toothed island, spun backwards, then collapsed over the falls on the Virginia side, the worst side. The first drop catapulted Ricky into the air. When he fell back into the bilge, the floor of the raft peeled back like a sardine can, depositing Ricky into the depths. I continued to paddle alone, my feet dragging in the current where the floor had been, my neck spinning looking for signs of Ricky. The roar of the rapid muffled as I strained to hear Ricky's cry. Hours later, or so the seconds seemed, Ricky resurfaced 50 yards downstream, all smiles. Climbing back on board, we paddled to our take-out at Chain Bridge on the Virginia side, where my mother was waiting with the Oldsmobile and a prayer.

I discovered the lack of floor didn't make much difference in the tiny Taiwan boat, and continued to use it for runs down Little Falls in the following weeks with various members of the Raft Club, even Steve Hatleberg, who thought he saw God during one capsize. For us it was the ultimate thrill in a suburban existence conspicuously short of same.

I fell in love with the Potomac that summer and wanted to know everything about her: every dimple, every curve, where she came from, and where she was going. I began to study her serpentine mysteries in my free time. She trickles forth at an altitude of 3,140 feet just downhill from the crest of Backbone Mountain in a deep fold of the Allegheny Mountains in West Virginia. There she seeps from a spring beneath a chunk of rock called the Fairfax Stone after the colonial landowner Lord Fairfax. The fledgling river soon becomes the Maryland-West Virginia border, loops back and forth around Appalachian ridges in the region of the Paw Paw bends, and then bursts through the Blue Ridge Mountains at Harper's Ferry, where she is joined by the Shenandoah. Here the plunging slopes and rolling rapids make "perhaps one of the most stupendous scenes in nature," Thomas Jefferson wrote, "worth a voyage across the Atlantic." Continuing her journey, the Potomac levels off, now alive with geese and eagles, oysters and shad. She eventually becomes a seven-mile-wide tidal giant, easing majestically into Chesapeake Bay as she stretches between the Maryland and Virginia shores.

As summer faded to fall the frequency of our trips decreased because of cooler weather, school commitments, and a new diversion: women. Ricky and I were both taken by a tall blonde named Arlene Wergen. The air surged with the dull clacking sound of soft, young antlers in nervous ritual combat. Since he shared homeroom and some classes with her, Ricky had the advantage and he exploited it. He took Arlene caving, camping, and bought her an expensive friendship ring. I had an ace up my sleeve, however—the river. I just had to wait for the right moment.

It came in mid-December. We were in the midst of an unseasonable heat-wave, and the weatherman said the upcoming weekend would be warm enough for outdoor activities. I asked Arlene if she'd like to go canoeing.

I picked out a run I had always wanted to do, a stretch beginning in Bloomery, WV, on the Shenandoah, running to the confluence with the Potomac, and continuing below Harper's Ferry, the place where John Brown's body lies a moulderin' in the grave. The ten-mile run was supposed to be beautiful, with some challenging rapids and good camping—all important ingredients in what I perceived to be an important weekend.

Saturday morning was clear and crisp as we loaded the blue canoe and headed downriver through an arch of sycamores and silver maples. The river here had sawed away at the mountains as they rose up beneath it, imbedding itself 1,200 feet and more in the Blue Ridge. I was wearing my new letter sweater, which I had been awarded for the dubious honor of managing the soccer team. Still, it was a badge and I wore it proudly with hopes it would impress Arlene. It was a beautiful day brimming with a sense of adventure and romance, and I could tell Arlene shared the thrill of a live vessel beneath us sliding gently over brawling water. An ad for Canadian Club had been running that fall showing a couple canoeing the rapids. The woman in the bow looked very much like Arlene, and though I bore no resemblance, I felt like the man in the stern.

As we eased our way down the river, the sun's rays reflected off the water, and I started to warm. I took off my letter sweater and bundled it in front of my knees. At lunch we pulled over beneath a spreading willow, and I prepared a sumptuous repast with Pouilly Fuisse and brie and French bread. As we took our first bites, a pint-sized bark came from behind, and a little puppy bounded into our picnic. He was a mongrel, but with the biggest brown eyes I'd ever seen and a wiggly, irresistible appeal for affection. For Arlene it was puppy love at first sight. She fed the little mutt all of her meal, and then some of mine, and asked if we could bring her along. "But she must belong to somebody," I protested. "Please go check," she implored, and I got up to make a search. Sure enough, I could find no evidence of owners within a mile of our mooring, and came to the conclusion that the puppy was indeed hopelessly lost.

So we perched the puppy on my letter jacket and continued downriver. As the day wore on it began to cloud and the temperature dropped. The puppy was asleep, so I didn't bother to put on my letter jacket, but instead, paddled harder to keep warm. By late afternoon we approached the river-wide ledge of Blue Falls, which the guide book rated as difficult but doable and recommended a portage for less-than-expert boaters. Checking my watch, I saw that we were at least an hour behind schedule; the puppy incident had taken precious time. The guide book said the portage around Bull Falls took over an hour, an hour we didn't have on a short mid-winter day. If we portaged, we'd have to paddle the final miles after dark, a dangerous proposition in the cold of December. And after a full summer of canoeing, I figured that I was more than less-than-expert and could make the run.

So, we rammed ahead into Bull Falls. The entry was perfect, gliding between the boulders as though on a track, slipping down the drop as though by design. At the bottom I held the canoe paddle above my head and screamed, "We made it!" But I was premature. The tidal waves at the bottom of the rapid continued to wash over the bow of the canoe and the boat filled with turbid Potomac. By the time we reached the last wave we were swamped

and the canoe phlegmatically rolled over, dispatching us into the icy river. The current was swift here and the cold punched my breath away. With one hand I hung onto the canoe, with the other I tried to paddle, all the while yelling for Arlene to swim to shore. Then I saw my letter jacket surface a few feet away. That jacket meant the world to me, so I started paddling toward it. Then, a feeble yelp. The puppy was spinning in an eddy in the opposite direction. For a quick second I weighed my options. I could retrieve only one. I went for the puppy.

A few hundred yards downstream I managed to grapple the canoe to shore with the puppy still held above my head in my one free hand. Arlene was there, shivering violently, yet she gave the puppy a hug that would crush a bear. Both Arlene and I had lost our paddles in the capsize, though I had one spare strapped to the center thwart. I emptied the canoe, turned it over, and tried to tell Arlene to get back in, but my speech was slurred; I could barely form words. I was becoming hypothermic. So was Arlene. I knew we couldn't stop here— we had nothing dry and it was getting dark. We'd die if we stayed. I pressed Arlene into the bow of the canoe and she crouched over the trembling puppy while I pushed us off. I had just the one paddle, but I dug in with all of my strength. The sun dipped behind the trees and a chilling wind blew up the valley. Barely able to see the rocks, I propelled us into the last rapids, the mile-long Staircase. We scraped and bumped and banged every few seconds, but somehow we emerged in one piece at the Route 340 bridge below Harper's Ferry, where my car awaited.

My plans for a romantic campout were scrapped that night. Rather than a hero, I was a bungler who almost cost us our lives, and worse, the life of the puppy, who won the contest for Arlene's heart and became her constant companion. Still, I remained hung-up on Arlene, as did Ricky. But it was unrequited love. As the school year wound down, Arlene started dating a Young Republican, a radical act in the Vietnam era. When Ricky and I independently asked Arlene to the Senior Prom, she turned us both down for the right-wing radical. We'd been left high and dry. Neither of us found alternative dates for the most socially significant event in a teenager's life. So we turned to one another and said, "Let's go run a river."

We picked the Smoke Hole Canyon section of the South Branch of the Potomac in West Virginia for two reasons: we'd never done it before and it was as far away from the prom as we could get and still be on our favorite river. It was a section described by George Washington as, "two ledges of Mountain Impassable running side by side together for seven or eight miles and ye River down between them." So, as the senior class was slipping into crinoline and tuxedos, we were fitting our kneepads and lifejackets. And as carnations were being exchanged, we were trading strokes on the upper Potomac. Mockingbirds called from the wooded cathedral through which we passed, hardly giving us any solace. It was springtime and the delicate pink blossoms of the laurel and the notched white flowers of the dogwood dappled the greening banks. We moved to music, but not the Motown our peers were enjoying, rather the haunting whistle of the lordly cardinal. The river here was shallow, stinging cold from the spring runoff. Some miles below our launch we struck a moss-encrusted rock jutting out into the current like some miniature Lorelei. The siren rock punched a hole the size of my fist in our fiberglass hull.

We didn't have the materials or the time to properly repair the hole in our boat, so we stuffed the puncture with spare clothing and continued downstream. It was slow going. We'd paddle ten minutes, then pull over for the same to bail. When we emptied the canoe for camp at twilight, we discovered our neoprene duffel bag had not been waterproof; all of our gear, sleeping bags, tents, and food had been soaked. We dragged everything up a knoll of weathered limestone overlooking the Potomac, erected the wet tent, and laid the rest of our effects out to dry in the waning minutes of daylight. It was quickly evident that our attempts to dry the gear by natural means would not work and that it was going to be a nippy night. We had several packs of matches, but they were all saturated and wouldn't light. We gathered wood and with our knives trimmed paper-thin shavings that would light at the least spark. But we went through several packs of matches and couldn't get that spark. With nightfall, the air became brittle and we jumped up and down, slapping our sides to keep warm. Our classmates were doing the jerk in the Whitman gym and we felt like the dance as we flapped in the dark. But it wasn't working and we knew we couldn't do the Freddy all night. We needed to build a fire as much as Jack London ever did. If we didn't we could perish and we both knew it.

Then Ricky literally got a bright idea. The flashlight still worked, so why not unscrew the lens covering the bulb and put the remaining matches inside the glass, against the filament bulb, where they could dry from the heat of the light? We had five matches left and inside they went. The flashlight was going dead. We unscrewed the top, took out the matches, and tried to light the first one. In my haste, I tore off the head of the match. The second actually lit, but before I could touch it to the kindling it blew out in the cold wind. I cupped my hand around the third as I struck. It spat to life, and as I touched it to the shavings, the fire took. In minutes we had a bonfire around which we sat and dried our clothes and sleeping bags. We bathed in the warmth all night, continuing to feed the fire and occasionally looking down the hill at the Potomac meandering in the moonlight in curves that looked somewhat like Arlene's. As with our classmates, that was a special night filled with danger and promise, with rites of passage, and with friendship and warmth.

The Potomac had dealt us some blows since our first assignation, but she had given me some of the most exquisite moments of my existence. On that prom night, high on a limestone ridge, I realized I really loved the river, deeply, and that I had found a consort for life. I discovered, as Tom Sawyer finally said to Huckleberry Finn, that all I really wanted to do was "have adventures plum in the mouth of the river." On that prom night I lost and found a certain innocence and readied for the adventures of tomorrow—the great adventures cached just around the next bend, just out of sight, on the river.

The Tragic Summer of 1997

by Eugene Buchanan

Flags flying half-mast at the Olympic Training Center. A scale-model dory, engulfed in flames, carrying ashes down the Grand Canyon's Lava Falls. A Chevy Chevelle, topped with flowers and kayaks, making one last shuttle to the Roaring Fork's Slaughterhouse run. A riverside service during September's World Rodeo Championships.

Rich Weiss. Dugald Bremner. Henry Filip. Chuck Kern.

Like a word-association puzzle, lines can be drawn from the above scenarios to the above names. Doing so, however, reveals a startling truth: the summer of 1997 will go down as one of the most tragic seasons in the history of whitewater kayaking.

Other people have died kayaking. A total of 15 in the U.S.1977 alone, to be exact. But never have as many high-profile paddlers perished within such a short time frame. Weiss, Bremner, Filip, and Kern. The names rattle off the tongue like a law firm. They were among the best of the best, well-known throughout the industry. Weiss, whose death caused flags to fly half-mast at the Olympic Training Center, was a two-time Olympian. Bremner, whose friends floated a flaming dory as a funeral pyre down Lava Falls, was a popular outdoor photographer and Grand Canyon guide. Filip, whose flower-covered Chevy stayed with him until his last shuttle, was a leading figure in Colorado boating circles. Kern—remembered by rodeo competitors with a blue ribbon tied to their lifejackets at the '97 Worlds—was Perception's western technical rep who had earned a berth on the U.S. rodeo team. One eight-week period; the deaths of four high-profile paddlers.

The unsettling part is that they all died on the water, pursuing a sport they loved. And they all died paddling Class V. "It's really sobering," says Perception's Risa Shimoda Callaway, personal friend of Weiss and Kern. "Hopefully it will make people think a little more about what they're doing." The problem, she adds, is a simple case of numbers. "The sport's no more dangerous than it was before, it's just that more and more people are running harder and harder rivers," she says, admitting that the summer's deaths have caused her to reassess running difficult drops. "The number of difficult rivers being done is staggering, especially compared to a few years ago. Everybody has an off day, and if you have one when you're paddling difficult runs four or five times a week, you're putting yourself at risk.

"What's scary," she adds, "is when you start counting all the close calls, the ones people don't hear about. That, and the fact that it could happen to anybody. There's no reason it should have been Chuck instead of someone else. And in Rich's case, ten other people would have made the same decision in the same situation."

That, of course, is exactly what is sending ripples of uncertainty throughout top-level players in the industry. "It definitely makes you think twice about what you're doing," says Ed Lucero,

Rich Weiss

Rich Weiss and John "Tree" Trujillo put in on Washington's Class V Upper White Salmon River on June 25. The river was running four feet (about 2,000 cfs), almost a foot above average. The two knew the river well, having run it at 4.5 feet two days earlier. After three quarters of a mile, they pulled over to scout Big Brother, a 30-foot waterfall with a small lead-in drop of about two feet, followed by a 28-foot waterfall. The falls are shallow on the left two-thirds, with most of the water going over the right one-third into a hydraulic. Mist rising from river right makes it difficult to see what is going on below. On river right about six to nine feet out from the base of the falls, but still in the backwash of the hydraulic, is an undercut cave visible at 3.5 feet but not visible on the day of the accident. Below the hydraulic is a pool, followed by another 15-foot waterfall. The correct line is a wide peel-out from river left two-thirds of the way across the river, enabling you to move from river right back to river left following a seam away from the hydraulic. John went first, flipped at the bottom, rolled, and eddied out on the left. Rich did not get left soon enough, dropped into the hydraulic on river right, and was immediately back-endered.

When John saw that Rich was stuck in the hydraulic (he couldn't tell whether Rich was still in the boat), he exited his boat and proceeded upstream along a narrow bank jutting five feet out from the wall, getting as close to the hydraulic as possible. During this period Rich's boat washed out, but there was no sign of Rich. John started throwing his throw-rope into the falls and into the underwater cave, to no avail. When he saw this was not working, he hiked out to the road, hitchhiked to town and called the sheriff. When the sheriff arrived, John led him and two rescue team members to the river, where they found Rich's body 100 feet downstream of the second falls, washed up on river right against a ten-inch-diameter log. His lifejacket and helmet were still on. He had a slight cut over his left eye, with a second small cut on the right temple. No other marks were noticed. The cause of death was ruled as drowning, but there is no way of telling whether a blow to the head caused unconsciousness first, or whether he drowned before the head injury.

a prominent hairboater and friend of Kern's. "I didn't paddle hard stuff for a few weeks after Chuck died. Richie's

death I could write off as sort of a fluke, but with Chuck it was just too much."

Dugald Bremner

On June 3, 1997, outdoor photographer, kayaker, and Grand Canyon river guide Dugald Bremner and three companions found themselves on the Silver Fork of California's American River. By early afternoon they reached the most difficult rapid and stopped to scout. High flows poured over a ledge, obscuring a sieve of faults siphoning much of the water through the bedrock. Dugald entered the current and lined up on what appeared to be simple turbulence at the head of the falls. In reality, the turbulence marked a submerged fissure cutting into the bedrock with water folding in from both sides. As he followed the flow, his nose hit a shallow piece of bedrock and stalled, causing his stern to snag in the crevice. The current dragged the boat down quickly, and Dugald asked Eric Brown, standing on shore, for help. While the other kayakers were downstream scouting, ready to assist possible trouble encountered on a series of lower pourovers, Eric waded across the fast-moving water, expecting only to give the kayak a nudge. But the situation rapidly turned serious. A strong current ran beneath the surface, drawing the stern downward and jamming it tighter into the crevice. Eric straddled the crack and used his body to deflect the water while grabbing Dugald's boat and lifejacket. Ralph Michlisch came over to assist, but the river pulled him

into the crevice and out through an opening in the rock. Bill Morse rescued him below and then both climbed back up to help rescue Dugald. As Dugald sank lower, the current pinned him forward against his boat, trapping his legs inside. The river then pulled the stern deeper into the crevice, causing the bow to rise higher. Dugald reached a hand out of the water and Eric grabbed it before feeling it relax. Seeing no other option, Bill jumped onto the stern of the kayak by bracing himself on the bedrock and yanked at Dugald's lifejacket, tearing it apart. Then he reached for Dugald's helmet, breaking the chinstrap, before he too was sucked under and eventually rescued by Eric.

After they paddled out for help, word of the accident reached Dugald's close friends and family, who quickly descended on the Silver Fork. On June 8, an expert team gathered at the site under the direction of rigger Mike Weis, with Lars Holbek and Eric Magnuson handling the in-river work. Within a few hours they completed the recovery of Dugald and his boat. His friends brought the kayak home to Flagstaff, AZ, and leaned it against the wall of Dugald's photography studio, where it still stands, bow skyward.

Adapted from a tribute by Scott Thibony that appeared in Boatman's Quarterly Review, Vol. 10, No. 3

Henry Filip

Colorado's Crystal River was running approximately 1,250 cfs (a medium-high level) on June 28, 1997. Local boater Henry Filip scouted Meatgrinder Rapid before putting in, even though he probably had run this drop about 50 times during his lifetime. Meatgrinder is divided by a large boulder, known as the "Island," which splits the river into a right and left channel and marks the middle of the rapid. The upper half is the more technically demanding section, with pourovers, wood, and the need to move right or left to avoid the rock-island obstacle. Two kayakers and one spectator were stationed along the river left bank with a throw rope and a video camera. Henry ran the upper half of Meatgrinder without incident and eddied-out in the river left channel.

The lower half is not as technical, but includes three holes in succession before the rapid ends. Henry waited while long-time paddling partner Gordon Banks set up to film the lower half of the drop. Henry peeled out and then went over a pourover and another hole he didn't have momentum to penetrate. After getting windowshaded in the hole, he recovered, but was then knocked over by the next cluster of holes. He floated out of this second group of holes immediately but his roll attempts were disrupted by another pourover and rough water. Henry floated into the third group of holes, marked by a cliff on the river left bank, still attempting to roll. He most likely took some head blows from underwater rocks in the process. Upon exiting the holes, Henry didn't show any more movement, nor did he attempt to roll. Slow-motion video replays vaguely show him letting go of his paddle after he drifts out of the third set of holes, next to the small cliff.

On shore, only Gordon was positioned to see the lower part of Henry's run. His perspective was limited, however, because he was looking through the viewfinder. As a result, he could not tell where Henry was. He presumed Henry had finally swum from his boat. The three spectators, now rescuers, searched the bottom area of Meatgrinder unsuccessfully before regrouping. Two of them then searched the river right side of the river while Gordon searched farther downstream. Gordon went down to Penny Hotsprings (one mile downstream), where he saw Henry's kayak floating upside-down in the middle of the river. He went down to the river to retrieve the boat. As he got closer, he realized Henry was still in the boat. Gordon and another rescuer could not get Henry out of the river before he slid into Narrows Rapid, just downstream of the hotspring. Henry floated through the Narrows section in his boat as well. Two miles later and after multiple attempts to get his boat to shore, Henry dislodged from the boat. Gordon reached him at an island and attempted resuscitation. By that time, Henry had been under his boat floating down the river for approximately 45 minutes.

Indeed, those tracking whitewater's accident and fatality rates point to 1997 as one of kayaking's worst. "There has definitely been a spate of high-profile, well-known accidents this year," says Charlie Walbridge, former chairman of the American Canoe Association's safety committee. "It's not so much an increase in the number of deaths, but a spike in the number of qualified boaters killed on Class V.

"The only cause of these deaths," he adds, "is the demanding nature of Class V, which is brutally intolerant of errors in water reading, boat handling, and judgment. We're getting to the point where kayakers are pushing the envelope the same way mountaineers have been doing since the 1930s. Just as in climbing, skilled, competent people are cutting their margins too fine. The really high-end stuff can't be run forever. Eventually statistics catch up with you."

Out of 45 whitewater fatalities reported in the U.S. in 1996—which includes everything from low-head dam accidents to heart attacks—ten kayakers died paddling Class IV-V whitewater (excluding the deaths of Steve Fairchild on Chile's Futaleafu and Washington's Justin Casserly in Mexico). Two of those in particular, says Walbridge, caused

Chuck Kern

On August 14, 1997, Chuck Kern, the western technical rep for Easley, SC's Perception Inc. and member of the 1997 U.S. Rodeo Team, drowned while paddling a narrow section of the Black Canyon of the Gunnison River in Colorado's Curecanti National Recreation Area. Paddling with a group of six experienced boaters, including his brothers Willie and John, Kern began his trip at East Portal early that morning. As the group entered a mile-long, generally portaged section of the canyon, they opted to run the more conservative drops. The accident took place just upstream of "Cruise Gully" on a five-foot sloping ramp of water. After everyone scouted and picked their respective lines, Kern opted for a run down a ramp on river left. What appeared to be a single rock just under the surface, however, turned out to be a rock bridge, creating a sieve not visible from the group's van-tage point. As Kern paddled over the drop, his bow went under the bridge and became vertically pinned in the sieve, with the water pressure pushing his boat out of sight. The rest of the group reached his side of the river within three to five minutes and set up a rope through his stern grab loop. They set up a Z-drag and attempted to pull the boat out from various directions, breaking several prussiks in the process. After an hour of trying to move the boat with no success, the group paddled the remainder of the river to contact the National Park Service. Through the rescue efforts of a team headed by Vail, CO's Mike Duffy, the Park Service arranged to drop the water level enough to enable rescuers to retrieve Kern and his boat. Private services were held August 23 in Kern's hometown of Stowe, VT, with a service for the paddling community held Sept. 3 at the Chutes des Plaisanc near Ottawa, Canada.

Kayaking vs. Other Adrenaline Sports?

Kayaking is not the only adrenaline-based sport to see high-profile participants pass away. In recent years, the sports of climbing, surfing, and skiing have all seen top-level players perish while pursuing the sport they loved.

Grief struck the skiing world in February 1996 when extreme skier Trevor Petersen died in an avalanche in the French Alps in 1996. The industry was further saddened by the death of long-time skier Allan Bard while guiding clients up Wyoming's Grand Teton; and again by the death of photographer T.R. Youngstrom, who died in a helicopter crash in the Andes of Chile. For former *Powder* magazine editor Steve Casimiro, the similarities between those risking their lives kayaking and those risking their lives skiing are striking. "It's the fact that you're dealing with objective dangers," he says. "At ski resorts, those objective dangers have been dramatically reduced. But as with kayaking Class V, if you're on a 50-degree pitch littered with rock bands, the objective dangers are big. At that level, it's just not enough to be great. You have to have the ability of discernment, to back away. You have to be able to say, 'Whoa, there are too many things going on that I can't control.' That's the commonality between these sports."

The big-wave surfing world also has lost a few top players. The highly publicized death of Mark Foo on California's Maverick break shocked a community as tight-knit as the Class V kayaking crowd. Then came the death of pro surfer Donnie Solomon in Hawaii, followed by the death of pro surfer Todd Chesser, also in Hawaii. "But I don't think these deaths have stopped anybody from surfing big breaks," says *Surfer* magazine's Evan Slater. "You just have to evaluate it and continue on. If I'm going to die, that's how I would want it to happen."

Climbing hasn't been immune from such fatalities either. "It's been a rough year in climbing also," says Dugald MacDonald, editor of *Rock & Ice* magazine. He is referring to the climbing death of Bard, and that of Doug Hall, who died in an avalanche while ice climbing in Utah. "That kind of thing is going to happen in high-risk sports," he says. "And as these sports become more popular, more accidents are going to occur."

Is kayaking more dangerous than these other sports? It depends who you ask. Skiing an avalanche-prone couloir above a cliff band and surfing waves with the power to demolish small ships are certainly every bit as consequential as paddling off a waterfall. As Casimiro points out, it comes down to recognizing and evaluating the sport's objective dangers. MacDonald feels that many climbers would rather take their chances clinging to the side of a mountain than subject themselves to the potential of drowning. "Many climbers perceive kayaking as being extremely danger-ous," he says. "But at the same time, there are plenty of kayakers who say that about climbing."

If anyone can assess the differ-ence between kayaking and climbing, it's 62-year-old Royal Robbins, a world reknown climber who also has 30 kayaking first descents to his credit. In his 40 plus years of adventuring, Robbins has seen a lot of things hap-pen in both sports. "Sometimes you have a rash of things happen all at once," he says from his office in Modesto, CA, where he heads his Royal Robbins clothing line. "Deaths like that happen in climbing, and hopefully that's all we're seeing in this recent string of kayaking deaths.

"But it's still rather shocking," he adds. "And these deaths do show that risk is there in extreme kayaking. I don't know if it's more dangerous than climbing or not—it's probably more comparable to mountaineering where you're dealing with more objective dangers—but I can say that I've come closer to getting killed kayaking than climbing." Robbins admits that the ante has been upped since his day. "Back then, we were all sufficiently afraid to run hard stuff," he says. "People are doing things now that we never dreamed of. But just as in mountaineering, because of better equipment the casualty rate hasn't really gone up. Still, once you start pushing things to too high of a level, the nature of the sport changes."

One similarity climbing shares with kayaking is the recent growth in playboating—where paddlers show up at a hole or wave, paddle for a few hours and then leave—and sportclimb-ing, which takes place at man-made gyms and on bolted routes outdoors. "The gear for both is a lot better now, and it has led to substantial growth," says MacDonald. "But the bottom line is more people are doing it, and that's opening the door to more mishaps when they pursue their sport in a less-controlled environment."

One way to compare the dangers of the two is to look at the numbers. According to reports filed with American Whitewater, kayaking fatali-ties in the U.S. totaled eight in 1995, ten in 1996, and fifteen in 1997. Climbing, says Jed Williamson, who edits an annual journal called *Accidents in North American Mountaineering*, has seen an average of 28 domestic deaths a year for the past decade. But Williamson is not discouraged by these figures—especially since they include everything from mountaineering acci-dents to those involving "non-climbers in a climbing situation." "With the increased number of participants the sport has seen, these figures are actual-ly encouraging," says Williamson, who, like Robbins, has spent a fair amount of time behind a paddle. "And I have to think that given the number of peo-ple taking up kayaking that it too is also doing pretty well."

nearly as big a stir as this summer's deaths. In September '96, Scott Hassan, a long-time Class V kayaker, drowned in a drain-type sieve on West Virginia's 400-foot-per-mile Meadow Creek, a run he had paddled more than 30 times. "That really shook a lot of people up," says Walbridge. "He was as well-known in the East as Dugald was in the West." The curve continued in December when well-known eastern boater Todd Smith died on West Virginia's Possum Creek near Chattanooga, TN.

This year's trend of paddlers dying on difficult water established itself well before the deaths of Weiss, Bremner, Filip, and Kern. Of the year's 15 kayaking deaths reported to the American Whitewater Affiliation (AWA) as of September 1, nine involved experienced paddlers on Class IV–V whitewater, and at least six of the victims were considered experts. Adding to the expert count are the May 12 death of Joel Hathorn, who missed a do-or-die eddy during a first descent of Idaho's Warren Creek and the June 5 death of New Mexico's Brian Reynolds, who took a Class IV–V swim on Idaho's South Fork of the Payette at high water.

"The percentage of hardboat fatalities on Class V has definitely increased over the past few years," says Lee Belknap, chairman of the AWA's safety committee. "And when charted as its own category, Class V fatalities show a striking increase over the past two years, despite an only moderate rise when measured as a percentage of all hardboats. The only consolation is that whenever we spiked like this in the past, the succeeding years were typically much calmer as paddlers learned from the accidents." Learning from this summer's

accidents, however, isn't easy—especially since, as Callaway points out, they could have happened to anybody. "Maybe that's the underlying lesson," says Walbridge. "When you have accidents involving mainstream paddlers, you're getting into a whole new realm of dangers. It's one thing to educate people who are unprepared. It's another when you're dealing with people at the top end of the sport."

The situation is certainly not unique to kayaking. Compared with tragedies in the climbing world, including recent disasters on Mt. Everest and in the Alps, the number of kayaking casualties is a drop in the bucket. But since they're coming from a smaller pool of participants, the numbers start carrying more weight. And for a tight-knit sport still emerging into the mainstream, the deaths of its top-level participants have left ripples of grief extending far beyond the surface.

As well as stirring up people's sentiments, the deaths have also stirred debates as to the direction of the sport, bringing up issues and concerns that until now have rarely been voiced. As with any tragedy (as illustrated in the death of Princess Diana) people want answers and the assignment of blame. In the case of Weiss and Filip, did a blow to the head come first or the drowning? Would Bremner have died had he been in another boat? Would Kern have made the same decision had he scouted from below? No one will ever know. The easy way out is to blame these deaths on errors in judgment. But that's like pinning an airplane crash on pilot error. Judgment is an esoteric term that doesn't take into account hidden rocks throwing you off-line or hidden sieves capable of swallowing boats whole. "Chuck had the best judgment of anyone," says Lucero.

"I probably would have made the exact same decision, and that's what's so scary."

Fingers are also quick to point to a breed of new, easy-to-paddle designs that are putting more people on harder runs faster. But that's hardly the case in the deaths of Bremner, Weiss, Filip, and Kern. For them, skill wasn't necessarily a factor. All were seasoned Class V boaters with more than 50 years of experience between them. No one can say that Weiss didn't belong on the White Salmon, that Bremner didn't belong on the Silver Fork, that Filip didn't belong on the Crystal, or that Kern didn't belong in the Black Canyon. If they didn't belong there, no one does. "It's not a skill question," agrees former U.S. Canoe & Kayak Team Coach Bill Endicott, who coached Weiss to his first Olympic appearance in 1992. "No one is going to have more skill than Richie. I think maybe we're just starting to bump up against the upper limit of what can be successfully run."

As for the role new equipment plays, Lucero adds that, if anything, new designs are making the sport safer as they encourage recreational "playboating" over running Class V. At the same time, however, they present somewhat of a Catch-22. Just as beginners and intermediates are using new designs to pursue playboating over river running, many

The Hairboater's Perspective

Editor's note: To find out the effect this summer's deaths had on paddlers who regularly ply Class V waterways, we went to some of the nation's leading hairboaters and asked them to share their thoughts:

Clay Wright, Ducktown, Tennessee

The terrain has changed so much in the last few years—we are so much better that we are routinely paddling in places where siphons, undercuts, terminal hydraulics, and logs occur frequently. While we are all routinely making good decisions, running clean lines, and having loads of fun in places few people ventured just five years ago, the cost of mistakes in these places is very high. There are so many more kayakers venturing into Class V water that there are bound to be more of them discovering Class V consequences as a result of mistakes. My friend Scott Hassan had run the Lower Meadow more than 30 times. He was showing a friend down in September 1996 and flipped above a sieve he had had a close call with the previous spring. This time he and his boat were sucked in completely. It is not a tough rapid, but it is Class V for a reason. It is a downside to our sport, but one we must be willing to recognize and live with. Scott and Chuck knew the stakes and paddled anyway. I plan to as well, but anyone who thinks it could never happen to them needs to wizen up. It could've been anyone. I don't think these deaths were the result of pushing the envelope. The Black Canyon, Meadow, and Little White are no longer the cutting edge; all these paddlers had run tougher drops before. You put enough people in a K-mart and someone will slip on a wet floor. Even experts slip occasionally and the more they go to the store the greater their chances of a fall.

Eric Jackson, Washington, D.C.

I got to the White Salmon for the Gorge Games a week after Richie's funeral and a lot of people were shaken up and didn't want to run the falls. But it was just as fun for me as it ever was, and the fact that Richie died there didn't seem too material. I didn't think the drop was jinxed or anything. Weird things happen, and everyone reacts differently. You're playing the odds, and the chance you could die running hard whitewater is greater than when you're running easy whitewater. But if you're paddling within your ability level, the odds are good you'll be fine. Overall, I think Chuck's death had a much more profound impact on people boating Class V than Richie's death did. Chuck paddled difficult whitewater all the time and that's what he was known for.

Dan Gavere, Salt Lake City, Utah

It definitely shakes you up when someone you know dies on the river. You can't put the death of your friends behind you, but I don't think it's going to change my style of boating. Chuck and Rich both knew where they were, knew it was dangerous, and paid for their actions. All the upper-level guys can accept those dangers—that's the bottom line. We wouldn't be out there pushing the envelope if we weren't willing to die on the river. If you're going to boat

that kind of water, you just have to be willing to accept the consequences.

Paul Tefft, Aspen, Colorado

Henry (Filip) was killed on my wedding day. He died on Meatgrinder of the Crystal, and we got married upstream at Crystal Mills Falls the same day. It's been a terrible year, and it definitely makes you take a step back and analyze if it's all really worth it. I still went out the next week and boated some hard stuff, but I analyzed the consequences more. It, and the other deaths, humbled me a little—especially when you lose someone so close. But people seem to have pretty short-term memories; the younger guys are likely to continue pushing the envelope, while the older guard who knew these guys might take a step back. It comes down to this: is your sport worth dying for? The answer is no if you enjoy life.

Lars Holbek, Coloma, California

This has been a tragic kayak season. I am reminded how easy it is to drown, and how amazing it is that more of us don't. In the '80s, we often identified places where we thought one could die in rapids. Then someone would run it and our predictions seemed overcautious. Now it seems that people are drowning in places no one would have predicted. In the case of Dugald (Bremner), we portaged the rapid only a few weeks before with little hesitation. There were warning signs everywhere, and lots of water flowing into bad places. We saw the line he chose, but it didn't look very sure and not too gratifying—more like bouncing down granite steps hoping you guessed the physics right. Still, factors stack up and combine to kill people all the time. We can look at the details of these deaths, say this or that would have prevented them, and yet kayakers will still drown in the future. Some of it is ego-driven bad judgment, some testosterone male craziness, some just being at the wrong place the wrong instant. Anyone who runs Class V passionately has been there at some time. For me, these deaths just drive home (again) the reality that life happens *now*. The sadness anyone feels who knew these four spectacular people can only help us to realize our own mortality.

advanced paddlers are using them on harder runs, and as a result they're having more close calls. "The sport needs to slow down and catch up with itself," maintains Tamara Robbins, one of Kern's close paddling friends. "In many cases, boat designs have eclipsed skill levels."

Fate might well have dealt a different hand had any of the deceased been in different boats. Then again, the cards may have fallen just the same. Kern was in a Perception Arc, one of the company's more forgiving models. Weiss was in a Perception Whiplash, a boat he had been paddling all year. Filip was in a New Wave Mongoose, perfect for the steep, rocky riverbed of the Crystal's Meatgrinder rapid. Bremner was in a Dagger Freefall, designed specifically for steep creeks. "The way Dugald pinned wasn't due to the boat," says Mike Bader, a close friend who helped retrieve the boat and body. "He would have gotten pinned no matter what he was in—he just misjudged the depth, which slowed him down and threw him off line."

These variables are what have old-school paddlers like Endicott so concerned. "In my opinion, this whole extreme game is getting carried too far," he says. "People need to think about their actions more. Part of good judgement is leaving more room for margin of error. When I started paddling in the '60s we had glass boats and there was a self-limiting factor. Run something you didn't belong on and you ruined your boat."

No one can deny that compared to Endicott's fiberglass days, modern boats are largely responsible for putting paddlers on more dangerous runs. But people will push the envelope no matter what boat—or sport—they're in. It's human nature. What concerns the likes of Endicott is when that envelope gets pushed because of external factors. "When you get more people involved, they begin to influence each other," he says. "Someone will run something and make it look easy, and others will base their judgement on that instead of deciding for themselves. And then there are those who encourage other people to sidestep their judgment by staging races, shooting videos, and taking pictures."

Most top-level paddlers, however, realize that the final decision to run something comes from within. "For the most part, people don't run hard stuff they wouldn't otherwise run because of races, videos, or any other external factors," says Eric Jackson, president of the World Kayak Federation, which stages an annual Class V race on Washington, D.C.'s Great Falls of the Potomac. "Most people paddle within their ability level, and if you do that, the odds are good you'll be fine."

It's not likely this summer's deaths will stop people from paddling Class V. As with skiers progressing from green circles to black diamonds, as boaters get better they will continue to push themselves. "When you reach that upper skill level it's an extremely fun challenge to paddle difficult whitewater," says former USCKT member Steve Holmes, who had a co-worker involved in a recent fatality on Colorado's Arkansas River. "And as much as we all hate to admit it, it's sort of an ego thing, matching yourself up against someone else. But the river's a fickle thing; it doesn't care who you are or how good a paddler you are."

If nothing else, this summer's deaths have caused discussions that otherwise might not have been brought to the surface. And that, says AW's Belknap, is a step in the right direction. "The most effective action is to talk about it and discuss it within the boating community," he says. "That's the only way for whatever lessons can be learned to really sink in."

Even though egos and adrenal glands may have been tucked aside for a while, life, and paddling, goes on. And no matter how stirred up people's emotions have been, it's a safe bet that all four paddlers in question would want every-

one in the paddling community to continue to live life to the fullest. "It definitely shakes you up when someone you know dies on the river," says Dan Gavere, an extreme boater who has been pushing the envelope for years. "But I know they died doing what they loved. If I die, I'd much rather be in my boat than anywhere else, and I'd much rather die because of my own mistake than because of someone else's actions. At least out on the river I'm in control of my own destiny. For us, it's a lifestyle. We don't do it for the money, we do it because we love to be out on the river." Although he still grieves about the deaths of his cohorts, he adds that it's not likely to change the way he paddles. "You can't put the death of your friends behind you, but I don't think it's going to change my style of boating," he says. "Chuck and Rich both knew where they were, knew it was dangerous, and paid for their actions. All the upper-level guys can accept those dangers—that's the bottom line. We wouldn't be out there pushing the envelope if we weren't willing to die on the river. If you're going to boat that kind of water, you just have to be willing to accept the consequences."

In the Shadow of Quartzite

by Eugene Buchanan

By the time I saw the pull out, everyone else had already climbed the steep, cactus-lined slope to the vantage point overlooking the falls. Angling my boat, I ferried towards shore, crossed the eddyline, and ran my bow up on the cobblestone beach.

As if to remind me why we were all here, a large "Danger—Falls 1/4-mile!" sign, painted in faded white letters, rose out of the eddy on a cliff above the pool, catching my attention like a Surgeon General's warning on a pack of cigarettes. Unlike the ever-present dangers of nicotine, the falls didn't need to carry a cautionary message anymore. They were destroyed the year before in an act of environmental vandalism even the Monkey Wrench Gang would have a hard time condoning.

This, of course, is exactly why I found myself scrambling up an innocuous, saguaro-filled slope above Quartzite Falls on Arizona's Salt River. At the top was the rest of the party, an odd consortium of river runners lured here by filmmaker Kristin Atwell, 27, who was making a documentary on the life and death of the falls. She had already taken several journeys down the river for her project, most recently with cinematographers Gordon Brown and Allison Chase, each trip adding new insights to the film. This time she stacked the trip with interviewees she thought would add more color to the production: Mark Dubois, co-founder of California's Friends of the River (FOR) and Oregon's International Rivers Network (IRN); Pam Hyde, director of Southwest Programs for American Rivers, a Washington, D.C.-based river conservation organization; and Roger Saba, a long-time private rafter from Phoenix. I was there to explain what the falls' destruction meant for paddlers, and my friend Pete Foster, a hydrologist from Flagstaff, AZ, was there to explain the basics of hydrodynamics.

At the top of the ridge, Paul Atkinson, a cameraman from Channel 8, Phoenix's PBS station, focused on Pam, the falls barely visible in the background. "I feel violated," she said, the tone of concern easily readable in her voice. Atwell, holding a reflective shield, shifted it so a faint beam of light caressed her face. "Not only for the loss of the falls," continued Pam, "but because it happened in a wilderness area. To do something like this defeats the whole purpose of what a wilderness area stands for."

Hers was a stirring performance—far more than mine on what the falls meant to paddlers or Pete's on how reversals trap their victims. After Pam's soliloquy, which caused even the neighboring saguaro to bend an ear, Paul Mischud, president of the 150-member Central Arizona Paddlers Club, took the stage, echoing sentiments expressed by others. "It's a travesty," he said, blinking into the lens. "I feel like a part of me is gone."

What is gone is Rocky Balboa's left hook, the Salt's knock-out punch that has caused trepidation for paddlers ever since it was first run. A frothy, white monster that had killed and would kill again. William "Ken" Stoner (also known as "Taz"), 37, who confessed to the crime, simply took matters into his own hands to put the beast to rest. While Paul continued, I climbed up to the top of a rock where Roger was gazing intently at Quartzite's remains a quarter mile away. "You used to be able to line your boats down at certain levels on the right, but it was a dicey move," he said, pointing to a pile of boulders. "Otherwise you had to wait in line with everyone else trying to portage." I followed his gaze to see a large quartzite dyke disappearing into the river and re-emerging on the other side. Harder than the surrounding layers of sandstone, the dyke withstood everything the Salt threw at it over the years, from sun-beating droughts to 100,000-cfs floods. But it could not withstand the Hand of Man. Proof came a few minutes later when two rafts rounded the corner, preparing for what used to be the climax of the Salt's 58-mile canyon run. Instead of catching a must-make eddy and beginning an arduous portage—which sometimes took several hours—they

followed each other to the right, took a splash or two across their bows and emerged unscathed downstream.

Their runs were exactly what Stoner envisioned they would be like in the aftermath of the explosion. But instead of getting a pat on the back for making the river safer, he was chastised in a wave of public outcry. News reports surfaced throughout the country labeling him an eco-terrorist on par with Hayduke of Monkey Wrench fame. "He was a little reluctant to talk to us, for obvious reasons," said *LA Times* writer Paul Dean, who hiked with Stoner to Quartzite for an interview. "He had been beaten to death by various media and assumed we were part of the assassination team. He wasn't talking to the media, which is what made him attractive to us."

Once Dean and Stoner made it down to the falls, Stoner explained his rationale. "I did it to save lives," he said. "To make it safer for the public to pass through." He then referred to the deaths the year before of two Californians, Richard Panich and Jerry Buckhold, who tried to run the falls and failed. "That made me want to take the killer out of it," Stoner continued. "Quartzite Falls is a hazard, and has been for a number of years. If I'd thought about it (demolition) before, I wasn't serious. After the drownings, I was serious." He faxed a copy of the story on the deaths to his friend, explosives and hazardous materials expert Richard Scott, who used an $800 cashier's check to purchase commercial binary explosives—inert ammonium nitrate that, when mixed with nitro methane, can create an explosion 30 percent more powerful than gelatin dynamite. At first, even that was not enough. "The first two explosions—28 pounds the first time, 30 pounds the next—there wasn't a whole lot of damage," Stoner continued. "The third was 68 pounds."

The third time proved to be the charm. Subsequent detonations were simply a matter of fine-tuning. "We definitely worked pretty hard to blow that thing up," admitted Scott, one of seven accomplices Stoner brought on board to carry out the task. In all, various members of the "Quartzite Eight," as they were dubbed by the media, hiked in on four occasions, detonating 154 lbs. of dynamite over three months in the fall of 1993. With a drought coming to the Salt the next spring, no one noticed the change until March 1994 when a rafter reported the falls had all but disappeared. A portion of a fuse left at the site led investigators to Scott, and fingers soon pointed to Stoner.

"I kind of knew we were doing something wrong, but I had no idea you could go to jail for it," Stoner said. "But I made something safer and lives will be saved. That outweighs the destruction of a natural resource in my mind. We removed a rock, we didn't obliterate a pretty waterfall. Sure this may have taken something away from a very few people who were qualified to run it, but we had a purpose that will benefit people for years to come, and ultimately save lives. And if we're guilty of anything, we're probably guilty of weighing out human life as being worth more than a rock."

To this day, Dean believes Stoner was speaking from the heart. "After decades in this business, I'm a pretty good judge of character," he said. "And he surprised me in that I was initially quite impressed with him. I like the guy."

He seemed to be a person of genuine emotions. I'd certainly go down a river with him, and I'd certainly go have a beer with him. The major sense I got from him was that he didn't realize this was going to get out of control and that he could go to jail for it. I don't think he bargained for that. But this isn't the first time in the history of crime, major or minor, that people didn't realize the consequences of their actions."

Although Dean painted an objective picture by reporting Stoner's side of the story (to the point where letters of criticism streamed into the *Times*), Stoner wasn't ready to deal with the publicity or consequences of his actions. In fact, after Dean's story appeared in the *LA Times,* the *Arizona Republic* picked it up and ran it in Stoner's hometown of Phoenix under the front-page headline, "Ecoterrorist or Hero?" Stoner reportedly stole it from his construction company's meeting room before any of his co-workers had a chance to see it.

To this day, Stoner maintains he did the Forest Service a favor by ridding it of a potential liability. Forest Service officials, however, aren't so sure. After a similar drowning in Quartzite in the early 1970s, the public asked it to correct the problem. "People said the obvious solution was to destroy it," said Pete Weinel, co-author of Tonto National Forest's guidebook to the Upper Salt. "We looked at it and said, 'No, that's not really the solution. The solution is to be careful and be warned.'" Besides, Quartzite wasn't the only rapid that had killed: Island Rapid killed someone in 1973 and Reforma Rapid did so in 1986. Stoner's plan of "doing the Forest Service a favor" might well have backfired. Now that the Salt's main obstacle is out of the way, and fearing increased use in an already fragile ecosystem, the Forest Service issued a permit system for the river a year later, introducing the same logistical problems and paperwork that accompany all permitted rivers. The new permit policy has also created new headaches for private users. Although Quartzite's disappearance makes the run easier, many longtime regulars are now finding they can't get on the river at all. The filming expedition with Atwell was the only river trip private boater Roger Saba—who has been running the Salt privately for 25 years—could get on last year. "No one I know got a permit this year," said Saba, still perched on his vantage point overlooking the falls. "And all of my friends applied. We used to be able to run it whenever we wanted."

Some suspect that Stoner—who has worked for three different Salt River outfitters—had other motives as well. Outfitters can now make better time by not having to deal with an arduous portage, and some believe it was Stoner's two-day marathons down the canyon, and the frustration and time delays the portage caused, that led to the falls' demise. "He came up with that line of BS that he was trying to save lives, but the problem was overcrowding," said George Marsic of Phoenix's Sun Country Rafting, one of two outfitters running the wilderness section of the Salt. "If there's anything good to be said of it, it served as an awakening for the Forest Service as to the need for a permit system. You used to have up to 20 trips going into the wilderness area at one time, with up to six different parties trying to portage Quartzite at the same time. Now it's regulated." Marsha Blumm of Phoenix's Desert Voyagers,

whom Stoner worked for while running trips in the wilderness area, feels the portages weren't that much of a problem. "Our guides knew how to portage and had a system where they could get through in 20 minutes," she said. "That's why we never suspected him (Stoner)." The relationship between Stoner and these various outfitters was not lost on investigators, who beat the streets looking for a connection between the area's outfitters and the culprits only to come up empty-handed. Stoner and Scott denied any such connection, and passed polygraph tests to prove it.

One of the main issues, it seems, regarding Quartzite's fall (the working title of Atwell's documentary) is what kind of price tag can you put on the value of wilderness? According to the Forest Service's restitution report, it was $313,000, the amount they figured it would cost to "replace" the falls (which Scott claimed could be done with concrete and reebar for about $30,000). Calling the Forest Service's pricing methods "antiquated," Judge Earl Carroll reduced the restitution amount to $75,000. For those who ventured to the Salt for its wilderness values, it's not that cut-and-dried. No formula can replace its loss. "Quartzite gave you the opportunity to find out how you dealt with adversity and fear," said kayaker Mike Stamps, a Salt River regular. "It gave you the opportunity to die. And there's no replacing that. When you take emotional experiences away from people, you can't measure what you've removed from their lives."

Just like many of those who decided to run Quartzite, Stoner and the rest of the Quartzite Eight have had to pay for their actions. The maximum sentence for repeatedly blasting in a wilderness area is 5 to 20 years in jail and $250,000 in fines. James Lewus, who helped on two of the trips in to the falls, received a $6,000 fine and 36 months of probation. For his help in hiking into the falls three times, Michael Meehl received three months in a work-release rehabilitation program, a $15,000 fine, and had his truck impounded. For helping with the explosives, Scott was sentenced to 366 days in prison, a $15,000 fine, and, along with Meehl and Lewus, is responsible for the $75,000 restitution. The four who made only one trip—Stephen Cortwright, William Kelley, and Chris and Mark Meehl—slipped felony charges by completing 120 hours of community service.

Stoner, meanwhile, who pleaded guilty to destruction of federal property by means of an explosive, and was due to be sentenced in March 1995, broke his plea agreement by fleeing the country to Australia. After working for various outfitters down under, he was picked up by Australian Federal Police in Sydney and was detained for eight months before being extradited back to the U.S.—where he faced a 29-count indictment for everything from destruction of federal property to bank, mail, passport, and federal home loan fraud. "He clearly made it worse for himself," said Paul Charlton, Assistant U.S. District Attorney for Arizona. "It's a unique case in that it is an individual who was once a professional and who would have probably served out his sentence by now."

Stoner spent the next 11 months in a Florence, AZ, correctional facility—where fellow inmates adorned him with the nickname "Dynamite"—before pleading guilty to seven of the 29

charges in a plea bargain: mail fraud, bank fraud, interstate transportation of stolen goods, failure to appear in court, passport fraud, and conspiracy and destruction of federal property by means of an explosive. On November 17, 1997, U.S District Judge Earl Carroll sentenced Stoner—who was brought to the courthouse in handcuffs and a green prison suit—to three and a half years in prison (out of a maximum five), recommending he be placed in a minimum security facility. Stoner was also slapped with $20,000 in fines from the U.S. District Court and another $10,000 from Australian courts, and was ordered to pay $10,000 towards Quartzite's $75,000 restitution to Tonto National Forest. He was also ordered to pay $58,000 in back taxes and return more than $140,000 to the banks and other institutions he committed fraud against before fleeing to Australia.

As he left the courtroom, Stoner allegedly turned to Assistant U.S. Attorney Charlton and said, "You won this time." Charlton, as quoted in a story the next day in The *Arizona Republic,* disagreed. "There are no winners in a case where we lose a great natural resource," he said. "My hope is that there is no next time, and that the lesson learned from this case is to leave the wilderness wild."

"I remember hiking up here with Stoner after he blew up the falls," said Atwell, referring to a hike she took up Phoenix's Camelback Mountain with Stoner after the blast. "He offered to take me down to the falls to show me how he had blown them up. My mom thought I was crazy to accompany him into the desert and that I shouldn't be spending my time with an indicted terrorist."

Dusk brought the flickering lights of Phoenix and the mountain's blood-red slabs of granite to life as we made our way down Camelback, a lone spire rising out of the city's swimming-pooled suburbs. Despite objections from her mom, Atwell and her father (Salt River guide Bob Finkbine) took Stoner up on his offer and journeyed with him to the depths of the canyon to the scene of the crime. Once there she videotaped his confession in front of Quartzite's remains to help tell the story of what happened.

After we finished our hike, we hopped in Atwell's borrowed Isuzu Trooper and drove to the local Price Club to shop for our upcoming trip. From there we headed back to her dad's house to sort gear and pack coolers for the next day's departure. Atwell's dad had guided with Stoner on several occasions, and even had him over to his house a few times during river guide parties (with a volleyball net strung outside and metal rocket boxes littering the yard, the house looked as if it had just hosted another.) It was at one of these parties that word got out as to who destroyed the falls. "They (members of the Quartzite Eight) couldn't help but start talking about it," said Finkbine, 68, a retired history professor who guides on the Salt and Rio Grande. "We all knew who did it pretty quickly. It's too bad . . . it caused a lot of problems for commercial trips, but it was a great rapid and I looked forward to dealing with it every time I went down the river."

Quartzite aside, the rest of the river is unchanged. Located in the Upper Salt River Canyon Wilderness Area 100 miles from Phoenix, the Salt still flows unimpeded from Mt. Baldy in Arizona's White Mountains to Roosevelt Lake.

Although a Class V–VI kayak run exists on its upper stretch above Apache Falls, the main whitewater run starts at U.S. Hwy. 60 and flows through a quagmire of different political regions, from the White Mountain Apache Reservation to Tonto National Forest and the Upper Salt River Canyon Wilderness Area. On the 58-mile bridge-to-bridge run from Hwy. 60 to Hwy. 288 lie more than 20 rapids rated Class III or higher.

At the put in, we paid our $10-a-day user fee to the White Mountain Apache Reservation and began rigging the boats while waiting for the rest of our party. The Salt lapped at each craft as we lowered the rafts to the water. Although we were in the middle of a desert, cold temperatures caused runoff to dwindle and forced us to break out apparel normally reserved for trips farther north. By noon the rest of the group arrived and I quickly introduced myself to Mark Dubois, the trip's token environmentalist. Dressed in homemade conveyor-belt sandals, cut-off blue jeans, and a brown wool sweater with the knitting coming undone at the shoulders, his attire was about what you would expect from someone who chained himself to a tree for eight days to stop the damming of California's Stanislaus River. While we continued rigging, he hopped into an 11-foot AIRE Super Puma and solo paddled it across the river, his experience evident in every stroke.

That afternoon gave us our first taste of the Salt's rapids and landscape. The canyon's infamous salt banks— orange and yellow sculptures complete with saline springs—showed themselves on river right, as did fields of saguaro cactus, standing like sentries with arms raised high. Protected as Arizona's state flower, many of the cactus reach more than 10,000 pounds—nearly 100 times more than the amount of dynamite used to destroy Quartzite. At camp, perched on a beach across the river from a series of Indian granaries high on a cliff, talk around the fire centered on the river's beauty and its fragility as a wilderness area. "Wilderness is meant to be wilderness," said Dubois. "Some of its danger is exactly what makes it a wilderness. The underlying question is how do we live with nature, and can we live with it as it is? The tough thing to get a handle on is that Stoner was a river guide, and river guides are usually sympathetic to the wilderness. To have river guides blasting away a rapid like Quartzite is kind of an oxymoron. I remember people, river guides, on the Stanislaus years ago going in at low water and chiseling the sharp razors off a rapid called Razor Back, and people were aghast.

"The debate hasn't happened enough," he added, the fire crackling off the canyon walls. "Do we let nature be what it is and live with what's there, or do we put handrails on everything?"

Dubois paused only long enough to reach down and, with the same poise he showed while chaining himself to a tree, brush a scorpion—as if it were nothing more than a ladybug—from halfway up his bare calf back to the desert sand. We would count three more scorpions on our campmates by morning, most of which had burrowed under sleeping pads to escape the cold of the desert night. After Atkinson and Atwell's interview with Dubois the next morning, interrupted briefly by a rattlesnake slithering onto the set, we shoved off to face the Salt's rapids that have remained intact. Rat Trap, Eye of the Needle, and Black

Rock—all in their natural form, all unmolested by man. As their roars came and went, the current carried us deeper and deeper into the Salt's fragile ecosystem. At one point, while waiting for the rest of the group to catch up, Dubois counted 20 flower species in a patch of ground no bigger than a 7-11 parking lot.

We reached Quartzite the next day on our final afternoon in the canyon. While Atwell finished with her interviews, I climbed back down to the river, pulled on my sprayskirt—dried from the desert air—and pushed off into the river. Quartzite was about a quarter-mile distant, but its horizon line appeared quickly. I tried to envision what used to lay beyond the horizon line, a deadly, churning hydraulic that commanded respect from everyone traveling the river. Then I tried to envision the explosions that rocked the waterfall onto headlines nationwide. Images filled my mind: a fuse sparkling at the end; a series of resounding thunderclaps; a vein of quartzite, older than the surrounding desert walls, buckling up and yielding to something stronger than anything Mother Nature had ever thrown at it; a loud roar echoing off the canyon walls; pieces of quartzite flying through the air.

Paddling to the lip, I felt a tingle of anticipation, the same feeling earlier river runners must have felt every time they approached the falls, the same feeling when approaching crux moves on other rivers—a tightening in the stomach, senses primed and ready. Until now I hadn't truly been able to sympathize with those mourning Quartzite's loss. I had never seen it or its surrounding wilderness. Like waking from a bad dream before things get out of hand, however, I knew the tightening in my stomach was

unwarranted. What had once killed without prejudice was now a simple Class III.
Before its destruction, a line of portagers
would have greeted me on the left bank.
Now the only line came from the empty
eddy meeting the river.

Pointing my bow towards the drop,
I dug in with my paddle and soon found
myself sailing through Quartzite's
remains, riding a tongue of water to an
innocent eddy below. I had done it. I had
kayaked Quartzite Falls. But it seemed as
hollow as the canyon walls, which will
never echo with its roar again.

Reconnected on the Selway

by Jon Turk

Dancing, floating, flying . . .

I aimed towards Steve, who was standing near the bottom of the first steep pitch with his camera, motor drive whirring. My skis were carving gracefully, and wonderful whiteness washed across my face, biting at yesterday's frostbite scars.

I watched, first with almost abstract curiosity, then incredulity, and finally terror as the snow wrinkled, churning into angry surf. Avalanche! Steve's body rotated, rose, and tilted. I looked over my left shoulder to see if I could race to the ridge, but I was deep in the gully and there was no escape. Somersaulting, cartwheeling— out of control. Heavy pressure, a sudden pain, I swam for my life, and then the slide stopped and I was at the bottom of the mountain, on top of the snow. Alive. Alone.

Shaking from fear and adrenaline, I zipped open my jacket and turned my transceiver from transmit to receive. I picked up a faint signal and I was certain that Steve was beneath me, under the snow, struggling to breathe air that didn't exist. Find him! Dig! I tried to stand, but couldn't. I lay back in the snow and told myself, "You've broken something. It hurts. But you can't afford the luxury of listening to pain. Steve is dying. Stand up! Find him! Dig!"

I carefully tried to curl my legs under me, but they wouldn't move. "Oh my God, I broke my back!" I saw a dull picture of myself forever in a wheelchair. Then I wiggled my toes and felt them press against my boots. My spinal column was intact, and I told myself, "It's bad, but not that bad."

Voices. Steve had washed farther down the gully and was on top of the snow, calling to Mitch, Linda, and Chris. I lay back, relieved. I looked around at the snowy peaks with their jagged limestone outcrops, and spoke to them as old friends, "I'll miss you guys." But then, with an upwelling of resolve, I promised myself that by springtime I'd be in my kayak, playing on the melting snow. I thought of rivers that I love. The Selway.

The Selway hovered around me as I bounced behind the snowmachine on a toboggan. As the ambulance sped through town, I saw myself in the center run on Ladle, dancing past holes. At the hospital they cut off my clothes, inserted IVs, and the doctor told me, "We've called Life Flight. We're flying you to Calgary." Separated pelvis, internal bleeding, hypothermia, dislocated shoulder. Two weeks in the hospital; a month more in bed and the La-Z-Boy recliner. Then the therapist put a wide belt around my waist and helped me to my feet. I was shaky; I needed crutches—but I could walk. The next day I was in the gym, lifting light weights, thinking of the Selway.

My friends joked that we'd have to mount a rack on the back of my kayak to hold my crutches so I could walk from the take out. I smiled, put the crutches in the back storeroom, and hobbled back to the porch. "I don't need crutches any more."

We paddled the Class I West Fork of the Bitterroot. My hips felt locked, but I shouted commands down the nerves and the joints reluctantly responded. The next weekend I tried the Pine Creek stretch on the Salmon, Class II. I did a practice roll in an eddy but it hurt so much that I boated conservatively the rest of the day. Then the Lochsa, and the Lochsa again. Time was running out. My put in date approached.

Hot weather was melting the 180-percent-of-normal snowpack. At the put in, the gauge read 6.5 feet, 20,000 cfs. I'd run the Selway 20 times, but never when it was this high. I was thankful for my three friends, all strong boaters, all familiar with the river. I didn't tell them that I hadn't done a combat roll yet this year. I wanted them to have faith in me. I boated scared the first day, but with no problems. That night the river rose another foot. This small Idaho stream was probably running twice the volume of the Colorado through the Grand Canyon. The water overflowed the shallow bank and trees grew out of the eddies. If I needed to, I could fly out

from Selway Lodge. No, the mental intensity reminded me of an old friend—me. I resolved to kayak the river.

I ran Ham, the first Class IV, on the right, punched the lateral, moved center, and passed easily above the hole. The waves were big and powerful but I whispered to myself, "Piece of cake." Double Drop didn't go so smoothly. A huge wave broke and surfed me backwards. There was no time to recover and I dropped into the hole. If I swam here, I might lose my boat, swim the next half a dozen rapids, and then have to walk the 25 miles to the road. But I couldn't walk 25 miles. No way.

The hole embraced me with aerated foam and violent moves. Then the turbulence subsided and I bobbed down the wave train upside down. I reached my paddle out. My body remembered and I rolled easily. As I paddled into the eddy, Charlie laughed and said, "You're in your boat, right side up, with your paddle in your hands. I guess you had a good run." I smiled weakly.

The right sneak in Ladle Rapid was blocked by a log. The center was mayhem. But I thought the left would go—maybe. Two of our group elected to portage. No one in the universe would care if I walked this one. I looked around at the ancient ponderosa pines on the south-facing slopes and the dark firs across the river. Spring flowers bloomed. This is my home. I'd chosen my lifestyle a long time ago. I knew that if I ignored my fear long enough it would retreat into a dark corner where it could watch but not rule. I waited. Then I slipped into my cockpit and pulled my sprayskirt tight.

I made the ferry cleanly, eddied out, and tried to relax. Then I entered the narrow slot between the rock and the hole, drifted too far right, and pried out of the hole. I was too far center to make the second eddy, but turned my boat in time to catch the green tongue. Time to move right, but the lateral had a nasty curl. I forced myself to wait and watch the scenery until the current carried me beneath the lateral. Then I pillowed off the big rock and I was home free.

Only four more rapids in quick succession and we would be out of the canyon. I ferried hard left between Puzzle Creek and No Slouch and saw a phantom motion in the cliffs along the shore. I paddled into the bouncy eddy and stared up into the eyes of a yearling doe. The river had eroded a small cave into the rock, and the spring moisture dripped off the almost Day-Glo green moss. The doe had an ugly wound on her right shoulder. She probably fell into the river and swam Ladle. She was undernourished and mucus oozed out of her nostrils. I guessed that she had clambered to shore and then was trapped in the cave, afraid to swim one more boiling rapid. I couldn't tell how long she had been there, but she was starving, sick, and hurt.

I whispered quietly to her, "I've been where you are, Little Mama, I know the abyss you feel." She backed up against the rock, cold water trickling over the protruding ribs and clotted blood. Her big eyes stared, ears stretched out as far as they could reach. I carefully climbed out of my boat and lifted it onto a narrow ledge. She tried to step backwards again, then looked nervously side-to-side, but she had nowhere to go.

"You'll die if you stay here. I had snowmachines, ambulances, helicopters,

doctors. All you've got is me. I'm going to give you a chance at life. I would have taken the chance, if that had been my only hope. I know I would have. I'll throw you in the water. You'll have to swim one rapid. Hold your breath when you go into the hole on the left. Then head for shore. Understand?" Her ears twitched. I lunged. My left hand pressed against the sticky wound on her shoulder. My right tried to grasp her hind leg, but motivated by the contact, she leapt.

A rear hoof bashed painfully against my ear. Her front legs glanced off my boat and then she was in the water, swimming strongly. As she disappeared around the bend, I reminded her one more time. "Remember to hold your breath." Then I was alone in the damp greenness of the cave. As I eased back into my boat, I whispered to myself, "Everything is going to be all right."

Jon Turk was recently awarded a grant to paddle from Hokkaido, Japan acros the Bering Strait to Nome, Alaska. Tales of his other adventures can be found in his recent book, Cold Oceans.

Why Am I Like This?

by David J. Regela

Regardless of how deep I scrunch into my sleeping bag, it is impossible not to hear the river. Filtered by goose down, the muffled rush is somehow more sinister and my head pops up like a dull-witted prairie dog in the path of a buffalo stampede. The Middle Fork of the Salmon River is really ripping this year. And it's raining.

Most of the commercial trips have canceled. All of the other private trips have scrubbed as well. The twisted, punctured bones of a couple of 30-foot sweep boats are somewhere downriver. So what am I doing here? Why, indeed, am I like this?

Earlier this afternoon we assembled at Boundary Creek from all over the West. Some of us good boaters with decades of experience. But the river was going like a banshee, and maybe going higher. We rigged our boats in a hailstorm, a quixotic mix of ice and sun. Gallows humor haunted the conversation. We repeated oft-told tales of past disasters large and small, we laughed, we jested, we performed for Cynthia, the permit holder and abject novice. "Just how high was it," someone wondered, "when the Brokaw party crashed?" No one knew.

Morning is clear, warm. Yet even Tom, the little general, seems distracted, subdued. I learn that during the night one of our number has surreptitiously escaped. He must have pushed his truck well beyond the perimeters of our camp before firing the ignition and beginning his thousand-mile retreat. Or else the white noise of the river simply swallowed the disturbance, conspiring to keep the rest of us on the menu.

We have a flip. An injury. Johnny is forced to evacuate his teenage daughter not quite five miles from the put-in at Boundary Creek. My passenger, fortunately, is a rowing fool and takes on Johnny's boat and his son, who wants to continue despite his fear. A ritual develops between the boy and me. Each night he asks, "David, what do we have tomorrow? Any big rapids?"

"No," I lie, "tomorrow's easy." The boy has been here before and he knows the river. Still, he wants some reassurance. I think it comforts us both . . .

So, why am I like this? It's a good question with an elusive answer. For me, the eternal bedlam clash of water and rock is both baptism and communion. The insistent tug of gravity is bewitching, irresistible, addictive. Call me Ishmael, for I am spellbound in the presence of moving water. Why am I like this? The adrenaline, the perception of risk is certainly a part of the attraction of whitewater boating. In point of fact, however, everything else, all of the other components, may be far more important.

The crazy flood-stage run on the Middle Fork is not completely representative. I recall another, calmer, saner descent just as vividly. The water was a translucent, living green, the Idaho weather idyllic. We watched a family of otters at work. That is, the adults faced the daunting task of teaching their pups to eddy-hop against the current. The lessons were punctuated with the almost continual chirping protests of the babies. Otters can be serious. The session lasted until the light was nearly gone, but they got the hang of it.

Moving water evokes my purest sense of reflection, my moments of greatest clarity. Witness my merely mortal form rowing the Salt River canyon, toiling against a headwind. A miniature cyclone, or dust devil, grows to ominous proportions at the mouth of a side-canyon. As it slips over the river's surface it exchanges its sediment load for a full measure of suspended water. The waterspout spots my boat and churns like a determined, demented assassin. Other boats are blown willy-nilly, yet I settle into the very eye of the beast. Sunlight, bent and refracted by the rotating water, separates into prismatic bands. For several seconds I am inside the rainbow. Literally. It is noiseless, windless, dry. Simple magic. River magic.

That evening at camp I announce my decision to take, henceforth, the Indian name Dances-With-Wind. Several companions suggest profane variations on the "Wind" theme and I concede that perhaps the name change is not in

my best interests. The experience could be no more profound had I been abducted by space aliens.

River trips beget small miracles on a fairly regular basis. Ask almost anyone. A sudden downpour in the sandstone cleft of Slickrock Canyon on the Dolores finds us sheltering under a large overhang amid the artwork of the ancients. As absorbed as midwives, we attend the birth of a score of ephemeral waterfalls from the opposite rim. The ghost-pass of a remnant grizzly on the Selway . . . and a black bear cub vacates a ponderosa in the middle of our camp with all the speed and purpose of a furry little fireman. Same trip.

The Flathead River in Montana is a glacial myth of a hue so surreal that one tends to disbelieve the sugar-coated Livingston Mountains as well. Snow and Christmas carols on the Salmon on the evening of the first day of summer. Somber, brooding stone ruins on the San Juan that whisper on the breath of evening in lost, archaic tongues, just beyond the scope of our understanding. On the Snake River in the Tetons, we watch a russet moose calf nursing with so much determination and force that the stoic gaze of its mother speaks more eloquently than mere words. A bridge exists between our disparate species—if only for a moment. And then a lion materializes and vanishes before our eyes as effectively as any character in a Star Trek rerun. My wife and I marry on a twilight beach at the entrance to a great cathedral canyon called Santa Elena. One side is Texas, the other Mexico. Other cultures, in more romantic times, would have called this place Avalon or Eden or Valhalla. In Hell's Canyon, not so very long ago, a jetboat operator mistimed his high-powered attempt to ascend Granite Creek Falls in direct line with our own descent. Scant seconds and an abundance of grace saw us safely into camp that day. I will forever carry the image of my wife talking and laughing with trip-mates in the lemon light of sunset. A beautiful sight. A gift. We read aloud from the journals of John Wesley Powell on the Green and Colorado rivers and try to camp in the shadows of their camps. Without fail, someone solemnly kisses the Tiger Wall on the Yampa in return for safe passage through Warm Springs Rapid not far below.

These small ceremonies are important to us. A part of our religion, our system of beliefs. And people are a large part of the equation. I am endlessly intrigued by group dynamics. The cooperation and conflict mirror life in the largest possible sense. People disappoint. They inspire. Warriors emerge. Friendships cut across class and tribal lines. Bonds are forged, rooted in our interdependence, that will endure. A week spent in Cataract Canyon one September stands as metaphor for the whole issue of camaraderie. No one had pitched a tent until the very last night when a fragmented low pressure system delivered rain and thunder and lightning. I refused to bother with a shelter and stayed awake in the warm rain, enjoying the storm. Two other tentless fugitives wandered over and we shared a flask of bourbon. I stared from one to the other of these good friends, in the intermittent illumination, realizing that they could not be more polarized. A hulking former superjock and a skinny introspective Rasputin. An odd couple

to say the least. Only on the river. Or in a war zone.

I have this capacity to forget things. Like the five days of dawn-to-dusk gale-force winds in Desolation Canyon that caused us to add 48 hours to our planned itinerary. What I recollect instead is the motor-rig that blithely passed us a hundred yards from our intended camp, damning us to row grimly into the gathering, gusty nightfall. We were rewarded with the experience of an emergency camp we affectionately called the La Brea Tar Pits. Great story. Especially veiled by the gentle benediction of time.

Lost amid these reveries, some sacred, some not, the great "Why am I like this?" dilemma seems redundant, irrelevant. But its season will come again. When courage falters, my whiny, strident little inner voice will demand a response, affirming that the question will always remain. Revived, perhaps, on the occasion of my next unplanned swim, spin, and rinse cycle—or in that electric moment when the boat is committed to the big drop at Rainie Falls. Just give me a minute. Allow me to dry off a bit, get my pulse rate down to normal, rediscover my sense of humor. I really do have a pretty good answer.

David Regela is a frequent contributor to Paddler *magazine. His stories have appeared in* Sports Illustrated, *among other national publications.*

Why Paddle Class V?

by Doug Ammons

I started paddling because I loved the water. I learned the basic skills and after a couple of times on the river, I found it was the wildest, most fun, most playful, and most beautiful damn sport I'd ever done. The people were great, the rivers beautiful, and every horizon line stirred fun and questions anew. There seemed no limit to where I could go. By my second or third time on the river, I was hooked. By the end of my first year, I was a fanatic.

I ran my first Class V rapid after I'd been paddling about two months. I was with a group of older guys on a wilderness river they knew well, and we came to a rapid they had always portaged. They said it was unrunable and at first I believed them. But after looking closely I realized there was a line, and I ran it with no difficulties. It was a little scary, sitting in the eddy above and feeling the river surge beneath me. But what led me to paddle over that horizon line was a quiet sense of certainty. I knew what I'd seen and I realized then that if you looked just right you could find a thread of truth that carried you through all the dangers and right into the heart of the river.

By the end of the first year, I was doing Class V with regularity, paddling with the best guys in the area. With good role models and great rivers, you can bootstrap yourself up pretty quickly. I went looking for new places, mostly steep creeks tucked away in remote canyons. There was exploring, topo maps, recon, first attempts, failures, waterfalls, complex portaging—all to find wild lines down beautiful sparkling streams. Sometimes we'd get thrashed, but we always came back. Who could ask for a better world? I found a place clean and pure, where the sun and snowmelt laughed with you as you paddled over the edge of the drop. We solved outrageous puzzles of movement and timing, played games of speed chess with the water, just at the edge of what we could handle. We wove ourselves completely into the river and lived for those moments of clarity when you were committed to the line, to that thread of truth. And all those days of friendship, worry, concentration, and smiles melted together into a great feeling.

I also went on more committing trips. In some ways it was more of the same, but with the greater commitment came new territory. The places got more spectacular and dangerous, and the trips changed their tenor. It was one thing doing first descents near home. Even on the most remote runs at least you weren't far from people. But doing it up in the wilderness of Canada, the jungle, or farther away still, was another thing. The fun of a clean line becomes less the point and something else steps in. The moves might be similar, but a new set of emotions becomes important out in the middle of nowhere, deep in the bottom of some canyon, alone with a friend or two. You look up at the vertical walls. The river disappears around a corner in front of you, all you can hear is a roar, and you know the game has changed.

You pay attention to different things when you're totally committed. Every sense comes alive. Your awareness heightens in every way. The water is your life, and you see and sense everything about it. You stretch yourself out and there's no dividing line between you and the beautiful, dangerous place you're in. Every decision you make has huge consequences and so you treat it with care, with a delicacy and intensity that puts you entirely in that moment. Each surge of the current, each paddlestroke, each word has a renewed importance. And for those minutes, hours, or days, you become a different person.

At some point over the years, I realized that for me kayaking was more than a sport. I found I needed the water and its beauty, its power and subtleties. I needed the friendships it had helped me make. I trained like mad, concentrated on every skill, and committed myself to my judgment. The harder the trip and the more it stretched us, the more humbled and small I felt. Each time it was like seeing a little further into a special

world and sharing something beyond friendship with my partners.

I have a lot to thank my friends and mentors for, not just their help in approaching Class V, but what it means. They taught me how to look at more than the hard whitewater; that it was a privilege to be in those spectacular places. How important it was to respect and meet the river on its own terms and never to lose sight of the fact that it is bigger than you in every way. Most of my best friends are people I've spent those times with, and I can't separate them from the feeling of approaching the horizon line. So friendship is a part of Class V too.

I've messed up and been hurt. In 17 years of Class V paddling, I've had three serious accidents. I dislocated my shoulder the first year I was paddling in the middle of a long Class V rapid. My paddle hung up on a rock and I didn't let go. Luckily, I was able to roll and get to the side. My friends reduced the shoulder there on the talus with a foot in the side and a couple of yanks. It was a good lesson that lasted for 12 years of healthy paddling, but sometimes you forget even the best lessons.

I had a bad season a few years ago. Maybe I wasn't in the best shape. Maybe my time was up. A moment's distraction left me plastered upside-down at high speed on the front of a sharp boulder, with a dislocated collarbone, separated shoulder, crunched ribs, and more. The distraction wasn't directly the cause of the accident. Really, it was a dividing line, because perhaps 20 seconds later and hundreds of yards down the river its consequences put me in a situation where I had no options. After I hit and the current peeled me off the boulder,

I struggled through another 200 yards of hard Class V, barely making it into an eddy, paralyzed on my right side from the pain, and unable to get out of my boat. Sometimes an accident isn't caused by an outright mistake. A lack of care for a second or two became a year of rehab. It could easily have been a lot worse.

I have also had friends die on the river. I'm left with a deep ambivalence, that something I love as a celebration of life can also lead to death. In every case, their decisions overlooked some invisible or seemingly innocent detail which made all the difference. The river's flow magnifies the consequences of all decisions and all mistakes; it is the flow of time itself. Nowhere else do you see so clearly how one small detail can cascade into the future with terrible consequences. The art of staying alive on difficult rivers is in choosing a line that has a future beyond the river.

If you seriously go looking for your limits, eventually you'll find them, but you might not like what happens there. The problem is you might not realize you're there until it's too late. We get away with a lot because water is almost always forgiving. We call that luck. I'm certain that most of the time we can get away with more than we realize, and people will always be plumbing this margin. We'll never find a clear edge because there isn't one. The river's beauty and danger come from the same source, and they can meld into each other from second to second. You can't understand all the strange things water does no matter how closely you look or how cautious and skilled you are.

I've run lots of rivers and thousands of hard rapids over the years, and many were first descents. I've faced a lot of questions about whether something was runable or not. I go on a careful analysis of what I see, but mostly I go on an intuition that comes out of my relationship with the river, my feeling that day, at that minute, on that run. There are several times when I've been broached, pinned, or tangled with submerged logs which could never have been seen no matter how long we scouted. Other, more bizarre things have happened. I've needed help from friends. I've helped them too. I've pulled bodies out of rivers, which was not enjoyable, but it was a damn good reminder of what happens when luck runs out.

The most upsetting thing I've ever experienced didn't happen to me. It was watching my best friend go for a horrible thrashing and thinking he was dead when we were running something we thought was clean. That was just the start. We were in a deep canyon, his boat flushed away, and he was left stranded against the wall with the choice of trying to swim through a series of huge ledge holes or climb a 500-foot, vertical, rotten cliff to get out. He climbed. I watched. The scariest thing is being helpless. It's an empty, terrible feeling. It took him a long time to get up and I decided during that climb that I don't like being a witness. He made it, finally. That was many years ago and we both have scars. I'm sure his are much worse than mine, but mine bother me too. After experiences like that you have to ask yourself where to put the balance point. And you've got to realize that sometimes there are things you might not see which turn out to be the point of the whole show.

I've always pushed to do harder runs, but I consider myself a careful paddler.

I've run things that are very intimidating, but I have never run a rapid I was afraid of. On really hard rapids, I make my decision if, as I analyze it, an intuitive feeling of clarity comes over me, a certainty that the moves fit and that I can do them. Sometimes it feels as if I've poured myself right into the river. If I don't find that feeling, I walk. I listen closely to any sense of doubt, even if I can't see its source, because the whisper is two decades of intuition reaching into a world beyond the rational. It has saved my life and the lives of two friends at least once.

The thought above depends upon having a choice about whether you'll run a rapid or not. Twice, I've been in the first descenter's nightmare: alone and in the wilderness, walled out with no portage possible, and being forced to run what looked like it a potentially fatal rapid. These situations were caused by decisions made long before reaching the actual rapid. In a sense, they were inevitable once the ball had started in motion days before. The point is, however, that I didn't deliberately go looking for them. They were hidden consequences of the path I'd chosen for other reasons.

These are the only times I've ever headed into something I wasn't sure I could run, but had no choice except to try. I can only assure you that you feel pretty damn small at that moment of truth and pretty lucky afterwards. Both turned out, neither was pretty. Maybe when all is said and done, those rapids weren't as hard as they looked. All I know is each one looked really, really bad from the one place I could scout. I know that after facing those questions about the unknown you find yourself climbing over a lot of emotions and ask-

ing a lot of questions about what led you into that situation.

I've seen people get a lot of different things from the river and from Class V. It's all in what you bring to it. If you go looking for challenge or for mystery, you'll find them. Treat it like a snowboard in a halfpipe and that's what it will be. If it's for bragging rights, looking for a rush, being cool, enjoying beauty, celebrating friendships—it can give these too. It can give you a magic you never will reach otherwise, and it can kill you. It's such an incredible gift it should be used with the utmost care. It's the greatest balance of fun, seriousness, and truth I've ever found.

Most Class V from 30 years ago is Class IV now, or less. We've upped the ante a lot as we kept looking for the edge. Disregarding all the grays about ratings, the way we use the term "Class V" just means whatever the edge of runability is at a given time. Each time we do another harder river, nip off another portage, find a steeper run, go for a higher water level, that's water under the bridge. Pretty quickly, we look for something higher, bigger, faster, or weirder. We change and the Class V changes. We never stop exploring, both it and ourselves.

Class V is also a word for a special kind of learning. It says, "Push hard, but remember—what you do in the next few seconds may mean everything." Class V is a rapid, a physical place with a beginning, a set of moves, and an end. It is also all the things that the physical place touches inside you, all the ripples of meaning it has for you, and those are things which go on as long as you live.

Class V is about your limits. It is about what you can control, and what you can come to with a steady, clear mind. Those limits change within you, even on a single run. They change with equipment and experience. They change from person to person, and year to year. For those who continue, there's always a new set of people who will try to take it past anything we ever thought possible. When the new guys push as far as they can, the next generation will already be hungry for more. After you're around for a while, you realize you've received a baton from the past, and at some point you'll end up passing it to others and stepping out of the way. Over time, however, everybody who steps up to the plate probably asks the same questions. And take my word for it, there's always some wild stuff going on. You might not hear about it because it stays where it matters most—between a few close friends and the river.

Whenever you enter the game, whatever door you come through, that's what you accept as your base. If you have the desire to find answers, the river will present the questions. I always keep in mind that no matter how hard we push, there is no end and there are no limits. The river will always have more.

—"With thanks to the rivers I know and my friends, including John Foss, Joel Hathhorne, and others who stepped over the line. We remember you."

Doug Ammons is a long-time expedition kayaker with several first descents to his credit.

EXPEDITIONS

Taming the Toltec

by Peter Heller

Garcia Bodellio asked the question no one could answer. He was a small, neat man in a huge hat, in the middle of the most beautiful country on earth.

Along the New Mexico/Colorado border west of Antonito is a province of meadowed hills, scattered ponderosas, bunched aspen, and sandstone caprock—folded and cut deeply by small streams. Now, in a wet July, the hills were sprayed with monkey-flowers. Cattle, some of them Garcia's, grazed.

Pushing his cowboy hat back, Garcia rested his elbow in the window of his two-tone truck. He let his eyes travel over the line of Japanese cars, pausing when he came to the purple and yellow kayaks. "Where?" he said gently.

"The gorge. Toltec Gorge."

He raised an eyebrow politely. "Maybe you don't know what that is like down there."

"We got an idea today."

He shook his head. "I've been here a long time. No one ever did that."

"We want to try."

Garcia looked thoughtfully at the bottom of his steering wheel. Finally he looked up. "Why?" he asked.

There was an awkward pause. A fly buzzed. The silence sounded a little like one hand clapping.

First Attempt

Earlier that afternoon I had been asking myself the exact same question. We had driven upstream to a place called Osier, at the head of the Gorge, to scout whatever we could. There were five of us: Landis Arnold, John Mattson, and Mark Lane, all from Boulder, Colorado, Dave Eckardt from Aspen, and myself. Landis and John had been there with another friend, Sascha Steinway, in June, and had made an attempt to run the canyon. Half a mile in, on a raucous, quickly steepening and constricting hair run, they came to a blind corner and a roar like the Blue Angels. They decided they'd rather spend the rest of the afternoon rock climbing out and hauling their boats up 50 feet at a time on throw ropes than run the blind corner. Further on, the walls became more sheer anyway and it looked like you couldn't climb out if you wanted to, even with rock gear.

So now, in late July, low water, they were back. And this time I was with them. The gorge was intriguing. It may well have been the last spectacular deep gorge in the Lower 48 that had never been paddled.

On Fishing

Osier, the put in, barely makes the maps. It sits between grassy ridges at 9,680 feet above sea level. It's a lunch stop on the Cumbres and Toltec Scenic Railroad, which runs along the rim of the canyon. There's a weathered, yellow water tower spouting leaks, harried by swallows who nest under the roof; an abandoned station house, circa 1880, boarded shut; and a new tourist building under a shiny red roof. From the station the Rio de Los Pinos looks like a quiet creek, winding out of a fold in the grassy northern hills, a deep blue, failing into the cleft beneath us. Less than a mile downstream, the river disappears into the pink rock walls of the gorge.

We parked on the mud road beside the station and set off down the railroad tracks to scout. A dense overcast crowded down over the country and broke into a fine rain. Just before the tracks disappeared into a tunnel, a gash in the rock fell all the way down to the river, affording a comforting view of a ribbon of white froth working its way through a sieve of rocks. We clambered out to the end of the buttress. I was relieved. Through binoculars nothing was visible on the river far below but a string of four

rocky waterfalls culminating in a jumble of seething boulders. The rest of the rapid was hidden coyly behind an abrupt twist in the walls. No sweat, I thought. Tomorrow I'm going fishing.

We walked through the tunnel and scrambled into the gorge. The gorge is more than 1,000 feet deep, nearly vertically walled at river level, cut with couloirs, rough buttresses, scree falls, and scattered over with spruce and pine which crowd the gullies and cling to ledges. It is labyrinthine, narrow, and steep. We estimated that in the one-and-a-half to two miles of gorge the river dropped 600 to 800 feet per mile. It twists and spills through the uplifted bedrock; in some places less than a hundred yards may be glimpsed between corners.

The rock was wet and slick, mottled with lichen, and we took great care. We split up and got to river level at a couple of different spots. Where I stood, the view upstream was not heartening; it was blocked by a 25-foot, unrunnable waterfall crashing into an aqueduct of sheer rock walls. How to get around? River left, depending on what the lip of the falls looked like, there might be a possibility of bouldering down to a seal-entry from a ledge beside the falls. In the tunnel of rock below was a hundred years of easier rapids. These culminated in a double cascade. The line was a three-foot-wide slot between a sharp undercut and a splat rock, which angled you across a seven-foot waterfall. Then surf across the hole at the bottom and line up on the far side for a 12-foot free-fall over an overhanging lip. No easy portage around this: once here, the only way not to run would be to rock climb to a ramping edge and rappel with your boat from a small dead tree.

John Mattson, a veteran mountain man and a trusted friend, looked at the tree. "Piece of cake," he said jauntily. "Rappelling with kayaks is fun." His intense blue eyes sparkling, he enthusiastically described the series of slings and harnesses that would go around me and the boat during the portage. I thought about trout. I wished I was with my father, knee deep in some gentle New England stream, making long casts in the shadows of maples.

It didn't matter that my father does not fish.

More on Fishing

That night, at the take out, we camp in a grassy bottom beside the alders. The sky clears on a beneficent, round, full moon. In the middle of the night, I crawl out of my truck to pee. I look at the moon. The grass is wet and cold beneath my feet. The river riffles and breathes. The ridges cup the valley, washed in light, speckled with pines. I love life. I am not going in the morning. I really will fish. Why should I jeopardize it all for a portage fest? It will be an equal act of courage to tell my old friends that I do not feel up to it; to fish and feel okay with my decision. Done. I slip back into bed relieved.

Jazz

Fat chance. Three cups of coffee. Sun. Cloudless sky. Impeccable morning. Everybody lingers over breakfast. Lingers over boats. Rigs throw-ropes, foot braces. Landis displays state-of-the-art rescue gear: a telescoping grab-hook that clamps to the end of a paddle, a mini throw bag, lightweight Z-drag pulleys, and folding saws. There is an unspoken understanding that nothing bad can happen simply because it would be a nightmare trying to get an injured paddler out of the gorge.

Carabiners clink and ring. Ropes are coiled and stuffed into dry bags. First-aid kits packed. Hip pads trimmed. Bivvy gear and extra food closed into stow floats. Break-down paddles set aside. An excitement hums through everything. It is irresistible. There is a kind of jazz that sets up before a first descent—or any run, really—that looms as a great challenge to the paddler. Music in the key of A: adrenaline, anticipation, action. It's transporting. It's like B.B. King playing Lucille.

At the put in, I hustle into my dry suit and carry my boat to the river. Strangely, I am even more relieved than when I decided to go fishing. It's amazing how fear and other considerations can vanish as soon as you launch into the water and begin to paddle. I think I know why: it's because there is nothing more expansive than releasing oneself to the music.

The Run

I won't describe the run in great detail. For me, there was something intimate, maybe sacred, in that day of paddling that resists elaboration. We named the drops, less for elucidation than because we love our names, but the list should in no way be taken as a guide, nor presumed to possess a high degree of accuracy; we were all blissed-out and addled with adrenaline when we made it. I asked Mattson what we should rate the run. He swallowed two Oreos and shot back "HARD!" John Mattson is a very good and experienced paddler, and I leave it at that. We estimate that on

July 27, the day we paddled, there were only 150 cfs in the river, and that was plenty pushy.

We were all surprised at how much superb paddling there was in the gorge. In something like 15 sets of drops, there were only five portages. We got into the fine rhythm of running, scouting, and running. We entered through a winding, shadowy section of smooth overhung granite walls we called Canyon El Dulce, and emerged below the double set of falls described above. (It turned out to be the sweetest of all drops; everyone ran it, and we named it the Toltec Two-Step). At one point in the heart of the gorge, at a place we called Lolita's Lap, we realized that there was no way out but down.

Everybody paddled well; all used Prijon T-Canyons. There were a few dicey moments, a few short broaches, but there were no swims and no mishaps. We were all a little awed to be moving through a place where perhaps no man had ever been. And Mark Lane blew our circuits by running the most unrunnable-looking 30- to 40-foot funnel waterfall I have ever seen paddled. I thought he was kidding when he got out to scout it. When he finished I wondered if he had a terminal disease.

Just before dusk, we paddled out of the gorge into an eddy-hopper, 250-feet-per-mile stretch and then out onto a stream of quiet, shallow water. The sun was setting upstream. Clouds of mayflies fluttered over the river. Alders, Chinese elms, and cottonwoods rustled along the banks. Lovely meadows opened along the bottom with here and there a quiet ranch house. We paddled steadily. After sunset, the sky upstream turned lavender, held in the tops of the spruce, and the Dog Star shone brightly. Everything had a rare clarity.

Mark and I, paddling ahead, came to a small wooden bridge. There were two fishermen on chairs, their backs to us and their lines in the water. Their cigar smoke drifted into the evening. In a few moments they would be very surprised; no one had ever paddled out of the gorge before. But now they were peaceful. Fishing is also a great way to spend the time.

The Temptation of Turnback

by Ken Madsen

March 1988

We splay out in the California sunshine. After the Yukon winter my skin looks like tuna fish. The sun feels great. We've just run Friday the 13th and Death Ferry, in Burnt Ranch Gorge. I'm wondering who thinks up the names.

"Have you paddled the Alsek?" asks a man who used to live in Alaska.

"No."

"That must be some river," he says. "Walt Blackadar died there, in Turnback Canyon."

"Actually," I say, "he drowned on a river in Idaho."

He shakes his head. "That Alsek must be an incredible river."

Kayaking is a sport where last week's achievements are passe. Yet paddlers still sit on riverbanks in California, around campfires in British Columbia, in pubs in England, and discuss Walt Blackadar's exploits in Turnback Canyon.

December 1988

Nine o'clock in the morning, but it's still dark as I walk into Whitehorse. My shoes squeak against the dry snow. I see pencils of smoke rising from houses and smell the sharp tang of burning wood.

The world outside the streetlights is inky black. The radius of my knowledge about the Alsek River is as well defined as the light from the street lights. I've paddled the rivers that form its headwaters—they are bright in my memory. But the Alsek is dark and mysterious. I open the door of the Yukon Archives, find a table, and cover it with my mitts, sweater, wool hat, and jacket. I pull out a topo map and trace the blue line of the Alsek. It begins in Kluane National Park in the Yukon, flows south through British Columbia, and reaches the Pacific at Dry Bay, Alaska.

I flip through the Xeroxed copy of a *Sports Illustrated* article almost 20 years old, "Caught Up in a Hell of White Water." The author is Walt Blackadar.

I think it's exaggerated. Hope it's exaggerated.

Blackadar was the first kayaker to paddle Turnback Canyon. His solo trip in 1971 gave him, and the Alsek, a legendary status. The canyon didn't have a second descent until 1980, and only two groups paddled it during the ensuing 10 years. A young French kayaker drowned during an international expedition in 1981.

Summer 1989

I talk to Kluane Park wardens who say Turnback Canyon is unrunnable when the river swells with summer melt, who say it's bad at any flow, who say, "Why don't you run the Tatshenshini instead? It flows into the Alsek below Turnback Canyon."

I decide to paddle the Alsek in late September when the cool nights will turn off the taps of glacial melt from the St. Elias Mountains and the river should be low. Some of my friends can't get the time off work, some stare at me as though I'm nuts. It looks, like Blackadar, that I'll have to go solo. It isn't until the end of August that I finally find someone interested in the Alsek. Derek Endress has just finished a summer of smoke-jumping and he's enthusiastic at the thought of a wilderness trip. "You're on your own in Turnback Canyon though," he says.

"My birthday—49! Looked in the mirror and realized I wasn't getting any younger. Decided to paddle the Alsek alone, though it is against sanity and all safety codes. I've tried for six months to get others to join me. I have left a letter at home with instructions to spend up to $5,000 to prove me alive or dead . . . If I am found dead, the pilot has been told to bury me there . . . "
—Walt Blackadar

September, 1989

We drive west on the Alaska Highway. It's the first day of autumn, but in the north the change of season comes earlier. On the mountains, the edge of new snow is just above us. A few stubborn leaves still cling to alders bordering the river.

It's sunny and cool and the river looks low, but cirrus clouds signal a change. Thick clouds build. Soon we are paddling in a driving rain. Gusty winds blow sand and grit across the river. High on scree slopes, Dall sheep and mountain goats seem impervious to the storm. Mountains, shrouded with shifting mist and curtains of rain, keep a tenuous hold on hanging glaciers. Waterfalls spout from gloomy cliffs.

On the third evening we arrive at Turnback Canyon, sandwiched between Mt. Blackadar and the Tweedsmuir Glacier. The edge of the glacier is a moonscape of jumbled boulders and gluey muck. Boisterous squalls shake our tent and fling my paddle into a newly formed lake. The downpour loosens refrigerator-sized boulders and chunks of ice from an ice-fall. They somersault into the river.

I huddle in my sleeping bag. I've never felt so insignificant.

In the morning the storm is gone, leaving a pale sky and a river that is a flooding sea of chocolate milk. The rapids look awful. Looking down at the whitewater from the canyon walls, Blackadar's journal doesn't seem so farfetched. Our portage is a two-day slog across the ice—and through the 20-square-mile chaos of shifting boulders and gluey mud that forms the glacier's terminal moraine.

Winter 1990

Winter arrives at the same time we fly back from Dry Bay. Ravens squat in the snow, feathers fluffed. I ski beside the frozen Yukon River, thinking, "Turnback Canyon didn't look that bad . . . " Derek is also eager, and two others catch the Alsek virus. Ian Pineau is a graduate of the crash-and-burn school of paddling. I remember watching from shore as he drifted broadside towards a turbulent slot between two huge boulders. He glanced up and said calmly, "This is not the way to run this rapid." Rod Leighton is the last word in exercise fanatics, never fully relaxed unless all stores of muscular ATP are depleted. Rod is a solid kayaker, but he hasn't paddled since the summer.

"Forget finesse," he says as we discuss Turnback Canyon. "I've been working out, I'll just paddle full speed ahead."

"Suddenly, I was in a frothy mess that was far worse than anything I have ever seen . . . very narrow—like trying to run down a coiled rattler's back, the rattler striking at me from all sides. I was shoved to the left bank about an inch from the cliff where a foot-wide eddy existed. For perhaps a mile I skidded and swirled and turned down this narrow line. I kept telling myself, 'You can roll in this,' but all the time I knew I couldn't."

—Walt Blackadar

May 6–9, 1990

The water temperature is barely above freezing and I'm grateful for the sunshine. The sky is blue but brittle-looking, as though it will shatter and rain as it had in September. In the four days it takes to reach the canyon, the river rises steadily with snowmelt. I'm worried that it's already too high.

Winter flexes its muscle as we near the Tweedsmuir Glacier. There is no sign of the moraine, just snowy humps that flatten into a 10-mile-wide ramp flowing

from the mountains. Only in the still air does the intense sunshine feel warm. We find a wedge of sand and gravel just wide enough for our tents, a desert island in an ocean of snow and ice.

May 10, 1990

Ian rolls over in his sleeping bag. Struggling for more sleep is futile so I unzip the fly and look out. The Tweedsmuir Glacier looms above the other tent. The river seems peaceful.

We've decided that fully loaded boats would be too sluggish in the canyon. We pack tents, sleeping bags, and enough food for the day. The bulk of our stuff is heaped on the gravel spit. Tomorrow we'll hike back across the glacier to retrieve our baggage, dragging a kayak as a cargo sled.

No one is in a hurry to start paddling. Rod sits on his kayak and slices duct tape to protect the raw spots on his hands. Ian brews another pot of thick coffee. Derek and I wander between the pile of gear and our kayaks, making minor adjustments that don't matter. Finally, there is nothing more we can do. We squeeze into our boats.

Caffeine and adrenaline make a potent mixture. We pinball down the Alsek, bouncing from eddy to eddy and loosening our muscles—but our nerves remain taut. The rock walls grow, blocking the sunlight. We gather in an eddy. The Alsek is big, the first rapid in the S-bends is big, the canyon walls are big. I feel small.

Zooming towards a huge surging hole, I cut right on a tongue that surfs me through the boils. Rod joins me in the eddy, then Derek.

"Good paddling," I say, but Derek is looking upriver.

"Ian's over!" he yells.

Ian's kayak bounces over a wave. He rolls up. Flips. Rolls up. And flips again as the surging river flattens him against a rock wall. The boat, held firmly by the current, twitches erratically as Ian tries to right himself. Finally he wallows up, escapes the boils, and joins us. He looks serene, as if he's been splashing in a warm bath.

The next few rapids are manageable, but I can't shake the awe of being in the canyon. The vertical rock walls pinch in. We find an eddy, but there is no place to wriggle out of our kayaks. I stretch my neck for a look downstream. The strong upstream current in the eddy floats me to the others, clustered under a rocky ledge. "I can't see anything horrible," I say. "I'm comfortable paddling until we find another eddy. What do you think?"

"I'm comfortable with that," Ian replies. Rod and Derek echo that they're comfortable. We're all comfortable.

An eddy is a safe, social place. A secure place. A place to temporarily shake off the isolation. I leave the eddy, and for the moment, I'm only concerned about myself.

I look for a place to stop, but there isn't one. The Alsek accelerates and the waves are growing. I sink into a trough and look up at the next wave. It's too rounded, too regular—but there is nowhere else to go. I reach the top and stare down—a long way down, into a wall of white that spans the river.

With instinctive hope, I drop into the hole and reach downstream with my paddle. Next thing I know, I'm riding it sideways, its crest foaming over my head.

One by one the others eddy out and arrive at the hole at regular intervals.

Rod gazes down at the top of my helmet. He powers into the right side of the maw, avoiding jackhammering me into the depths. Ian gets a great vista—the underside of Rod's boat, and me, still hanging on.

The current's right-to-left kick bounces me into boily upswellings against the wall. I've never been in a hole that big, and I'm shaky. Rod's kayak flushes out, but Ian is spending quality time in the hole. The end of his kayak spins like carrot in a blender until eventually he submarines downstream. Derek is the last to drop into the hole. He joins the upside-down parade. I follow.

"I ran the first mile of rapids with tremendous respect—found myself upside down twice . . . slammed into the cliff once and was pinned there for a lifetime . . . flipped and hung upside down while the boat was tossed out of the most violent boils before rolling up . . . "

—Walt Blackadar

The cross waves and boils seem friendly compared to what's ahead—tons of water nozzling through a 15-foot slot. Ghastly froth hugs the wall on the right. Balancing on a tiny tongue of downstream current, I claw to escape, but get sucked back, slam into the wall, cartwheel, and roll up. Once. Twice. I wash out and roll up, relieved to be in control, in calmer water. But just downstream, Derek is swimming, clutching Rod's grab loop. His kayak vanishes around the corner. Ian's spray deck is off and he's up to his armpits in water. It looks as though his pulse-rate has finally reached three figures.

The sun shines brightly. Silty water ebbs and surges impersonally. But Derek is on the wrong side of Turnback Canyon, without a boat. He sits despondently on a sloping shelf of gray rock.

"What do we do now?" he asks.

The past few minutes have brought a reawakened respect for the Alsek. We are all healthy—not necessarily happy, but healthy. I look downstream. The river pillows off a headwall and slams into another constriction. I'm not willing to chase Derek's boat without scouting.

Ian upends his kayak and water gushes out. Derek scrambles up a promontory. "The rapid is short," he yells. "It empties into a calm bay."

"I'll go after the boat," I say to Ian and Rod, "while you ferry Derek over to the moraine."

The next couple of rapids are easy, short chutes that punctuate the widenings of "The Hourglass." There are big eddies, but no kayak. The rock walls pinch in again. Not the place to split the group further. Besides, I'm nervous. I pull into shore to wait. Meanwhile, Derek leaps into the frigid river. Rod and Ian tow him to the other side.

I walk back to meet Derek while Rod and Ian scout the next rapids. Derek looks lonely trudging across the rock and ice in his dripping spray skirt, clutching a paddle.

I try to think of something reassuring to say, but all I can remember are the words of a veteran paddler, old enough to be able to rise above the embarrassment of swimming but perceptive enough to understand how it feels. "There are two types of boaters," he'd said in a grizzled voice. "Those who have swum and those who will swim, and they're the same thing."

I know something like that would sound banal right now. I keep quiet.

Derek says he'll meet us downstream, and starts walking across the bleak moraine. I feel drained of adrenaline, of energy. Even the caffeine has worn off. The last rapids are straightforward. Fortunately. Our adventure quotas are filled for the day.

Ian looks at Rod and me. "Congratulations," he says.

I smile, but without the euphoria I had expected. We are the first all-Canadian group to paddle "unpaddleable" Turnback Canyon, but we're four boaters with three boats—in the middle of an icy wilderness. I worm through the underbrush and onto the moraine. I whoop and hear an answering shout.

Derek slumps on a boulder and stares at his feet. "Now what?"

"It's not an emergency," I say. "We have plenty of food and gear at our cache." I'm trying to imagine how I would have reacted to a potentially lethal swim, to the cold, to the sight of us successfully paddling the canyon while he walked along the bank. He hasn't tried to hide his feelings, but he has maintained his composure.

"What about my kayak?"

"Someone will have to stay here while the others paddle out for help. Hopefully, we'll find the boat along the way."

Derek's face sags at the thought of waiting by himself.

"Look," I say, "I don't mind staying here. You can paddle my kayak."

"Let me think about it." His expression says that it's settled.

We search the bedrock shelves overlooking the glacier, and find two snow-free tent sites. The clear sky brings a dry night but plummeting temperatures. Derek's sleeping bag is in his kayak. He borrows a Therma-rest and swaths himself, mummy-like, in spare clothing.

"There's one huge horrendous mile of hair (the worst foamy rapids a kayaker can imagine), 30 feet wide, 50,000 cfs and a 20-degree downgrade going like hell. Incredible! I didn't flip in that mile or I wouldn't be writing."
—Walt Blackadar

May 11, 1990

A ptarmigan flutters over the tent, its guttural croak mimicking Ian's snores. I hear the quavering whistle of a varied thrush. The border of alder buffering the river from the glacier stirs with life—a contrast to our last camp. There, only wind, rock fall, and river rumblings punctuated the silence.

We zigzag over the moraine, heading back to our base camp at the head of the canyon. Fearing snow blindness, we fashion glacier goggles from slitted duct tape. Derek ranges ahead in wetsuit booties, scouting for the best route. Rod and Ian shackle themselves to my kayak, like prisoners in a chain gang, and drag it. The crust of snow supports us for a couple of steps, then collapses and we sink to our hips.

When we reach camp, Derek burrows into Rod's sleeping bag to catch up on sleep. I light the stove and brew coffee. Rod lolls back on his sleeping pad.

"Where does Detour Creek flow into the Tatshenshini?" he asks.

"Not sure," I answer, feeling lazy.

We sip our coffee. The sun heats our strip of exposed gravel and heat waves distort the mountains at the head of the glacier. Ian takes off his shirt. "How far it is up the Tatshenshini to Dalton Post?" Rod asks.

Neither Ian nor I know.

"I wonder how long it would take someone to walk to the highway from here?" Rod has a far-away expression in his eyes.

"A hell of a long time," Ian says.

We laugh, but I look at Rod and realize where this is leading. He is determined to solve our boat shortage by climbing over the mountains to the Tatshenshini and upriver to civilization.

In the afternoon Rod puts on his drysuit. We shake hands. Ian gets in the kayak and ferries him across the Alsek. He walks out of sight to the north. Five days later, Rod hobbles onto the Haines Highway. Five days of sinking to his armpits in soft snow. Five days of crawling through willows and alders, and scrambling up rotten rock pitches. Five days of watching the slopes for spring avalanches and the thickets for grizzlies.

Derek, Ian, and I lurch across the moraine one last time. We squeeze our gear, and Rod's extras, into our boats. I duct tape the extra paddle to my stern deck, like a mutant rudder left behind by the march of kayak evolution.

I don't expect to find Derek's kayak before the river widens at Alsek Lake, but a few kilometers below the canyon we see a familiar yellow shape. It bobs under an ice floe, brimming with sand. We take turns towing it.

The Alsek wilderness casts a powerful spell. Soon Turnback Canyon is a memory, an image of dark rock walls and surging whitewater. Winter turns into spring as we escape the refrigerator chill of the Tweedsmuir Glacier. Snow retreats to higher slopes. The green of new leaves lies in delicate mists over the trees.

I'm wondering about Walt Blackadar. Turnback Canyon didn't jibe with the description in his journal.

Others who have run the canyon have said the same. The questions go round and round during the next four days as we paddle towards Dry Bay. Where was the "30-foot drop into a boiling hell?" The "40 mph" current? The "20-foot-deep hole?" Is it wild exaggeration? Or, as has been suggested by some, complete fabrication?

August 1990

Five of us, myself, Wendy Boothroyd, Poco Bartels, Fraser Rowe, and 16-year-old Jody Schick, have just made the first descent of the Bates River. The Bates flows into the Alsek a day's paddle above Turnback Canyon.

Jody has a long acquaintance with the canyon, even though this is his first trip here. His father worked as Chief Park Naturalist in Kluane Park and had a consuming interest in the Alsek. Several of the early groups to run the river used the Schick home as a base camp.

In 1981, when Jody was 7, he talked with members of an international expedition intent on a first European descent of Turnback Canyon. Thierry Giorgetti, the youngest paddler, talked with Jody and showed him his kayak. A few days later, Giorgetti drowned in the canyon's violent rapids. The expedition was aborted and several kayaks helicoptered to the Schicks' back yard. When I returned from the Alsek in May, Jody grilled me about water levels. The flow had been about 15,000 cfs, similar to the highest levels the canyon has yet been run at—with the probable exception of Blackadar's descent, before flow data was collected.

Jody was unimpressed. "You haven't run the real Turnback Canyon unless you do it at high water," he said.

Now it's mid-summer and the Alsek is booming with glacial melt from the St. Elias Mountains, home of the most extensive, non-polar icefields in the world. We have no intention of running the canyon, but hope to shorten the grueling portage by putting in above the Last Major Constriction, the final big rapid. If I remember right, we can portage it at river level.

We struggle across the Tweedsmuir Glacier's terminal moraine. Two strenuous days later, dehydrated and hungry, we lower the last kayak to the water. Fifty thousand cfs of silty water is slamming through the canyon. The Last Major Constriction looks nasty. We'll need to ferry across the smoking current to a small patch of calm water. Wendy's face looks like the underside of a halibut, "I have no strength left," she says. "Let's camp here tonight."

"I'd rather do the ferry now than first thing in the morning," Poco says.

"What about supper and a rest first?" suggests Fraser in his thick Australian drawl.

Wendy wanders off. She returns with a resigned expression. "There's no place to camp in this jumble of rock. Pass me some chocolate."

We lean against our kayaks. "What should I do if I end up in the rapid?" Wendy asks through a mouthful of Mars bar.

"This has been a day! I want any kayaker to read my words well! The Alsek gorge is unpaddleable! Believe me . . . I'm not coming back. Not for $1 million, not for all the tea in China. Read my words well and don't be a fool. It's unpaddleable."

—Walt Blackadar

"You're bound to flip," I say. "Count to ten. Hopefully you'll flush through the boils and whirlpools and you can roll up."

We squeeze into our kayaks and look dubiously at the far shore, several hundred yards away. I follow Wendy, yelling encouragement. The banks slip quickly upriver despite her grim strokes, but we reach the "calm" water. Ocean-like surges fling Wendy and Poco into a rocky alcove where they wedge themselves like corks in a bottle of cheap wine. They crawl out and drag their boats to safety.

Fraser, Jody, and I are confident that we can paddle to an eddy just above the rapid, where portaging will be easier. We peel out.

Fraser and I hit the eddy, but Jody turns upstream on the eddy line and washes backwards. A boil catches his boat, flips it, and spits him into the main current. He rolls up, glances at me with an "Oh, hell" expression, and disappears downstream.

I yell to Fraser, "I'm following him," and peel out. A huge breaking wave picks up my kayak and upends me in a cauldron of boils and whirlpools. I spin in a succession of cartwheels. After 15 seconds that feels like 15 minutes, and four or five rolls, I wash out, totally disoriented. I see Jody wallowing into an eddy. Fraser manages to stay in the main current and only flips once.

Jody had cut to the inside, trying to sneak past the boils that burped like simmering oatmeal in a giant's pot. An invisible hand pulled him and his entire boat underwater. Everything went dark and the pressure ripped his spray deck off. He squeezed his legs against his knee braces to prevent being torn from

his boat and began to count, "One, two, three." Amazing self-control. At the count of seven he saw light, but finished counting to ten before rolling his water-logged kayak up.

I don't need to ask Jody what he thinks of the real Turnback Canyon. We both know.

I scramble across bedrock shelves to look into the lower end of Turnback Canyon. I think about Blackadar, a tiny splash of color in this huge mono-chrome landscape. Impressions and fears would be magnified. People are frail, and this wilderness is powerful.

I come to terms with the saga of Walt Blackadar and Turnback Canyon. His literal words might be exaggerated, but not the feelings they convey. If he had felt the Alsek's power, as I have just felt in Last Major Constriction, I understand why he wouldn't come back. Even for all the tea in China.

Latvian Style on the Bashkaus

by Eugene Buchanan

    *"**Among all the rest Altai** routes, this one is to be pointed out because of its unity and the combination of impressions of fairy landscapes and difficult and worth-overcoming rapids, leave alone the extremely high psychological tenseness connected with the danger and long staying alone in the isolated deep canyon."*

    Reading the description of Siberia's Bashkaus River does little to boost my morale. I pass it back to Bruce Edgerly, who is sitting on a pile of gear in the back of the bus. But he is preoccupied with his own thoughts. "The last thing everyone told me was to be careful," he says, shifting his weight to a sack of porridge. "And here we are careening down switchbacks on a Siberian pass in a broken-down bus with a group of complete strangers on our way to run a Class VI river on home-made equipment we've never even seen before."

    His words hit home; we are all a little nervous, especially about our shuttle vehicle. The red rug on the dash and centerfold on the wall do not hide the fact that it has already broken down six times. Glancing up front, I see water starting to spurt through the dash. It looks like once again we will have to dodge old Faithful, a geyser that forms every time the engine overheats. A year earlier we were lucky enough to win a grant from Gore-tex to run a river in Siberia. Now I am beginning to wonder if we were so lucky after all.

The Latvian Connection

    Our seats on Finnair are first class. And except for our river sandals, we blend in admirably, at least until we root through the complimentary ditty bags for items that might come in handy in Siberia. Sipping a tumbler of cognac, I plug my earphones in and settle on a radio station playing the Rolling Stones. I couldn't have found a more appropriate song: "I stuck around St. Petersburg when I saw it was a time for a change. I killed the Tsar and his minister, Anastasia screamed in vain."

    The first-class luxury does not last long. Windowless concrete greets us at the Moscow airport. Matching the bleak surroundings is our future; we are not sure who, if anyone, is going to meet us. The sign catches us by surprise. Taped to a paddle blade waving over a sea of heads is a piece of paper reading, "We look for four American kayaker to go Kalar River." I look at Bruce, Van, and Ben, counting with my finger. "That's us," I say. "That has to be us." At the end of the shaft is Boris, a full beard and ponytail giving him the air of a Berkeley professor. Joining him are Igor and Sergei, their eyes landing on our pile of gear.

"What is this?" asks Boris in a thick Latvian accent, pointing to a canvas bag housing the frame and cars.

"Our frame," admits a sheepish Ben.

Boris grunts and turns away. In a few seconds we see why: Sergei's two-door car has to carry seven people and all our gear. The car's lone mud flap is touching the pavement even before we all pile in. Squished in the back, we pass row after row of identical concrete apartment buildings on the two-hour drive to Igor's apartment. Two boys playing soccer with a flat ball wave as we head to an elevator reeking of urine. Igor presses the number 12, dodging wires sticking out of the control panel. In the crowded dining room, his wife brings us herring, bread, and vodka. Before we know it, our glasses are full. When Igor and Boris throw their heads back, we realize we have to do the same. Four shots later Boris is still telling us why we should abandon the Kalar and join his group on the Bashkaus.

Boris is a member of Team Konkas, a Latvian whitewater team that has been running rivers together for 12 years. And it was a fluke he met us at the airport; we were expecting someone else. Dialing Igor's rotary phone, we try to find out what happened to our original contacts. We soon learn that they are stuck at the Project RAFT Championships in Turkey, delayed by a storm on the Black Sea. Boris is meeting his group the next day at the train station. Still groggy from jet lag, we have a serious decision to make. Do we wait around indefinitely in hopes that our contacts will return, or cut our losses and join the Latvians? The decision is made tougher when Igor plugs in a video of a Bashkaus trip he took three years earlier. The rapids look horrendous, the homemade equipment even worse. Catarafts surf uncontrollably in holes above Class V swims. Eddyless rapids continue for what looks like miles. Igor then describes having to wait ten days in the heart of the canyon for the water to drop, witnessing three deaths in the process. His group finally hiked four days out to the nearest village.

I part the drapes and take in the rows of buildings that match the grey clouds. A lightning storm brews in the distance. "What do you guys think?" I ask when the four of us are alone in the tiny guest room. "I don't know," says Ben. "We don't even know these guys."

Tough Times in Latvia

In the end, we decide to join the Latvians on the train ride and agree to try calling our contacts again from Barnaul, which will have given them four days to return. To kill time before the train leaves we take rides on the Stalin-built subway. In one of the passageways we see a dead man, arm in a cast, lying on the stairs. People walk by without a second look. Over the heads of commuters we see the telltale homemade backpacks of other Russian river-runners setting out for their annual reprieves.

The rest of Team Konkas has already traveled 13 hours from Riga and now face a 73-hour ride to Barnaul. Theirs is the only team from Latvia taking part in a river expedition this year. Usually more teams do, presenting slides and videos at the end of each year in an annual contest which Konkas has won for three years. But times now are tough. "There will be no party or contest this year," says Olga. "People can't make trips when their money has to go to food." Konkas is lucky this year; Yevgheny, an industrial wire salesman, has helped subsidize the trip.

Long used to a Soviet umbrella guaranteeing employment, housing, and health insurance, Latvia—which seceded from the Soviet Union in 1991—is experiencing tough times. Factories are only open three days a week. Boris, a computer programmer, takes home $40 a month. Ramitch, the trip leader, is an unemployed chemist. Making matters worse is the decree by the government saying you're not a Latvian citizen unless your parents were born before 1940—the year Russia took over to beef up its troops against Hitler. So people like Boris—a Ukranian Jew whose grandfather was killed while hiding out during a World War II raid—have no real nationality, no longer Russians and no longer Latvians.

The Train

Accustomed to such confined travel, Sergei and Vladimir lay paddles across the top bunks to create a platform for the packs. Since Boris buys us tickets at the Russian rate, he cautions us to keep quiet whenever the conductress passes by. Although we look as if we could pass for Russians, Olga quickly sets us

straight. "You smile too much and your teeth are too good," she says. Andrew smiles, exposing three empty slots.

We bridge the cultural gap by speaking the universal language of whitewater. In a summit of sorts, Ramitch calls us over to his bunk and asks us of our plans for the Kalar. He says there is a reason no one runs it: it is a mosquito-infested bog. He also tells us the train we had hoped to take to the put in is not running, a victim of unstable permafrost. He then pulls out mylar maps of all 212 named rapids on the Bashkaus that he obtained from a river library in Moscow.

Still hesitant to join their group, we ask him about a river called the Ketoi. Perhaps it would be a better alternative. Ramitch says not with our equipment and not without someone who has been there. A few years ago, a group missed a mandatory portage. All six died. He then draws a picture of a skull and crossbones on a makeshift map where another accident occurred. "Very many people have died there," adds Olga. "We think you come with us." We return to our bunks, agreeing we cannot make a decision until we reach Barnaul.

Ramitch pours shots of vodka into 14 cups and we whittle the night away playing guitar. Ramitch starts off, and it is comforting to see that for someone who has rapids mapped out on mylar, he can still cut loose. Although they like our versions of Rocky Raccoon and American Pie, their songs have ours beat. One, Boris tells us, is about not being a man unless you've survived the Chulishman and come home with an oar in your leg and a broken nose. Another is a memorial to whitewater athletes who have died. Then Ramitch belts out a song comparing those who run the Bashkaus to tightrope walkers in a circus. All their songs hint of river folklore and everyone knows the lyrics.

Outside it is jet black. The door between cars slams shut, the conductress letting us know we're being too loud.

The next morning we are covered with welts. Van gets the bedbug award for most bites. It is hot and muggy, but the Latvians came prepared; they stole a key from a Latvian university that fits all the windows. When the conductress shuts them, they wait a few minutes and open them again. That afternoon the Latvians begin packing their food and cigarettes into plastic bags, designating them with tags for certain days. They are very organized and serious. One of the three Sergeis stitches a hole in his shoe.

The next stop is Omsk, once the largest prisoner weigh-station in Siberia. Until a few years ago, towns like this weren't open to foreigners; tourists had to take the 5,810-mile trans-Siberian railroad, the only land route between Western Europe and the Pacific Far East of Russia. We are paralleling it to the south on a train few Westerners have ever ridden.

That night we venture through the crowded cars to a makeshift restaurant at the end of the train. A man sits next to us and tries to make small talk. Prisoners in Russia gain clout the more tattoos they have. This man has tattoos on all ten fingers. We eat quickly and thread our way back to home base.

Barnaul

The best thing about the train ride is that we don't have to deal with our gear for four days. All that changes when we arrive in Barnaul. Van and I guard the goods while Ben and Bruce try to call Moscow. The call takes four hours. Our original contacts have still not arrived. We decide to join the Latvians.

Again telling us to lay low so we won't be charged a foreigner's price, Ramitch strikes a deal with a bus driver to take us to a village 100 miles north of Mongolia. With 14 people's worth of gear, we cram into the back ten spaces. When we arrive, I realize we are not far from the land of Genghis Khan; at the bus station, I watch a rough-looking redhead grab a cigarette from the mouth of a local Asian.

Camped across the river from the village, we have a final logistics meeting with Ramitch. The decision is to run the entire 200-km. Bashkaus, unless it is too high. Talk then turns to our equipment. We have too much, he says. The Latvians are a tough act to follow, able to carry everything they need for a 30-day raft trip on their backs. Ramitch then tells us our oar boat—a lightweight cataraft made by Jack's Plastic Welding —is too big. In the end we give in and agree to go Latvian-style. We had all seen John Armstrong's *Hard Labor* in Siberia, a video documenting the first western descent of the Bashkaus in 1986. And it was the Americans portaging oar boats that seemed to give the video its title.

Cook detail is divided into groups of two. Ben and Van are up tonight. Used to leading expeditions for the National Outdoor Leadership School, Ben feels Olga's eyes boring into the back of his head as he doles out rations. "Too much," Olga says. "Our boys don't need that much." Van fumes when

Olga tells him he put too much coffee in the pot.

Later that night, Van and Ben come to our tent with second thoughts. "I just have this feeling we're on a runaway train and that once it starts there's no way off," says Ben. After talking it over, we agree to continue on, but vow to have a say in expedition matters.

Outside by the fire Boris is singing, "We will, we will, rock you!" He asked us for the lyrics on the train, and since none of us knew them, we took the liberty to make a few up. When he bursts into "Baby you're a rich man, and you've got a suntan!" we look at each other and smile.

The Bus

Camp is packed early. While Ramitch searches for another bus to take us to a village 24 hours away we stash the leftover gear at the bus station. The last time the Latvians were here they had to wait four days for a bus. This time Ramitch pulls a coup. A self-proclaimed "tourist agency" official wants 4,500,000 rubles, or $4,500 for the 14 of us to travel here for 30 days. Although the Latvians are now tourists also, Ramitch talks him out of it, lining up a beat-up bus in the process. The official's attitude is not lost on Yevgheny.

"The whole country is like this bus," he laments after the bus has broken down for the third time. "And the government is like the driver." In front of the vodka-toting driver, the front hood bangs open, making me lean closer to hear him. "The country and government have it all wrong," he continues. "Instead of encouraging people to travel and then capitalizing on it by selling them things, they say 'You can come, but you have to pay'. So no one comes."

He then moves from politics to paddling, telling us that the Bashkaus is one of five Class V runs in the Altai Mountains known as the Altai Bars, meaning Snow Leopard. If you run all five—the Argut, Chulishman, Chuya, Chulicha, and Bashkaus—you have achieved your Snow Leopard. Although all five are located within 100 miles of each other, it is a difficult task. Each one boasts continuous whitewater that makes Idaho look like Ohio. Ramitch and Sergei have each notched three.

When we pass through a village on the Chuya, Olga shares a story from their last trip here when they spent 29 days on the Argut. They ran out of food and had to beg for bread in the village. Ramitch, she says, lost 20 lbs. The four of us exchange uneasy glances. She then relates a legend about the area's rivers. Father Altai had a daughter, Katun, who fell in love with a handsome man, Biya. The father didn't like this, and to stop her he threw stones into the Katun, creating rapids. It didn't work, and the two rivers eventually joined to create a daughter named the Ob. Another legend involves our take out at Lake Teletskoe. When Father Altai learned of enemies who wanted to take away his riches, he began to throw all of his gold into the river. The ensuing dam created the lake, which is rumored to contain vast amounts of gold.

After four dashboard geysers we pull over to camp at 2 a.m. While I head straight to bed, the Latvians go straight to work. A roaring fire cooks a pot of noodles and a pot of tea. Snug in my sleeping bag, I don't bother to get up. It is the last time I forsake food for 26 days. In the morning two sugar cubes rest atop 14 pieces of rock-hard dry bread. Rations have begun. Van figures out how to salvage more calories from his porridge bowl by swathing it with leftover tea.

The village of Ust Ugalon, meaning "Place where the River Starts," is as far as our bus can go. After making arrangements with the driver to meet us in about 26 days, Ramitch tries to flag down an army truck to take us to the put in. If necessary, the Latvians are prepared to hike. But they are not martyrs. If they can finagle a ride, so much the better, especially if it can be accomplished by trading vodka.

The Put In

After 182 hours of shuttling—involving three airplanes, five cars, a 63-hour train ride, two buses, and an army truck—we arrive at the put in. It doesn't take long to see that river running here has evolved much like wildlife in Australia, completely free of outside influences. The Western world got one of its first looks at it in 1989 at a raft rally on the Chuya. But not many have seen what goes on behind the scenes of a major expedition. Since most trips involve hiking to the put in, paddlers only carry what is necessary. Everything from frames to paddle shafts is reaped from the land. And the economy ensures that everything else is homemade: backpacks are made out of army cots; tents out of parachutes; raft pontoons out of old germ warfare suits and truck tarps; and life jackets out of soccer balls.

When we pull out our lifejackets, Yevgheny grabs one and holds it up for examination. Everyone else gathers around. "This no good," he says, shaking his head. No matter that we have Extrasports we regularly use kayaking.

Ours pale in comparison, in fashion, and flotation.

For the Latvians, the flotation doesn't end with the jackets, which have Ensolite strips sewn into the forearms, elbows, and chest. They also have nylon pants with Ensolite sewn into the shins, thighs, and buttocks. The result makes the wearer look like a cosmonaut. A few jackets boast inflatable collars that hint of Dracula, and Ramitch's even has two slots in back where he puts his and Olga's sleeping pads every morning. Most also have a film can containing survival gear: matches, fire starter, and cigarettes.

The Ensolite serves another purpose as well. Everyone also has a Sadushka, the Russian answer to the Crazy Creek Powerlounger. When you stand up, the butt-sized square of padding rests around the lower back. When you sit down, you slide it into place for extra cushioning. When he sees that we don't have any, Yevgheny measures us up for the right fit.

The three put in days are spent standing around in our underwear and Sadushkas chopping down trees to build frames for the rafts. Ramitch gives us the relatively harmless task of stripping wooden dowels to be twisted into loops of wet webbing to hold the frames together. During this time I learn a few new Russian words I haven't heard before, most of them hinting of profanity.

The days are also spent getting used to each other's food. For lunch one day we introduce the Latvians to peanut butter. They respond by introducing us to pork fat. For the first few meals I pass on it, dishing it off to a readily waiting Boris. But as the only energy source around, eventually I, too, learn to devour it down to the hairy-stubbled rind. At dinner one night, Boris shows us how to roast the rind like a marshmallow to make it more palatable. For dessert, we introduce him to popcorn. Before we can stop him, he pulls out a handful of unpopped kernels and crunches them in his mouth.

What we didn't bring is reaped from the land. Berries, mushrooms, and onions are gathered at every chance. And so are fish. One morning Van nearly breaks his ankle trying to land a six-incher. It doesn't take long to realize that anything with a heartbeat is a keeper, even though you usually burn more calories cleaning it than you get from consuming it. The fish are used to make hot fish-water, not to be confused with fish soup, with every day's catch simply dropped into a pot of boiling water, head and all. Like pork rinds, eyeballs mean extra calories.

Everything down to the last sugar cube gets divided into 14 equitable portions. Everyone gets good at sizing up which portions are bigger. In keeping with the food-dividing concept, Bruce and I once slice three PowerBars into 15 pieces. Pork fat meets PowerBars, East meets West. We then put a glob of peanut butter on each one, and top each morsel with two jelly beans. If they can allocate sugar cubes, we can do the same. But sugar cubes are a valuable commodity. After dinner one night, Van pretends to throw a sugar cube in the fire. Boris yells for him to stop. Then he throws it to Boris's main food rival, Sergei, which gets Boris yelling even louder.

The River

After the last dinner at the put in, Van gets the honor of raising the official team drinking flag. We toast one another with shots of vodka mixed with a tonic made from grass. The booze is especially soothing for Yevgheny, who earlier in the day cracked his tooth on a piece of dry bread. When the toasts are through, we discuss signals and what to do in case of a flip. We add our own questions, too, like what to do if you see three Latvians swimming and one American. Everyone laughs, but then Ramitch turns serious. "The river doesn't know or care if you are Russian, Latvian, or American," he says. "All she knows is you have to be strong to run her."

After another toast, they elect Ben to be trip meteorologist, which requires taking water and air temperatures three times a day to track weather patterns. Rains mean the river will rise. And if you're in the heart of the canyon, that can spell trouble.

The next morning another group rows past in a phlot, a craft with three huge pontoons running sideways to the current. The craft is steered with giant sweeper oars, one downstream and one upstream, requiring three people to handle each one. The blades are pieces of sheet metal and salami cans serve as thole pins for the oars. We quickly learn that it's a small world even in Siberia; it is the same group the Latvians met while running the Ketoi.

During a break in preparation, I look at the river description Ramitch picked up in Moscow. Runnable in July and August, the Bashkaus drops 4,143 feet before reaching the take out 130 miles later. The ideal flow is about 2,800 cfs. Ramitch says it is quite a bit higher now than when he first ran it. The description also rates it as the most difficult river in the former Soviet Union.

We pilot our own craft, and all eyes are on us for our inaugural run through a Class III–IV drop near camp. Kneeling on the pontoons, two per side, and paddling with homemade canoe paddles, we pass with flying colors and begin to be accepted as equals. Our stew that night contains a surprise: freshly butchered sheep. Earlier in the morning, Ramitch traded a bottle of grain alcohol to several gunned horsemen for a member of their flock. The horsemen would tell their boss the sheep got taken by a bear. Ramitch brought 12 liters of booze for bartering and partying. So far it had been used for sheep and shuttles. By the end of the trip, eight liters will have been used for such trading.

Between mouthfuls, Bruce and I ask Boris as many questions as we can where the answer starts with the letter V, just to hear him pronounce it. "We have wery, wery much willages here," he answers.

To see who has to run the rapids first, we play Russian Roshambo where the three guides throw out up to five fingers each. Ramitch counts them up and then counts around in a circle starting with the rapid. Whoever it ends up on has to go first. I lose three times the first day alone and begin to get a sneaking suspicion that it might not be just luck of the draw. The Latvians also play the fingers game for other things, from extra pork rinds to extra sugar cubes, In 1989 they even played it to see who got to join Yevgheny at the Project RAFT championships in North Carolina. Ramitch, Andrew, and big Sergei won, teaming up with the Nantahala outdoor Center's John Kennedy to take 11th. But they didn't play it to see who got to sit in the two first class seats; in

keeping with the team spirit, they took turns rotating to take full advantage of the food and drinks.

Scouting is as much a gamble as the fingers game. The only English Ramitch knows is left bank, right bank, camp place, carry things, and big stop. Asking him if he means ferrying above a certain log, then cutting left above a hole before running a slot on the right is futile. "Big stop, camp place, carry things," he responds.

As the days progress, we begin to see the rituals in their lives. They have never had the choices that come with capitalism; many of their decisions have been made for them. This same structure is evident on the river. Instead of getting to camp and unwinding, they immediately set about various chores. Even relaxing with a bottle of booze is a ritual, requiring the raising of the flag. Today everyone sets their watches to Ramitch Time. In a subtle control move, he set his watch an hour ahead to take better advantage of the sun.

The trip dynamics take on a microcosm of Soviet life: from each according to his ability, to each according to his need. All chores are for the betterment of the group, whether it's fishing, collecting berries, chopping wood, or bartering for sheep. Bruce and I do our part one day by gathering wild strawberries. Only if we gave each according to his need, we would be in for a lot of picking; each berry is probably only good for about a tenth of a calorie.

Life has begun to revolve around calories. One day, a bite of soup happened to have a fly in it. At home, I would have discarded it instantly. Here I was grateful. A few days earlier, Olga lost my lens cap while taking pictures. But

I ended up ahead as she slipped me her share of pork fat at lunch and dinner. The lifestyle would make the American Heart Association cringe: These guys live on salt, fat, sugar, caffeine, nicotine, and grain alcohol all while stressing out about Class V rapids.

Today we barter for more sheep. But when the horsemen return, they only bring two quarters. So Ramitch only gives them half a bottle. An argument ensues, gunned men on horseback vs. Ramitch in lifejacket. Ramitch quickly tells us to get back on the boats and we leave. That night, Boris tells us of a trip he took where drunken horsemen tore through camp trampling tents and cutting down tarps. Boris had to beat them away with a paddle. Another story recounts a group that was forced at gunpoint to break camp and run Class V rapids in the middle of the night. All eight people in the group died. I begin to question the idea of giving the horsemen booze to fuel their fire.

Later we barter for bread and jam in a tiny village. When we try to pay, the family turns its back; they are too proud to take anything in return. It is a far cry from our dealings with the horsemen.

Today is cold; 42 degrees according to our trip meteorologist. As with the pontoon shells, the Latvian's rainjackets are made from truck tarps. With everyone shivering, Ramitch decides to head to shore where we partake in the Latvian hypothermia cure: shots of vodka.

The rains stay for the next three days. After a quick breakfast of dry bread and pork fat at Camp Glum, I notice that my left knee is beginning to swell from kneeling on the pontoons. I savor the few extra calories I get from the sugar coating on an Ibuprofen.

Tonight is Sergei's birthday, and Ramitch raises the drinking flag. Sergei, 32, sings a song about his mother wondering when he'll find a girl and settle down. Van gets up and follows it with Camptown Ladies, although no one besides Boris, Olga, and Yevgheny knows what he is saying.

Sergei is in hog heaven. For lunch, several people slipped him extra pieces of fat. I could stomach three thanks to Olga's lens cap escapade. Sergei wolfs down seven without batting an eye, stopping to nibble each rind. And when the 14 pieces of dry bread are lined up, his is the only one with a small piece of salami.

After Sergei finishes licking the dessert bowl, Ramitch makes a toast: "This trip is special," he says. "It is our first time with American river runners and food has been strong. We toast also to running the strongest rapid any of us have ever run."

Gutsy call, considering these guys have run rivers all over Siberia. When the campfire dies, we learn they mean business; the plan is to spend two weeks in the 30-km-long lower canyon, just over two kilometers a day. We ask Boris about Ramitch's toast. "I like to prove myself a real man by running the hardest water I can," he explains. "Back home there is no way to prove yourself."

The next day dawns sedately. Thanks to recent rains, the water has risen 21 cm. The last time Ramitch was here the river was three feet lower. Two groups pass us: one is the group we saw before; the other is headed by Vladimir Grasanovich, at 49 considered the John Wesley Powell of Russian river running. He has been down the Bashkaus four times. This time he has vowed to run every rapid.

The Lower Canyon

We get our first taste of portage hell at a rapid called Barricade, where we carry our gear a half-mile to camp. It is our turn to cook again. So far that has been the only way to mark time: ticking off seven days until you have to cook again. Camp is about 30 feet long and five feet wide, interspersed with uneven rocks. The roar of the rapid is deafening. Ramitch shows us a boulder ten feet away that tumbled down when he was camped here four years ago. Looking up, I see a trail of snapped trees leading to its former home in the cliffs.

The next morning I see Yevgheny making a little, two-foot cataraft out of wood. He ties a rope with an adjustable knot to one end and then heads down to shore. He calls it the Little Ship and uses it to ferry rope across the river, much like flying a kite. The result is a taut line extending across the river for rescue, but one that is not tied off at both ends to create a strainer. It is positioned at the bottom of the rapid as a final safety net. Ramitch gives us an hour to decide if we'll run the drop. There is also talk of bailing out and hiking over to the easier Chulishman at the next camp. But that camp is still several Class V drops away. And the rapids are not one-move rapids. In this morning's obstacle I count eight specific moves needed to avoid holes and rocks. Three cups of coffee with an extra handful of grounds do little to settle my nerves.

We decide to portage the top section, but still have a hard run. I put my Sadushka around my chest for extra flotation. As usual I lose the fingers game and have to run first. Still not sure of the best line, I ask Ramitch what line

he's taking. "I watch you," he says with sign language, pointing to his chest, his eyes and then me.

A few days and countless rapids later, Sergei tests the Little Ship. After surfing a hole for the better part of a minute, he is thrown from the raft above a Class V swim. Five throw ropes miss him and he barely manages to grab the rope ferried out by the Little Ship. Playing leapfrog with the other groups, we watch Vladimir run the same drop. A rock stops his boat dead, but he immediately grabs a long log strapped to the side and pries the boat free. That night his group invites us down to their camp. But they make sure to add, "And bring something to have with tea." Food is scarce for both parties.

One of several cruxes greets us the next morning. Soon after camp we pass a memorial for a rafter who died where Sergei took his swim. Farther on is another one for a rafter who died on a rapid we face today. One group decides to hike out, opting for a five-day marathon to get to the nearest village instead of facing the remainder of the run. Camp is in a boulder garden, a flat area just big enough for 14 bodies. Yevgheny pounds sticks into cracks in the cliff to anchor a tarp against a pending storm.

Today we face four serious rapids. The upside is that tonight is Van and Ben's turn to cook dinner, meaning we will have bigger portions. The downside is that we pass four more memorials, three of them bearing tomorrow's date when we will face one of the toughest rapids of the trip.

Ever since a bad day a few years ago, the Latvians have always laid over on August 13. I'd vote we take our layover day tomorrow. We camp on the right after spending more time carrying gear than running rapids. And with heavily laden packs, the portage is not a stroll in Gorky Park. One slip means you join the August 10 memorials. Halfway through I pause to cool off at the mouth of a cave. Inside is a layer of permafrost complete with ice. Farther on we pass remnants of other parties: broken frames and a pile of tube material.

Below camp is another memorial, complete with a tiny jar of vodka, a stale piece of salami, and a letter from the victim's mother. As hungry as I am, I leave the offerings intact. Above camp is a register dating back to 1988. For the most part, the Bashkaus, which was first run in the late '70s, has only seen one or two trips a year. Last year and this year, however, the pace has picked up with three or four entries annually. Thumbing through the pages, my eyes land on a lone English entry. It is from Jib Ellison, founder of California's Project RAFT, from his trip here in '88. Boris then points out Igor's entry from a few years earlier when he witnessed three deaths. Boris looks even more downcast after reading through other Russian entries. "Let's just say there are a lot more dead men than there are memorials," he says. That night, Van, Ben, and I all have dreams about one of us dying.

Today's portage requires a Tyrolean Traverse. As Bruce points out, the day is like a classic Russian novel—tedious, complex and time consuming. There is a lot of unnecessary milling around as everyone pitches their two cents in about how to prepare the ropes. Captained by Vladimir, the phlot runs everything we portage. But it misses the eddy on river right where its gear

and extra passengers are. Vladimir's group also has to set up a Tyrolean Traverse.

We make it through August 10 without perishing. Our bad luck comes on the 12th when, after breaking camp, we are left with no choice but to run a semi-blind drop. Ramitch and I both flip. After the ensuing swim, I end up on the left with Sergei who pulls a pack of matches and a cigarette out of the canister attached to his lifejacket. Soon we have a roaring fire. Downstream on the right are Ben and Bruce, who stayed with the raft and have everything laid out to dry. Even though it is completely drenched, the tooth-breaking dry bread is still hard. The sweet bread doesn't fare as well, and dinner is nothing more than soggy dry-bread soup. No one can finish their bowl, not even Boris.

The next days are filled with rapids and variations of soggy sweet bread. In an unnamed rapid we get caught in a hole that spins us around nine times before letting us go. When you're on the downstream side, all you can do is dig your paddle in and hold on. When you get spun to the upstream side, all you can do is hang on and yell. Afterward, Boris explains another Russian safety device. Some boats, he says, have a pocket that houses a rock and a parachute. When the boat flips in a hole, the rock falls out and unleashes the parachute that fills up with water and pulls the raft out. "It worked once," he says. Sergei tells us he often attaches a similar parachute pocket to his life jacket.

Sergei's raft flips in an unnamed rapid, an undercut cliff breaking the frame. Where in the U.S. this might pose a problem, here we head to shore and chop down a tree for parts. That night, Ben cooks a cake in a makeshift Dutch oven, using a spare paddle blade for a lid. Having lost mine in the flip, I use the lid as a paddle blade the next day.

Before we know it, the river calms. Still in the heart of the canyon, the tranquility seems out of place. Trees sticking out of the water with driftwood in their branches seem even more out of place. Rounding the corner, we see why. The canyon is still young. Eight years ago a giant landslide careened down the canyon, completely blocking the river. The ensuing wall of rock backed up the river for miles until the water finally found a way through. The result is Perestroika, the worst rapid we've seen yet. There is no question about portaging, which requires several mile-long trips over steeply angled, unstable debris. The main drop, a 20-foot, river-wide pourover, has been run once, by a group in a bublik, a raft made of giant innertubes standing on-end. One man got killed, his memorial is tacked to a tree at the end of the portage.

A few days later we join the Chulishman. We are all feeling the effects of kneeling for three weeks in a row. At a village where we trade a throwrope for meat, Bruce hops off the raft and falls in up to his shoulders, even though the water is only knee-deep. He did not realize his legs were asleep. We lay over for two nights at the confluence, where half of the group joins Ramitch on a two-day death march to a waterfall. As with raising the drinking flag, there is a ritual to the hike: walk for 25 minutes, rest for five. We cover 36 miles in two days this way. Although it induces a severe case of trenchfoot, Valeri does it in the same black leather boots he wears on the river. When we return to camp, fresh sheep ribs are roasting Argentine-style over the fire

The next day we float down to Lake Teletskoe, where Father Altai threw his gold. Along the way we pass another group that has just finished the Chulishman. They lost a boat in the last major rapid and have everything crammed onto one cataraft. While they plan to sail and paddle across the 80-km. lake, we hope to catch a boat that comes once a week. At camp we find we just missed it. The shuttle used to run more often, says Olga, since the lake was once a popular vacation spot. But with the economy so poor, no one is travelling. Ramitch then pulls another coup by persuading the captain of a 28-foot sailboat to give us a ride.

With 19 people onboard and all our gear, the stern is awash in water. At camp near the village at the end of the lake, the final piece of the puzzle falls into place: still drunk from a night on the town, our bus driver backfires up to camp. Before saying our good-byes at the Barnaul train station where the Latvians will spend three days waiting for the next train, I see Boris talking to a member of Vladimir's phlot team. Vladimir ran Perestroika, he says, fulfilling his vow to run every rapid on the Bashkaus. His phlot disappeared completely, re-surfacing with a blown-out middle tube.

Our plane is over-booked, but Ramitch pulls another coup, telling the reservationist we are writing a Russian travel novel. We also play our ace-in-the-hole: a gold-bordered letter from the mayor of Jackson, Wyoming, saying we are his personal emissaries. These two lies and a $10 bribe get us onboard. They also get us seats; when we board, two people are sitting on their luggage in the bathroom and another couple is kneeling on their bags in the aisle.

Olga flies with us and will meet her group in Moscow when the train arrives. After the flight we find a hotel near the airport, a broken elevator lying outside the front door. As we insert the key to our room, the door opens and four Russians file out, a bottle of vodka on the coffee table and a cigarette burning in the ashtray. We head to a fancier hotel the next night, dropping two months' salary in Olga's eyes for two rooms. We drop another two months' salary at a restaurant. Igor joins us and listens to our tales.

During the telling, I think back to the countless nights around the fire, the guitar playing, the rapids, and the "fairy landscapes" and "high psychological tenseness of the long staying alone in the canyon." My recollections are interrupted by Olga, who, after spending two days with us in the city, realizes how far apart we are now that we are no longer on the river. "You men are like space-men to us," she says, holding back the tears. The next morning we pack our bags and fly away.

Cape Horn—Once More With Feeling
by Jon Turk

Fall, 1975:

One Wednesday evening, while drinking beer in a Montana bar, my friend Craig announced that anyone who rounded Cape Horn under sail could toast the Queen with his feet on the table. He wiped the foam off his beard, grinned, and the conversation drifted off to other subjects.

Spring, 1976

I struggled with the tiller to keep the 46-foot sloop straight as she surfed down the giant waves, but I couldn't stop her from plowing into the cross swell. Green water rushed across the cockpit and collided with the foam falling from the breaking wave behind us. My log book read, "From Anacortes, Washington, towards New York, via Cape Horn," but we were only a few hundred miles from Anacortes, and Cape Horn was thousands of miles away. Sometime during the storm a check valve in the exhaust failed and the engine filled with salt water. We sailed back to the marina and the mechanic told me I needed $10,000 for a new engine. I sold the yacht, bought a 1964 Plymouth Valiant, and headed to Colorado to ski.

Summer, 1978

The Cape Horn dream was like a lover who haunted my memory three years after she had packed her toothbrush and moved on. One afternoon, I read a story about Joshua Slocum's journey through the Straits of Magellan in the early 1900s. Fuegian Indians attacked his sloop and he protected himself by carpeting his deck with tacks. I put the book down. There was a message there I wasn't seeing. The story wasn't about Slocum, it was about the Fuegians. The Straits of Magellan are just north of Cape Horn. If people could paddle the Straits in bark canoes, it seemed reasonable that I could navigate the region in a kayak.

February 11, 1980

The wind intensified and the waves grinned white. To the south, I could see Isla Wollastan. Beyond lay Isla Hornos and Cape Horn. After 450 miles of solo paddling, my dream seemed close. All I needed was a sheltered cove and a camp where I could wait out the storm. The wind veered and blew me into the kelp. I fought for sea room but the kelp tangled in my paddle. Slowly, inexorably, the wind pushed me back toward land. The swells steepened, rising, preparing to break against the beach. Then a big one cradled me and effortlessly tossed me cartwheeling into the trough below. There were no thigh braces to hold me in, and I spilled into the water. I knew I should be cold, but adrenaline had shut off my temperature sensor. I swam toward shore and stood, only to have a wave knock me down again. I crawled toward the beach, suddenly aware of the cold, and began shivering.

How would I survive on this desolate tundra without dry clothing, shelter, or food? I ran back into the surf and grabbed the waterlogged boat, attempting to muscle it to shore. The undertow tried to pull it out of my grasp; I fought back, slipping into deeper water. A wave lifted the boat over my head and I somersaulted backwards. The boat raced faster than my body, twisted, and before I had the sense to let go, my shoulder dislocated. I had dislocated my shoulder before and had discussed the problem with an orthopedic surgeon. Lying under water, with the boat beating against my chest and the waves scraping me against the sand, I recalled my doctor's advice. Grab your elbow with your good hand, rotate and push. HARD! The shoulder popped back in, the wave passed. I salvaged a few survival essentials from the kayak, and staggered back to the beach.

October 6, 1995

It was a peaceful evening at home. Chris was kneading dough for biscotti; I had put on some music and was looking out the window. I was almost 50 years old. The phone rang. It was Eric Rice from The North Face. He asked if I would be interested in going someplace very wet to test some new gear. I said I would come up with something. I put the phone down and looked at Chris. "I think I'm going to try one more time to paddle around Cape Horn." Chris looked up from her flour and egg yolks. "Really?"

November 7, 1996

Mike Latendresse and I sat in the cockpits of our Dagger Apostle sea kayaks. We were grounded on the beach but the bows extended far enough into the water to rock gently in the surf. The hotel owner's son and a few onlookers stood by silently. "This is dumb," I thought. "They are going to push us off; I'm going to turn sideways in the first wave, tip, make a wet exit, look stupid, feel stupid. We should just go back to the hotel and wait for calmer weather." Mike looked at me; I shrugged and looked back at the waves. "Vamos," I called, and eager hands pushed me off. I took the first breaker in the chest, paddled outside the break and raised my paddle in the air, "Cape Horn, here I come!"

We had elected to start our journey from Puerto Natales on the west coast of Chile, about 500 miles from Cape Horn. Other kayakers have started from Ushuia, Argentina, or Puerto Williams, Chile, about 100 miles from the Horn. Those put ins seemed too close. Verlen and Valerie Kruger started in the Arctic Ocean 21,000 miles away, which seemed a little radical. Our compromise was arbitrary. We wanted to give the expedition depth, but as much as we admire the Krugers' journey, we didn't have three years to devote to the project.

A persistent storm made travel almost impossible, so we paddled only ten miles in the first five days. While we were hunkered down in a sheltered cove, some fishermen told us the natives had followed a passage through Canal Obstruction to a series of portages and fiords that led to the Straits of Magellan. We turned south and the next day paddled and sailed into a narrow canal where we were surrounded by the iridescent green mosses and dense foliage of the Patagonia rainforest. Just as a warm winter day on Canada's Baffin Island is (20 degrees F), and a rainy day in the Gobi Desert means a few dew drops, a protected passage north of Cape Horn—supposedly sheltered from swells and the winds of the "Howling Fifties"—is hardly benign. Packets of maritime air collect on the peaks, cool over the glaciers, and then drop down the precipitous slopes to form short, intense storms called *williwaws*. As Mike and I neared the end of Canal Obstruction, we encountered headwinds and hugged the shore using the lee of every small indentation in the coast. By midmorning, the clouds parted and the sun poked through just enough to bring welcomed warmth. But this same heat reflected off ice caps, creating temperature differences that stirred the air, collected it, compressed it, and sent it flying. We hid behind a point and watched small whirlwinds whip across the canal, spinning air and water together into waterspouts. The coast rose sharply from the sea, offering no place to camp.

"What do you think, Mike?" I asked about the possibility of bedding down somewhere. Mike shrugged, a body language that was to become common throughout our journey. It meant, "Sure this is dangerous, but there isn't much choice, or maybe there is, but who knows? I certainly don't know, we could wait and retreat, but . . . let's go."

He paddled off into deeper water, heading for the next point. I gave him space and followed. The wind rose and fell, whirlwinds danced and played. A waterspout raced down the channel, veered left, headed for Mike, and then engulfed him. First the edges of his body and boat became fuzzy, like the subject in a modern art painting; then he became misty like a ghost friend; then he disappeared. Terrified, I thought, "No, he didn't just vanish, my eyes are playing tricks. It couldn't lift him off the water! No, these aren't tornadoes. They're just little whirlwinds. Dammit, where is he?"

Finally he reappeared, first ghost-like, then Monet-like, then Mike-like, upright, paddling for the point. Another waterspout veered past him and headed straight for me. I wasn't sure what to expect so I held the paddle low and waited. The wind grabbed one blade and lifted, and I braced to the other side. Then the wind grabbed both blades at once, shook, and pulled. Rain and spray hit me on the face, pelted the back of my neck, flew into my ears, beat the underside of my chin and the top of my head. I tried to maintain a visual horizon, but all I saw was a white room, a cell of insanity padded with bubbly foam. Water smashed into my face with the force of horizontal hail and I shut my eyes. Like a blind man reaching out to the world with his cane, I felt the storm with my paddle. Then, suddenly, the paddle stopped tugging and twisting; the whirlwind had passed. I opened my eyes and saw the sky, a few whitecaps, and the dark forest a half-mile away.

We found an ancient trail at the portage site and followed ghosts of bark canoes up a river, across a lake, and then over two short ridges and two more lakes. After a day and a half, we returned to saltwater in a gentle rain. During the next three days we paddled past tidewater glaciers towards the Straits of Magellan, traveling southeast through the Straits and then south through the Tierra del Fuego archipelago. When I look back at that time, it's hard to be honest with myself. Maybe I should call Mike and ask him what happened, but I don't think he knows either. I've been on enough expeditions to know you're not supposed to take chances when rescue is remote. When winds build, you should go to shore. But sometimes we stayed out, and each day we rationalized our actions by saying we had to get to a protected camp, or the wind caught us by surprise, or it would be safer if we pushed on a few miles to make tomorrow's crossing during the early morning calm. We never admitted to ourselves—although I suspect it's true—that we broke expedition protocol and paddled the big water simply because the boating was so much fun.

Take, for example, our 15th day out of Puerto Natales. We woke up at 4:30 a.m. and launched by 6 o'clock into a flat sea, paddling as our reflections danced in the pastel lighting of a high-latitude sunrise. By 10, enough sunlight had bounced off the peaks to stir the air and generate a breeze. We raised sail,

and even though sailing was slower than paddling, we relaxed and watched the rainforest drift by. Within an hour the wind picked up, tugging at the sails and driving us along. I sat upright, steering with edge and rudder as the kayak skimmed across the surface, the hull hissing. Waves became steeper with the wind, showing occasional whitecaps as they compressed into the sinuous straits. We reached a rocky headland where our route led across the mouth of a fiord. I was beginning to feel a little scared, but Mike continued on course and if he could do it, I could. A gust charged out the fiord, hitting me on the side, rotating the sail so that it flapped wildly. I stabilized with a hip snap and a brace, tightened the starboard sheet, and felt the acceleration as I surfed along the crest of a swell. Another gust hit and my bow hung in the air as the kayak surfed under sail. Then the gust subsided and the boat settled into the trough. I looked behind me to read the wind ripples on the sea, reminding myself that I could never roll a kayak with a mast and 12 square feet of sail. A line of spray raced down the main channel and another sped out the fiord mouth. I couldn't imagine sailing through the confluence of these two winds, so I dropped the sail, and glanced over at Mike, who was doing the same.

We paddled the remaining distance to shore, ran along the beach to warm up, ate a meal bar, and then slipped back into the cockpits. If either one of us had said, "It's getting a little crazy out there," the other would probably have agreed, but we just shrugged at each other. We hugged the shore like two muskrats, then set off into deep water again, bound for an island a few miles away. Waves pushed us along, broke against our backs, occasionally rolled over our heads, and periodically caught us just right for surfing. Mike caught a wave and raced past me so fast I felt as if I was drifting backwards. Then it was my turn to accelerate, as a wave curled behind me and rustled gently. Eventually the kayak outraced the water, purled gently in the trough, then slowed sufficiently so the wave crest passed, embracing chest and armpits with a chilly farewell.

We continued south through the islands, focusing on each adventure, each wave. On November 28 we swung outside all protecting islands to round Peninsula Brecknock. About a half hour from camp, we felt the first deep-ocean swells rhythmically lifting and relaxing the boat. As we moved into the main channel, the waves grew taller and steeper. Whereas the previous storm waves were only five or six feet, these were two to three times that size. When I dropped into the trough of one of them, it seemed as if the water should crash on my head, but the wave politely adhered to the laws of physics and the crest gently eased under my boat. Riding high, I looked south across the open sea toward Antarctica, invisible across 400 miles of ocean. To the east, a shaft of sunlight pointed toward our next shelter, Canal Occasion. The kayak rocked erratically because the symmetrical southwest ocean waves were jumbled by four coastal influences: surface waves formed by today's west wind, yesterday's northwest storm swell, and outgoing tides from both Canal Barabara and Canal Occasion that undercut the waves on the northern and eastern edges. Such a confluence of forces, if magnified,

could produce a suicidal mayhem, but on this day they combined to form a manageable, even mesmerizing, motion. The kayaks rose on the big swell, rocked in several directions in response to surface effects, and slid into a quiet trough surrounded by improbable gray walls.

With a gentle tailwind and a lot of nervous energy, we paddled the eight-mile crossing in two hours. After we passed a few small islands that intercepted the Pacific swell, we rode the changing tide and the gentle western flow into the channel. Ahead of us, something black jumped out of the water. At first I thought it was a dolphin the way it leapt, curved, and frolicked back into the water. But it clearly had no dorsal fin; it was a seal. An instant later another seal jumped, then another, until a dozen or more seals leapt, dove, and swam in circles around us. We felt they were welcoming us and telling us to relax, "The danger is over; the ocean is a place to play, and the journey is a game, not a series of dangers and hardships."

We paddled east past the tidewater glaciers of the Cordillera Darwin, rested two-and-a-half days, then continued past Punta Guanaco where I had crash-landed 15 years before. Finally, on December 14, the 32nd day of our journey, we pulled to shore near the southern edge of Isla Hershal. We climbed a small hill and looked across the four-mile strait to Isla Hornos, Cape Horn. The land rose gradually from the north shore, then thrust upward to form a 1,300-foot bluff—the most southerly tip of the Western Hemisphere. I'd been dreaming of this place for 21 years, I'd failed twice, and now I was here. But *here* wasn't close enough, I had to be *there*, south of the rock, in the water, in my kayak.

High winds held us down for two-and-a-half days. I spent my 51st birthday huddled around a smoky fire and Mike presented me with a birthday candy bar that he had surreptitiously saved from his rations. At about 1 a.m. the morning of December 17 I was awakened by a strange sound. I sat up in my bag. No, it wasn't a sound; it was the absence of sound. The three-day storm was over and the air was still. I closed my eyes but couldn't sleep and woke Mike at 2 a.m. "It's time."

We packed in the predawn gray light and were in the water by 3:30. We followed south across the straits, then followed the north shore of Isla Hornos west into a gentle swell and headwind. After a few miles we rounded the corner, the compass swung south again, and our world changed. Huge swells rolled in from their journey, unimpeded, around the world. They crashed against jagged sea stacks and reflected back to form a turbulent, unpredictable cross swell. I thought briefly about all my years of kayaking—a few thousand miles in the Arctic ice, spring rivers in Idaho, Class V creeks, and now a month on this journey. Surely, I told myself, I had developed a feel for wave and hull so that my body would anticipate and react.

A kayak is the ultimate Judo master, drawing its strength from its vulnerability. The boat provides no resistance to the waves, allowing the water to roll under and crash against the rocks. I absorbed the gentle sideways motion with my hips and concentrated on paddling forward to the southern cape. After a few miles, the coast veered to the southeast and Mike and I followed it, turning enough so that the side swell now approached off the stern quarter.

The boat and paddle were the same, but the motion was different. It was like skiing a slope in a telemark turn and suddenly switching to parallel, or switching from a foxtrot to a tango as the band plays a medley. An hour later we turned another 30 degrees east and Cape Horn swung into view. It started to rain and the drops spread and dissipated in the calm lee between waves. A rainbow darkened and faded behind Mike's head. The waves pushed from behind, routinely rolling over the deck and burying us to our armpits. When I slid down the face of one I felt a wind in my face—not an east wind but the wind created by my own speed, surfing the giant combers. The early morning sun played hide and seek behind the waves, then lifted itself high enough to bathe Cape Horn in an orange glow. Mike looked inconsequential in his red boat, red suit, and familiar blue hat—appearing, disappearing, bobbing against the double rainbow in the background.

I saw the first Cape Horn navigation light, then the second. Rising on a high swell, I noticed an offshore break stretching into the sea. Mike asked, "Should we cut inside the break? We've got a quarter of a mile space." I thought of all the creek boating I've done; all the slots I've paddled with a few inches to either side of the boat. A quarter of a mile is wider than dozens of creeks put together; it's wider than a large river like the Salmon or the Colorado. Surely we could paddle through an opening as wide as an entire river. Then I tried to imagine a dropping tide lowering the waves until they tickled the top of a shoal. I saw the shoal holding the bottom of the wave just long enough to slow it down, while the top raced on ahead running over its foundation and crashing into the trough. In my mind I felt a kayak, my kayak, tumbling down the face of the breaking wave. We'd taken a lot of chances along the way, but the seas were so monumental here I lost sense of scale and I felt vulnerable.

Just when I was about to say something, Mike hollered, "There's not enough control in this dance!" We paddled outside the break and then turned into a protected cove at the east end of the island. Mike reached shore first, jumped out of his boat, and ran into the water to grab my bow and lift me onto shore. I stood awkwardly, stiffened by cold, took a step, and slipped on the kelp. Mike reached out to steady me.

There is a Chilean guard station on Isla Hornos and a flight of steps leads up the steep bank. The wooden staircase seemed improbable in this vacant land. We tied off the boats and started up the steps, back towards civilization. I had a toast to make to the Queen . . . with my feet on the table.

The Thule Bheri: River of the Hidden Land

by Doug Ammons

Icy water surrounds us, so cold it hurts to touch. The wind whips freezing droplets onto our hands and faces and our kayaks are covered with beads of ice. The sun is dazzling in the blue-black sky, but the wind and spray remind us it is late November high in the Himalayas.

We are gliding across the clear blue water of Lake Phoksumdo. Along the lakeshore, barren cliffs climb steeply out of the water 9,000 feet above to hanging glaciers atop the Kanjiroba peaks, sitting like a blinding white jewel in the sky. We peer into the depths, but the cliffs continue down under the water, disappearing into the sun-rayed darkness. We are 30 miles from Tibet at the very headwaters of the last big unrun river of Nepal, the Thule Bheri, and in a few days we will start our descent.

A half-mile across the whitecapped lake the Ringmo monastery stands on a rocky bench above the water. Faintly, bells and chanting can be heard, blending with the sounds of the lapping water and wind. Buddhist prayer flags dot the cliff faces. Charlie lets his kayak knock together with Scott's and mine, and gives us a smile. "We're here," he says. "We're finally here."

Two days ago our team of kayakers arrived by helicopter from Kathmandu. It took us only two hours to travel hundreds of kilometers over the roughest terrain on earth. It might have as well have been a trip to another planet. We took off in the 20th Century and landed at 12,000 feet near the shores of Lake Phoksumdo in the medieval land of Dolpo, the most remote and the poorest part of Nepal. Soon after take-off, we gaped through the windows at the jagged panorama of the Himalayas, including 8,000-meter-high Manaslu rising above hundreds of others. The Annapurnas and Dhauligiris came into view with impossibly huge ice ramps glistening white in the sun. Cruising at 15,000 feet, we passed Pokhara, with Machhapuchhare looming over the valley. Continuing west, we flew around the end of the Dhauligiri peaks, then turned northeast up the Bheri valley toward Tibet. Knife-edged ridges rushed by on all sides. We looked at each other crammed around our gear, then out the windows again. There was nothing between us and the ground, and it was a long way down. We landed in the village of Dunai and met Angad Himal, a friend of Charlie and Scott's from prior recon trips. After a quick greeting we arranged with him to bring porters to Lake Phoksumdo in four days. Then we were in the air again and headed up the tight canyon of the Suli Gad, one of the two main tributaries of the Thule Bheri.

In a couple of minutes Charlie shouted, "There's the waterfall!" over the whine of the engine. I peered down and caught a glimpse of a white cascade falling farther than any waterfall could possibly go. "It's over a thousand feet high!" Scott yelled. Danielle and I glued our eyes to the windows, awestruck at the beauty and absurdly huge scale. In a few minutes Charlie yelled again, "There's the lake!" The helicopter took a banking turn and orange-and-black cliffs rushed by. As we straightened out, Phoksumdo Lake slid into view, an astonishing deep blue with sunlight sparkling brilliantly on the waves.

We landed on an untended field in a cloud of dust and quickly unloaded the gear. The Russian pilot was in a hurry to get going. Everyone ran for cover as the machine wound up and disappeared in a storm of dust and whirling blades. In a few minutes all was quiet. We were left standing around a mountain of gear and six kayaks in a scraggly field, with curious Tibetans eyeing us. We just covered three weeks of walking and 1,000 years of civilization in four hours. Our plan was to spend four days at the lake, then head down the Suli Gad to Dunai, paddling as much of it as we could. From there we would to travel up the other main tributary, the Barbung Khola, and paddle down the Thule Bheri 250 kilometers to the first road.

A few hours later, we found out about a festival at the nearby monastery. The monastery has been here 65 genera-tions and represents the religion of B'on Buddhism, a mixture of Buddhism with the old shamanistic B'on religion of Tibet, now unique to the Dolpo. A ten-minute walk took us through a scrub pine forest along the lakeshore, where we reached the monastery and an age-less scene. The dirt-smeared herders and farmers of Ringmo gathered around the lama, who was dressed in a multicolored, high-peaked hat and robes. Prayer flags flapped in the wind as he chanted sutras from B'on scriptures. Along with the 50 or so villagers, we bowed our heads and were blessed by him. For several hours, whirling dances mesmerized the crowd. Monks wearing elaborate masks spun and jumped in dances depicting battling snow leopards and deer, celebrating the harvest, and warding away mountain demons for the winter ahead. From the monastery, the all-seeing eyes of Buddha gazed serenely across the remote crags. That night it was bitterly cold, with strong winds blowing glacial dust every-where. The stars were so bright they seemed to jump out of the sky. I wore all my clothes inside my sleeping bag, but my teeth chattered anyway. My water bottle, full of hot tea and carefully stuffed inside my bag, was frozen solid in the morning.

There's a rim of ice around the shore and the water is so cold its spray numbs our hands. We hear the bells of a yak herd coming around the cliffs near the end of the lake and paddle our kayaks over to watch. Driven slowly along the trail by the herder and his family, each yak carries wool bags packed with salt for trade in the lower valleys of the Dolpo. Suddenly, the final bridge collaps-es and plunges four yaks into the frigid lake. They struggle through the floating logs to the shore and lunge out, while everybody looks on dumbfounded. The bridge is gone, the herder and his family are stranded with the rest of their yaks, and several other herds are coming down. They all face a grueling, week-long trip back over two 17,000-foot passes and around the Kanjiroba mountains. It looks like a disaster.

Using hand gestures, Scott and Charlie convince the herder to load his salt bags onto their kayaks. He looks dubious, but is overjoyed when they bob around the corner and in a half-dozen trips ferry his year's labor to shore. The other two herds and families show up. For the rest of the afternoon we ferry salt bags, help the families cross the cliffs, and wrestle 60 more yaks off the ledges into the water. What first seemed like a disaster turns into a three-ringed circus, complete with a yak-diving contest. Cowboy Charlie rounds the strays up in his own 'yak and drives them to shore. At sunset we finish, soaked and worn out.

Angad shows up with the porters two days later and we prepare to descend the Suli Gad, a small river which flows out of the southern end of the lake. It forms the Thule Bheri about 15 miles downstream when it joins the Barbung Khola. We do this section in pieces with many gaps, walking a larger portion than we kayak. Two miles below the lake is the huge waterfall. Flowing out of the forest, the river pitches off a cliff then falls in cascades, arcing again and again into space, until it finally rumbles into a deep gorge below.

Large pine trees line the trail as it switchbacks down into the narrow canyon. Cedar trees five feet in diameter nestle in the shadowed hollows along the river. It all looks remarkably famil-

iar, and repeatedly I have the eerie feeling that I am within a few miles of my home in western Montana. Around a sharp corner, I come face-to-face with a Tibetan family. They look up from a temporary shelter of stacked salt bags, their yaks patiently lying around them like huge shaggy dogs. A large mastiff growls, wagging his tail but unsure of the intruder on the trail. The surprised, soot-blackened faces gaze at me from under the blankets, hair strung with red beads. "Namaste," I say, putting my hands together. Suddenly five sets of white teeth gleam and a cheerful chorus of "Namaste!" comes back. I smile to them and continue on my way. No, this isn't Montana.

The trail climbs thousands of feet in and out of deep gorges. In some places it is carved into solid rock, at others it is built by thousands of flat stones piled above the water's reach. It isn't until the third morning that we find it possible to kayak. It is a relief finally to get on the water. Here the Suli Gad is large and beautiful with continuous rapids. We are in and out of the kayaks, looking for routes. Zigzagging through steep boulder gardens and over small waterfalls, the stream offers brilliant Class IV–V technical paddling. The water retains the glacial blue color of the lake and is bitterly cold.

For the last two days the porters have obviously considered us crazy for lugging our kayaks along the difficult trail. Suddenly they are transfixed by our descent. They run along the trail, laughing and cheering like kids as we shoot over drops. All of us, porters and kayakers alike, are in high spirits when we reach the confluence of the Suli Gad and the Barbung Khola. In the strong afternoon wind, we get out and hike several miles upstream along the Barbung Khola to Dunai, the village which serves as the capital of the Dolpo.

We rest for several days in Dunai, working on the kayaks, packing food and supplies for the 200-km descent of the main river. We visit Angad's boarding school and tree farm, the small hydropower project and the hospital he has designed and helped build. Angad is unbelievably busy, yet always works in the same quiet, patient way, slowly chipping away at the problems of the Dolpo.

It is late in the year and our trip has brought a windfall to the local economy. This is not a popular trekking area because it is so difficult to get to and so poor. Charlie asks Angad to recruit porters from local villages, explaining that we will pay the going wage of 200 rupees, or roughly four dollars a day per man. For each of the 20 porters needed this will equal almost half a year's wages. Angad tells us the government has plans to build a road the entire 250 km up the valley, gouging it out of the bedrock. He is ambivalent about it, pointing out that this is a problem all across Nepal. Roads bring prosperity in some ways and disruption in others. His goal is to decrease the isolation of the Dolpo without destroying its unique culture and beauty.

We trek upstream along the Barbung Khola as the river cuts a deep, narrow trough north and westward behind the Dhauligiri massif. At the end of a long hike we reach the village of Tarakot, perched like a fortress on a ridge, and make camp on a terrace above the river. The next day we wait until late morning for the air temperature to rise near freezing, then put in. Immediately around the first corner we're out and scouting. There's horizon line after hori-

zon line, but Charlie and Scott are so hyped up about finally being on the main river there's no stopping them. They lead at a rapid pace, craning their necks from the last possible eddy above each drop.

Repeatedly, I am impressed by their lead in the continuous Class IV+ and V. The obvious thing we're all watching for are sieves, and several times the river is almost entirely choked off by boulders. But the two seem to have a sixth sense about the river, flawlessly weaving through one blind corner after another. A mile downstream, a bigger set of Class V drops bank up against a rock wall on the right. After scouting, Scott and Charlie shoot down through a maze of boulders, aggressively hit the lower set of ramps and slice through a final big diagonal into an eddy. Danielle and I follow. Gerry comes next, looking for all the world like he's in perfect control. He disappears into the big diagonal and abruptly ricochets back to the right, pitoning into the cliff. "Ugly," grimaces Scott, as Gerry shakes his head from the whiplash.

After several miles the gradient eases and the river becomes beautiful Class III and easy IV, looking exactly like the open Ponderosa forest and grassy hillsides of the South Fork of the Payette River in Idaho. The only thing that's different is the view of 24,000-foot Churen Himal up the valley. The sun is high and feels warm as long as we're sheltered, but it is desperately cold in the wind. On the sunlit side of the canyon the sidestreams dance and sparkle down into the river. Butterflies occasionally flit across the cliffs. On the opposite side in the shadows, the sidestreams are covered in ice. We reach Dunai late in the day, all of us shivering badly.

The next day we rest in the village and finish packing. Around lunch, Scott tracks down a soccer ball and soon has a pack of children dribbling and passing. An arm around one child, a big smile for another, he plays nonstop jokes with ball-handling. The kids eat it up. Afterwards, missing my own children, I pull out my bubble-making wand and start creating four-foot diameter bubbles for the kids. They crowd around, eyes wide as saucers, and stare amazed at the swirling rainbows in the bubbles. Suddenly, everyone bursts into laughter. A hooting mob chases behind the huge spheres as they wobble and rise across the courtyard in the breeze, then lazily head out over the river. Charlie and Angad, who have been deep in a serious conversation, can't stop laughing as the kids bounce up and down hollering for more.

When the packing is finished late in the evening, the cards and the sharks come out, as Gerry reveals his true forte. "Dirty Clubs?" he asks in his Scottish brogue, eyebrows raised. "Doctor, do you know that game? No? Ah, it's a wonderful game, let me show you . . ." The night spirals off into a haze of beer and cheating, as Danielle and Charlie do their best to keep Gerry in line while Scott and I try to figure out why it is that the rules never seem to be the same from round to round. The next day after saying goodbye to Angad and the schoolchildren, we head down the main Thule Bheri.

The first long day of Class III–IV travels down a wider valley and brings us to Tibrikot. We camp in the boulder-strewn yard of the "Hotel Famus," whose name is spelled three different ways. The hotel consists of four tiny rooms with filthy beds. As scabies, bed-bugs, and other unrecommended pets are endemic in the area, we set up our tents between rocks in the yard. High on a promontory above the river stands an abandoned temple with long banners streaming in the late afternoon wind. At sunset we climb up to investigate. Up the valley in the distance, the western-most of the Dhalighiri peaks rise like luminous phantoms above the clouds. The river is in deep shadow, but we can see that it makes a sharp bend, splits the earth, and disappears into a gorge. All has gone well so far, but the most diffi-cult sections lie somewhere ahead.

The next day, Rajindra paddles through the long Class IV+ lead-in rapid with us. He has been paddling intermit-tently along the river, and portaging the harder rapids. He handles this one very well. Afterward, his hand gestures and smile tell the story: "I came through down, nice and easy. It's okay. I pass through boulders smooth, and the waves. I did—I did success!" Just down-stream, the rapids increase to Class V and head into the canyon. Rounding the corner, we change worlds. Immense rock walls arch up out of the water on each side, and tall cacti are scattered about. The rest of the day we swap leads as the river alternatively perks up to Class V and calms down. That evening we're treated to a fantastic light show. As the sunset lingers thousands of feet above us on the walls, the spans of golden rock reflect the light back and forth until the entire canyon shines a lustrous yellow-gold. There are no shadows. Every rock and tree is luminous. The river, and even the air itself, glows.

For the next five days the river stays a delightful mix of everything from Class II to Class V. Again and again, we have brilliant technical Class IV–IV+ rapids from put in to take out. There's every kind of drop imaginable, with an occasional hard Class V thrown in to keep us on our toes. The late fall weather holds, and each day dawns clear and cold. Every morning we go through the same routine of prying frozen puddles out of the bottoms of the kayaks, and knocking the ice off our spray skirts and drytops. As the days roll on, all of us battle colds and injuries from the nonstop action. Tendonitis, muscle spasms, bruises, and nasty infections all take their toll. One night we all bemoan our ailments around the fire until Charlie breaks in, "You're a sad spectacle, gentlemen." He shakes his head in mock disgust, carefully cleaning his own badly burned foot. "Remind me next time I do a hard river to go with guys who are *healthy*."

On the seventh day down from Dunai, the gradient takes off. The continuous Class IV becomes solid Class V+. We spend an entire day on the opening rapid, nearly a half mile long. All of the scouting has to be done from the river terrace 100 feet above the water, and we know we can't see many of the subtleties. It looks runnable. There's only one way to find out. I go first and get all scrambled up, flipping right after the opening moves. I can feel the boulders whipping past my head, quickly crank a roll, then sketch into an eddy. After a few breaths, it's another 300 yards of piling into cushions, boofing, and punching holes. Scott enters, almost gets knocked over, but regains his balance with a deft flick of his paddle. He quickly cuts far left and over two big ledges, then back into the center to miss a sieve. Punching through a bizarre exploding hole, he tail-stands for a good

40 feet downstream before he gets the boat down and slices through the last set of moves. Danielle paddles strongly, but hesitates near the bottom and a hole typewriters her far left. She finishes the rapid with an awkward run over several ledges against the boulders on the bank. Charlie is next, and the rapid doesn't take any guff from him either. It violently jams his boat under at the crux until only the top of his helmet is visible. He pops out like a cork and rushes through the second half of the rapid, huffing and puffing into an eddy far below. Gerry is on-line too, but gets pounded back and forth by the holes. At the bottom he looks like someone who's gone a few more rounds in the ring than he wanted to. As we stuff our throw ropes and prepare to make camp, Gerry sums it up, "I think it's safe to say that rapid gave us a good beating." We go to sleep knowing the next section will be even harder.

Scott and I are up before daylight and head down the trail to scout. Charlie has already run ahead on his own. We're astounded as the river races around corner after corner, pounding though mazes of huge boulders. Every single section has big holes and wild, corkscrewy water. It is continuous Class V+ for at least five miles, but Scott and I agree it should go. It looks wild. We are back in camp eating breakfast when Charlie returns. He is amped. "This is it! This is it!" he shouts. "I recognized the rapid where we stopped scouting two years ago." He's practically hopping he's so excited. "The pieces are all here. This is the big section, the main gorge."

We start early in the morning. The first rapid has a snakelike lead-in through the boulders to a big ledge on a corner. Scott rockets down, cuts tight against the inside and plummets over. Hitting the hole at the bottom, his boat squooshes wildly upward like a watermelon seed. He struggles against a current seam erupting like a geyser, then whips into an eddy. Charlie's next around the corner, looking relaxed and composed. He rides high onto the cushion against the cliff and banks the corner like an Indy 500 racer. I try the same with less elegant results. Finally, Gerry romps into view, jaw set, arms pumping, and gets stuffed straight down the gut of the drop. We all cringe and groan, but after some creative flails of his paddle, he bounces up with a surly look and catches an eddy below us.

It's a wild, wild day. The river is one continuous horizon line. We're in and out of the boats scouting, bouncing possible lines off each other. There's maybe 3,000 cfs and a gradient of 350 feet-per-mile, but even big numbers don't do it justice. Truck- and house-sized boulders litter the riverbed, forcing complex moves in extremely powerful current. Sometime late in the afternoon, I turn and look up the river in astonishment, nudging Charlie and Scott. Behind us, the river stairsteps up into the sky. We head downstream. In some places the main channel is choked off or slams into a rock sieve, and we maneuver into the steep smaller channels. In one rapid, the river bounds down a frightening series of ledges directly into a monstrous undercut boulder. In another, there is a bizarre zigzag of four nasty ledges in a row, hammering us around like maniacal pinballs.

Charlie leads into a deceptive drop, spins on the corner, and disappears. Scott cranes his neck, suddenly stiffens and shouts, "He's vertically pinned!" and takes off like a madman, planing into a ridiculously small eddy just above the drop. Charlie flushes out, cranks a quick roll, and we see that his paddle is broken in half. Stroking hard with the single blade, he cuts into an eddy just above the next big drop. When we reach him he's not very happy. "Bow got hung up in the rocks under the ledge. Broke my paddle prying out," he explains, then looks sadly at the shattered fiberglass and adds, "New paddle, too." I give him my spare breakdown paddle and we continue. Near sunset, the rapids ease off, and we know we're through the crux.

After two days of mixed, difficult water, we camp at Rhadijhula. Pulling our kayaks up onto the bank, dozens of curious villagers crowd closely around us. "This is what a goldfish feels like," says Scott with a rueful smile. "There's only one show in town, and we're it." Gerry strikes up an animated conversation with several locals, laughter and gestures punctuating scattered English and Nepali words. Danielle says, "You'd think after 15 years over here he'd be fluent, but Gerry does things differently. I think he only knows 30 words, but he knows exactly when to use them."

A hundred kilometers of paddling are left, down a much larger and milder river. On the twentieth day since we landed at the lake, we say goodbye to our porters and head downstream. Every time we pass a village, hordes of children line the river, calling and laughing. We paddle past several cremation ceremonies and bow our heads in respect. Hour turns into hour and everyone settles into their own thoughts. The path downriver is clear. We slowly come out of the mountains and into the lower hills of the Bheri valley. In place of the barren mountains there is ever-thickening jungle. At nightfall we stop, exhausted from fighting a strong headwind, and sleep on the stones beneath the broad branches of a Bo tree. The following morning we're up before first light, paddling into the mist. After several hours, I see Charlie and the others climbing up a roadcut with their boats on their shoulders. It's the end of the paddling. After 21 days, 250 kilometers, and 10,000 feet of whitewater, we've reached the first road.

We trudge heavily into the small village that has grown up around the road-head. A large crowd surrounds a junker bus, its engine revving as black exhaust pours out. Gerry, who has hustled a few minutes ahead of us, yells, "It's the only one this whole week! We've got two minutes!" We rush madly, stuffing our wet gear into the boats, then tie them down on the top of the bus among the bicycles, baskets of vegetables, and squawking chickens. We hurriedly cram ourselves inside. The gears grind and the bus lurches forward, people shoehorned into the aisles and seats. I find myself looking into the dark eyes of three young children who peer shyly through a forest of legs. Outside, the morning mist is lifting softly off the jungled hills. We've traveled from the 10th century down the river to the 20th century, and made the only bus for a week by two minutes.

Passing out of the village, piles of garbage line the road, plastic, painted signs, and trash are everywhere. Sickly looking dogs forage, chased by small children who stop to play within a few feet of the passing bus. After weeks of beauty in the mountains, we're suddenly confronted with the problems of the Third World as it struggles into modern

times. "That's why Angad doesn't want the road into the Dolpo," says Charlie quietly, nodding toward the scene.

The driver turns on earsplitting Hindu pop music. Dust and exhaust come in the broken windows as we bounce past the bridge to Surkhet. We're headed home, a 30-hour drive. It won't be until sometime tomorrow that we rattle, bleary eyed and exhausted, back into the noise and dirt and crowds of Kathmandu. As the villages slowly bounce past, I'm not the only one thinking back to the clear water of Lake Phoksumdo. Now more than ever we're surrounded by the seeming opposites of this land—modern and ancient, dirt and beauty, poverty and spiritual wealth. It is the chaos of Nepal, and it remains as inscrutable as the all-seeing eyes of the Buddha.

Editor's note: This story is an excerpt from a chapter in an upcoming book, Whitewater Descents, *(Water Nymph Press) edited by Doug Ammons. An Emmy award–winning film was made of the trip, "Thule Bheri — River of the Hidden Land" for the Outdoor Life Cable Channel.*

Circling Mongolia's Dark Blue Pearl

by Nathan Taylor Ward

Birds whirled around shore, their soft songs filling the nighttime air. Not used to hearing birds at night, I awoke and crawled from my tent to find the source of this mysterious music. The full moon of a few days before had faded into near nothingness, letting the Milky Way shine like a huge, white river flowing across the sky. To the north the jagged Sayan mountain range marking the northern border of Mongolia was little more than a dim outline.

We were camped on the northern shore of Mongolia's Lake Hovsgol, at 125 km long, 36 km wide, and 262 meters deep, the 14th largest freshwater lake in the world. A week earlier we had set out in our sea kayaks to become the first people in the world to circumnavigate this remote body of water. One of us heard rumors of a big, remote lake in Central Asia—a place locals called the "dark blue pearl," saying it was the most beautiful spot in the country. A few phone calls later we found it tucked away in a corner of Mongolia. We had been working in Hong Kong for over a year, and, as ardent kayakers, visions of open water, mountains, and the legends of Genghis Khan quickly flew through our heads. While sitting in a crowded Hong Kong cafe, the thought of spending time in open spaces and experiencing a nomadic culture sounded too good to resist. By the end of the night we had equipment lists scribbled on napkins and a departure date set.

Lake Hovsgol lies about 700 km northwest of the capital city of Ulaan Bataar. The lake is the centerpiece of Lake Hovsgol National Park, an area set aside for protection in 1992 with funding from the United Nations Development Program. Often compared to Siberia's larger Lake Baikal, Hovsgol has escaped the environmental problems plaguing Baikal and remains one of the most intact ecosystems and purest bodies of water in the world. You can still drink straight from the lake with no ill effects. In addition to the lake, the 838,000-hectare park also includes vast tracts of high mountains, taiga forests, and forest steppes that harbor 244 species of birds, 750 species of plants, and 68 species of mammals, including wolves, brown bear, and reindeer. Natives that live near the lake remain equally diverse with four distinct ethnic groups (Khalkh, Buryat, Darkhat, and Tsaatan) living in and migrating through the area. The northwest corner of the park remains one of the last areas where the dwindling population of Tsaatan (reindeer herdsmen) continue their nomadic lifestyle after coming to Mongolia from Siberia.

Lake Hovsgol National Park represents a new era in Mongolian history. In 1921 Mongolia became the second communist country in the world after allying with Russia to drive out the hostile forces of a Chinese warlord who had taken over the capital city. From 1921 to 1990 Mongolia stayed intimately tied to the Soviet Union and the country remained off-limits to everyone but those from Eastern Bloc nations. When the Soviet Union collapsed, it threw Mongolia headfirst into the world's economic and political arena where it was left to fend on its own. Protests, democratization, and initial steps toward establishing a market economy soon followed. This radical transformation continues to cause problems for the Mongols, but it has also opened the country to foreigners. For the first time in 70 years, nearly anyone can come to Mongolia—fabled land of nomadic horsemen, Attila the Hun, and Genghis Khan.

We started our trip in Hatgal at the southern tip of Lake Hovsgol, and the dusty little town made us feel we had traveled back in time. The few streets were empty except for a couple of villagers, dressed in traditional long coats called *dels*, riding their horses on errands. Once in a while a government official drove by in a new four-wheel-drive on his way to tourist stops up the western lakeshore. The rest of the time a sense of quiet filled the air. Signs of the Soviet Regime still littered the town—half-completed buildings, faded propaganda posters showing men wielding wrenches, robust women holding a

baby in each arm. At one point someone installed streetlights along the main road. Today they are battered, the light sockets empty, and the wires cut down and sold as scrap metal—signs of a bygone era in a land turning back to its roots to regain its identity. Today locals have turned from agriculture to tourism and hope the national park will boost the economy.

Since only a narrow finger of the lake drops down into Hatgal, we could not get a feel for the lake's size from town. Once we paddled just a few kilometers up the mountainous western shore, the lake opened up and looked more like an ocean. For Mongols, the "dark blue pearl" represents a place of national pride. We soon discovered the reason for the name. As soon as the sun slid behind the clouds the whole lake changed from green and blue to an ominous gray. In the sun, the water along shore rivaled that of the Caribbean, but the deeper water always remains a mysterious blue. We watched mesmerized as our shadows played over the bottom of the lake, 15 to 20 meters down. Locals claim they can see the bottom of the lake even at its deepest point, 262 meters down.

Two days into the trip we realized that in our excitement to get on the water, we neglected to buy enough food. We faced a week of paddling on slim rations before reaching a place to buy more. Back in Hong Kong we had visions of catching fish with ease and cooking them over campfires. After two days without a nibble, we drew straws to see who would paddle back for more supplies. Luckily, Mongolia is a country of nomads who traditionally travel without food. Instead, they depend on eating with people they meet along the way, knowing that in time they'll return the favor. This hospitality has been noted in travelers' accounts for centuries, so we decided to try it—no one wanted to paddle back. We chose a *ger* (traditional felt tent) at random from the few on shore. A few minutes later we sat around its owner's fire drinking a bowl of salty milk tea laced with rancid butter. We were offered potatoes, turnips, wild onions, and blueberries picked that morning. We bought all they had to spare and traveled on with new-found faith, fascinated with the Mongolian way of life. That night the fish even started biting and we spent many nights cooking our *all-Hovsgol* meals over campfires.

The lake's western shore looks like a landscape out of a Tolkien novel. High peaks of the Saridag Range run the length of the shore—fractured, rocky red spires jutting from the ridgelines and fast-flowing streams cutting through forested valleys before joining the lake. Adding to the mystery were wild-looking Mongols occasionally appearing on shore, riding shaggy small horses and staring intently out at us before turning and disappearing into the mountains. After a few days we passed *Har Us* (black water), a mineral spring renowned for its healing powers. Mongols travel to the spring from all parts of the country, gathering the water in bottles to take home. Despite its importance as a spiritual site, there was nothing there but a large *ovoo* marking its location. Mongols still practice *ovoo* worship, a remnant of Shamanism that survived the communist crackdown on religion. An *ovoo* consists of a pile of stones and branches shrouded with prayer flags, locks of horse hair, money, vodka bottles, and anything else that can be conceived of as an offering.

When you come across an *ovoo* you walk around it three times clockwise before making an offering. This ritual brings good luck, so we walked around and made our offering, just to be safe.

From *Har Us* to the town of Khank, the trip took on a new personality. We didn't see anyone for days and existed only in the cycle of day and night—paddling, cooking, and sleeping. Thoughts of society faded as our minds became occupied with simple things like the direction of the wind, the intensity of the sun or rain, the cries of the birds, and the wind rushing through the pines. After such solitude, arriving in the village of Khank on the northeastern shore was quite a change. We read that it was an important trading spot between Russia and Mongolia and we had fantasies of well-stocked shelves. In reality, we were the big event of the week as children raced along the shore crying *"Nashir! Nashir!"* (Come here! Come here!). Their faces showed the ethnic mix of the area, from ruddy-skinned Mongols with dark hair to blonde children who looked more Russian than Mongolian. The stores were full of bare shelves, the old-style Russian canteen deserted and cold. The shopkeeper told us they were out of vegetables, jam, and flour for the winter, even though it was only late August. We picked up a kilo of rice from China, some packages of dried bananas from Vietnam, and some locally made biscuits. It was a first-hand lesson about the realities of life for people in that remote part of the world.

The full landscape around Khank made up for the empty shelves. We found an amazing wetland along the north shore full of seagulls and wild swans. Behind the wetland, green rolling steppes dotted with white *gers* blended into the towering Sayan Range, a string of mountains rising more than 3,400 meters and marking the Mongolian-Russian border. From Khank we paddled out into a still lake that mirrored the clouds perfectly. Days like this distorted time and distance. We experienced mornings when the next bay looked no more than five minutes away but took hours to reach. Other days we would paddle for hours with the sun never moving across the sky. Sometimes the wind would whip down from the north out of Siberia, bringing early morning frosts and gusts that threatened to rip the paddles from our hands. The wind kicked up swells that could transform the lake from serene to a frothing sea.

As we made our way down the eastern shore we found a more subdued environment. Even though it didn't have the visual awe of the western shore, it offered its own allure—enchanted mossy forests, bays full of volcanic rocks that teemed with spiders, and a view of the mountain range that stretched across the horizon. We continued to paddle and fish, experiencing a lifestyle and culture foreign to anything we knew before. For 14 days we felt like the area's early explorers—a time when there were no boundaries or maps, a time when food, weather, and mystery were the defining elements of life. And we realized that in Mongolia, the past very easily blends into the present.

Chasing Guinness:
Setting the World Canoe Record

by Neil Armstrong and Chris Maguire (as told to Allan C. Kimball)

So you want to set a world canoe record? Start off without ever having paddled a canoe before in your life; don't do any research about where you're going; get no sponsorships and go broke before you get halfway along; begin each day late and end early; pick up some frostbite on the Mississippi; portage 75 miles with an armed guard across a Colombian desert battling heat exhaustion; crash into rocky beaches; get robbed; dodge bullets and mosquitoes and biting flies and killer bees; and have an enormous amount of luck. Above all, don't set out to set the record.

That's the way we did it. After 9,966,420 paddle strokes we set a new world record by traveling 13,028 miles by canoe—from Medicine Hat, Alberta, to the mouth of the Amazon River at Belém, Brazil. And it only took us three years.

We know some paddlers do it differently. Don Starkell, whose 12,181-mile record of 1980–'82 we broke, had canoed most of his adult life and planned his trip from Winnipeg to Belém for ten years before he ever set out. Verlen Kruger, the world's greatest paddler, not only planned his every move over several incredible treks but even designed and built his own boats to do it.

We just drove to a canoe shop and picked up what looked good and what folks told us we might need. Verlen says he never carried a single thing that wasn't essential and it had to be the best quality. We just loaded up until we had 500 pounds of junk crammed into a 17.5-foot Clipper Tripper—Neil's father called it "fitting ten pounds of shit into a five-pound bag." We had about two inches of freeboard when we set out that grey, warm, 12th of July in 1993.

Looking back, we had everything but the proverbial kitchen sink, and we might have had that, too, if someone told us we needed one and we could figure out a way to attach it to the gunwales.

Throughout the journey, even though we threw out a lot of items (like the socket set someone insisted we needed), people would be amazed every single time that we could actually get it all in. It became an art to get everything in just the right place.

We named our canoe *Eileen*. That was Don's influence, since he had named his canoe *Orellana* after Francisco de Orellana, the first white man to navigate the Amazon River in 1541. We didn't know the name of any great adventurers because we hadn't done any research. We just wanted a name. We thought of *Yellow Banana* or something stupid, just hoping the canoe wouldn't turn into a yellow submarine, but it came down to a family thing. The beginning of this adventure was the first time that Neil, his brother Mark, who had been in Canada since the '80s, and their father had been together in many years. Neil's mother died when he was 16, so we thought, you know, maybe we should name the canoe in memory of her, which seemed like a really nice thing to do.

It was a mistake. Whenever we'd stop, people would gather round and we'd tell them stories about where we had come from and how far we were going, and things were usually light-hearted. Someone would notice the name painted on the bow and ask, "Who's *Eileen*?" expecting it to be the name of a girlfriend. When they heard who the canoe was named for, their laughter would cease. Everyone would become quiet and serious.

It was not a mistake to leave from Medicine Hat, however, but again not much thought went into that decision either. The original plan was to leave from Winnipeg, where Don started his record journey. If we had retraced his route, all we would have done was equal his record. By starting 847 miles further west, we would break that record, but that wasn't the reason we started in Medicine Hat since we had no idea at the time that we'd be going on to Brazil.

The real reason was that Neil doubted the canoe would survive on a rickety old rack on top of a rickety old car traveling the 800 road miles from Medicine Hat to Winnipeg.

Neil checked a map and saw a river running east. Well, if we can get to Winnipeg on the water, he figured, why not start right here. The South Saskatchewan flowed into Lake Diefenbaker, and on the map it looked like the Qu'Apelle River might connect the lake to the Assiniboine River which flowed into Winnipeg. Neil called parks officials to see if it was possible. One ranger said that although the Qu'Apelle was usually very low at that time of year, recent flooding might have given it enough water to float on. It was possible, but we wouldn't know for certain until we got there.

Originally, we were going to paddle from Alberta to the mouth of the Rio Grande in Mexico. Everyone made such a big thing about our lack of canoeing experience. What's so difficult about paddling? we thought. You just stick the thing in the water, pull it back and do it again. Even the distance didn't seem a real problem. After all, from Alberta to Mexico was only about the length of a pencil on our map.

By deciding to leave from Medicine Hat, though, we'd already altered the original plan. That many more river miles meant an additional month of paddling. The three-month holiday was suddenly four.

So here we were: two inexperienced 26-year-old Englishmen 7,000 miles from home, paddling an overloaded, fragile canoe on a strange Canadian river, hoping that our friends were wrong about Suicide Bend up ahead.

They kept coming up with dreadful names for this place, such as Deadman's Corner or Capsize Curve. These friends said we'd never get past that particularly nasty bend in the river. "So we'll see you in a couple hours," they laughed.

They wouldn't see us for three years.

Thinking our trip wasn't going to be too much out of the ordinary, we never gave much thought to getting sponsorship. Expeditions do that all the time, of course, and you see the resulting advertisements in all the outdoor magazines and on television, with adventurers of one stripe or another touting the benefits of this jacket or those boots or that port-a-privy. But we never thought of what we were doing as an expedition. To us, we were just another couple of Joe Blokes taking another canoe journey.

We discovered much later that what little skills we did pick up paddling were wrong. In fact, when we got to Houston we found out not only were we paddling incorrectly, but that we had the wrong length paddles. We were crushed to find that out, but once we learned the correct method and had the proper paddles, it was much easier.

Even though we didn't know what we were doing, simply because we were doing it people assumed that we were experts on canoeing. This happened whether we met people who had no real canoe experience or whether we met people with decades of experience. It was unsettling to have bona fide experts ask our advice on canoeing matters when we didn't have a clue. We'd just kind of laugh and turn the question back on them: "Well, how do you do it?"

When people asked us why, we had a difficult time answering. People wanted us to say it was part of some life-long dream, or perhaps some other personal quest with soaring aspirations. We really just wanted to have an adventure, to have a good time and do something a little different. Canoeing is a sport, it's healthy, and it's a great way to meet a lot of people. That's all that gripped us. And for Chris, it wasn't even that important. His view of the trip was just a couple months floating down a river, a little summer diversion. If he'd known the three months would become three years, well, he might have said that wasn't the sort of adventure he had in mind.

People were shocked when we talked about the distances, even when we were still just going to Mexico. When we'd say we were paddling to Mexico, there'd be looks of complete horror and amazement. Nobody could quite come to grips with this distance in a canoe. And why in a canoe? Why not take the bus or fly? Where's your motor? Why not a big boat?

People always said, "You'll never make it."

Even when we were around hardcore canoeists, people who we thought might have been a little more supportive, we'd hear negative comments. Like the time we spent in Minneapolis, which has a great canoeing community. Paddlers told us we'd get frozen in before we ever got out of Iowa. We ignored them. It wasn't that we had become arrogant, particularly, it was just that by that time we'd heard so much advice from so many people warning us about so many dangerous spots in so many rivers, and yet most of the time that spot would be nothing. Maybe ten years ago, someone's best friend's second cousin went out and overturned a canoe, therefore that spot's dangerous. It got to a point where we'd listen and be polite, but not pay much attention. We had more faith.

Of course, we didn't believe the Mississippi River could freeze. Wasn't it too big and flowing too fast? (Someone told us it flowed at 40 miles per hour. At that speed what barge would ever need a tugboat?) Then we saw these photos of barges stuck in the middle of the river and we said, yup, it freezes, but still we figured it wasn't going to happen to us.

Verlen's advice to us was to smile and approach strangers before they approached us; that it was the best way to avoid the troubles Don and his son Dana always seemed to get into in Central and South America. But that was our style anyway.

"I get a vicarious enjoyment out of anyone who goes out and stretches their horizons a bit," Verlen says. "They obviously did. Their thinking grew as they moved along. That's a good thing to see. I knew they'd succeed if it was urgent within them and they didn't think about how far they had to go but just that they had to get there. Most people do have what it takes, they either just don't know it, or don't want to pay the price."

Both Don and Verlen say that attitude and character have much more to do with success than actual skills. Good thing for us.

At first, we were still building up our stamina so as soon as one of us would suggest a rest stop the other would instantly agree. That was especially true when we'd spy what we began referring to as a "magic Budweiser sign." We would meet people who would buy us a beer, and sometimes the barman would even give us a free six-pack. It's

not that we asked, people were just offering it to us all the time and we're very polite, very British. It's rude not to accept. But that meant we were stopping early, drinking and telling tales until the bar would close, then not getting back on the river until perhaps 11 a.m.

Through Canada and much of the northern U.S., we plied our "water trick" in an effort to get the sort of creature comforts most folks take for granted.

This is the way the water trick worked: when we got to a city, we'd look for a safe, comfortable campsite. We'd look for signs of children, for example. We would go up and ask for water. If we knew they couldn't see the canoe, we'd put our life jackets on just so they'd know how we were traveling. Even if we had water, we'd empty it out and just go up there and look pitiful. The husband would always approach us first and we'd ask him for some water. When he'd give us the water, we'd ask if there was anywhere we could camp, get talking about our trip and ultimately get talking about his yard. We'd always pick where it was flat or a nice jetty or something. We'd ask if we could camp there, and he'd go back and check with his wife. We'd kind of joke about it, to see how long it would take the wife to come out. We knew if it was a long time, they wouldn't want us there. But no one ever refused us. It was always just whether or not they would invite us in for supper. Sometimes we'd spend a little longer putting up the tent, just in case they did, which was often. Many times we'd even get a hot shower or invited in to sleep in a real bed. We'd joke about it to ourselves because it happened with such alarming regularity, but we were very appreciative of it.

What struck us is that we'd feel ashamed for someone traveling in England because we couldn't imagine them getting this same kind of hospitality.

We certainly weren't very hospitable to the geese we encountered on Minnesota's Lac qui Parle in October. We stopped for lunch under a bridge that divided the lake. What we didn't know was that the first half of the lake was open to the public but the other half was a bird sanctuary. We saw no signs saying the lake was closed, so we paddled off. As we approached the end of the lake, the sky instantly became black with geese— tens of thousands of geese—who'd been disturbed by our yellow canoe. Then we heard the bangs of hunters' shotguns. We felt very guilty about sending all those geese to their deaths.

By November we were on the Mississippi and heading south. The weather was getting very cold and we finally worried that the river might actually freeze before we could get far enough south. Waking up in the morning, we broke ice from the tent, packed up, and cracked through ice with our paddles to make headway. We were miserable. Our original plan called for us to be in Mexico by December, but in mid-December we were only at St. Louis, where we stopped for a couple of days to get warm again.

Chris noticed his toes were swollen and one developed several interesting colors and a disagreeable smell. We saw a doctor who said the problem was frostbite. Chris was thinking the doctor was just going to inspect his toes and fingers, but out comes a scalpel and the doctor quickly sliced off bits of Chris's toe. He dug deep because you have to get rid of all the bacteria that's in there. Then he grabbed Chris's finger and starts cutting bits off that. Chris's only anesthetic was gripping the edge of the bench he was on. Maybe the doctor didn't like Brits. Now Chris has something to remember St. Louis by: no top to his big toe anymore and a rather sensuous indentation on his left index finger where flesh once was.

On Christmas Day we were still paddling the Mississippi. We were out of water—really, this time—and approached a tug boat anchored nearby. The crew aboard the *Kate Tully* was eating a Christmas turkey dinner and before we knew it, so were we. Sweet corn, corn bread, turkey, beans, fudge cake, and pecan pie. It was a feast and a Merry Christmas.

We arrived in New Orleans in February, and spent two weeks recuperating in the City That Care Forgot. We were just in time for Mardi Gras, a celebration we had never seen before. We attended several parades, just watching at first, but it wasn't long before we were diving for those cheap plastic beads along with everyone else.

Once we left New Orleans, we had a leisurely paddle along the Intercoastal waterway to Houston where we officially became the British Canoe Expedition, deciding to see if we could paddle to the Amazon.

The idea to go on had been floating in our minds for a couple of months, but Houston was where our journey became a business for six weeks as we successfully searched for sponsorships and got prepared to head south of the border. We visited consulates, printed up official T-shirts and postcards, and even got a public relations man.

Why not go on? Why not continue into different cultures? We knew 11 more countries lay ahead, and we could paddle the Amazon, the great Amazon River. All these countries we'd probably never have the opportunity to see again, especially the small towns inaccessible to regular tourists. We knew these were places we'd never see again, and very few people will ever see. Our families back home thought going on was great. And all the cold weather was firmly behind us. We'd come about 4,500 miles with about 9,000 more to go, so we were already a third of the way there. So why not? All we needed was a lot of faith and a little bit of ignorance. After all, ignorance had gotten us that far.

Spending time in Houston helped us significantly in going onward. First, Bruce Gillan, a canoe shop owner, gave us much needed instruction, outfitted us with paddles of the correct size, and helped install a rudder Verlen made for us.

We went on a radio show and just read off a list of things we needed. We got all we asked for from listeners, including vaccinations. We visited the consuls of all the countries we would be passing through, and the British consul, to get letters of safe passage. That idea came from Verlen, and it was probably the smartest thing we ever did. We used those letters all the time, and they got us out of many serious jams. And one of them helped save our lives.

As we paddled away from Houston we had about $1,000 each. Not much, but we weren't traveling like tourists. We carried our own transportation and lodging. Luckily, food was relatively cheap in Central and South America because we managed to catch maybe three fish in three years on all the rivers we paddled.

Many people we met thought we had rich families subsidizing the journey, asking us, "Hey, where's your Daddy's gold card?" and all that, but every penny we had we saved from working.

In fact, we ran out of money in Mexico. So we learned how to make hats from palm fronds, and that basically subsidized the rest of the trip. Of course, people weren't just buying the hats because they were wonderful hats—although they were quite stylish and well-made even if they were green—but it was a way of giving us donations and getting something back, a souvenir of our adventure, a way for each of them to feel they were a part of it. And we think they appreciated us more because we were willing to work for their money.

We made considerable money from those hats. Every day we'd go to a dock in Cancun where we knew American tourists would arrive, and we would sit in front of the canoe with a big sign behind us that said, "British Canoe Expedition: World Record Challenge. Donations Welcome," making it all quite official, so they could see we weren't just joking. We'd sit and weave hats and people would come up and give us money. We got some $100 donations, which was kind of surprising. And some people actually liked the hats.

When we got to a town, Chris, whose Spanish was better, was the one who had to find out where everything was. He was the one who had to explain, after the inevitable crowd would gather, that "OK, look, we've come from Canada. We're going to Brazil. We're camping here. That's a canoe. This is a tent. We've come so many miles. We need to sleep. We're going to eat. Good night. Any questions? No? Good." Of course, people would still come up and talk to us and we'd talk with them.

Being in the open ocean terrified us. That was something we had no experience in, and neglected to get much instruction, so every day when we headed into a beach was like a controlled crash landing. With a full load, the canoe was amazingly stable, so we would pick our spot and turn in. The breakers would pick us up and we'd backpaddle like crazy with the bow almost under, but we'd force it up. Chris would sometimes disappear completely from Neil's sight. At one point on every wave it seemed we had to wait to be dropped so we could paddle again, then near shore Chris would jump out and pull the boat in.

The adrenaline rush was incredible, the shouted directions were incomprehensible, and the jubilation once we landed never seemed to slack off. Sometimes we would lose equipment, but usually not much. Although one time we did lose a teapot in a capsize as we landed, and an Englishman should never lose his teapot.

The first time we were robbed was in November along the Mexican coast when a man came up to our tent at about 2 a.m., poking us awake with a stick and demanding "Dinero! Dinero!" When we stuck our heads out of the tent to see what was going on, he brandished a knife and repeated his demand for money. We'd never seriously thought about robbery before this.

Chris tried to get out of tent, but the thief was trying to come in at the same time. Chris finally pushed him out then shook six pesos out of a bag, hoping the man would leave. "No mas dinero," Chris said, showing the robber an empty bag. The thief then put his knife to Chris' throat shouting, "Mas dinero!" We didn't panic. We just kept asking each other how to get out of it, speaking in English, while the stranger kept a knife poked at Chris, now almost piercing his side.

We wondered if we should use our pepper spray, but thought if we did, the man might stab Chris in his panic. We thought of the flare gun and Neil went scrambling for it while Chris shouted, "Shoot him! Shoot him!"

But as Neil searched their equipment, the thief jumped him and put the blade against Neil's back. Neil slapped the man in the face and fell away to avoid the knife, his heart thumping and his face flamed with anger. Neil found the pepper spray and gave the robber a full dose. The robber and Neil ran off in opposite directions. But the spray didn't halt the stranger for long. He bolted down beach after Chris. The spray had burned Neil badly, but it didn't seem to affect the thief. Finally, Neil found the flare gun and tried to load it as Chris was yelling that the thief was gaining on him as they ran down the beach. Chris doubled back to our camp. It seemed a comical sight, Chris running by in his underwear yelling, "Shoot him!" as he's chased by a crazed bandied with a scarf over his head.

Chris tired of waiting for Neil to save the day and began running down the beach toward a camp of fishermen, trying to remember the Spanish word for help. What he got out was, "Socorro! Socorro! Loco hombre! Bandito!"

The fishermen seemed slow to catch on to what was happening. When they did, they ran the thief off. We returned to our camp and checked our equipment. Luckily, the only thing missing was the six pesos Chris had given the bandit. The fishermen laughed.

Looking back now, we laugh, too. That robbery was nothing compared to what happened in July near Sandy Bay Sirpi in Nicaragua, the most traumatic event of our lives.

We camped back in the bush as rain fell. Two men stopped by while collecting coconuts, but nothing happened. A little later three men approached in a motorboat, each holding a machete and acting very suspicious. They asked what was in the canoe, what was in our bags, demanding that we let them see inside. Our bright yellow camera cases held their attention as they shouted something about marijuana and cocaine. We told them we were just waiting for friends to return at any moment, but they demanded to search our bags. They wanted everything we had, our waterproofs, watches, cameras, but we kept refusing. Finally they left, saying they would be back with more help.

We quickly loaded up and launched through surf. We had two options, paddle far off-shore to pass town or go back north and hide in the bush. A storm was quickly approaching and they had a motor on their boat, so we knew we couldn't get by them. We headed back up the beach, paddling like crazy against the current and wind, looking for a clearing to hide behind. We dragged the canoe up the beach and about 300 yards into a mangrove swamp. Our plan was to wait until dark and load up and sneak past them.

We sat in the bush, whispering, drinking coffee, and eating biscuits. The rain fell heavier and we started shivering, then, as dusk arrived, so did the mosquitoes. We got the parawing out and laid it over us, huddling in the middle of that swamp, soaked, as the temperature dropped.

We heard a noise. Was it thunder or a gun? We sat up, frozen, waiting, then all hell broke loose. We heard two more gunshots and saw the flashes. We kicked off our shelter and ran.

As they chased us, firing their weapons, we got down on our bellies crawling over mangrove roots and struggling through vines in the pitch black. Before long, we couldn't move and just huddled against the roots in six inches of water. The expedition's over, we both said, assuming even if we survived the night we'd have no equipment to finish the trip with. No one could criticize us for stopping under these conditions.

As we shuddered for hours in the rain, providing a smorgasbord for mosquitoes, we hoped the marauders would just take our equipment and leave, but we feared if they found us they would kill us. Every time we thought they had gone, we would hear more gunshots.

We moved a few miles down the beach, planning on getting into the surf and drifting in the sea as far as we could. We moved as well as we could in the total darkness, holding on to each other so we wouldn't get separated. We stopped once to check the time, but as we switched on the flashlight more shots were fired. Now we were running for our lives.

We kept moving and praying, often crawling on our bellies like soldiers in war, heading to the sound of the surf. We scrambled down to the water's edge and slid in like turtles and let current drag us out. For the next two hours we drifted, swam, and crawled through the surf. Even though it was black, we were far from invisible because phosphorus trailed from our shoulders. We were exhausted but had to keep going.

At daylight, we dragged ourselves onto the beach and into the bush, deciding to head into the nearest town and hope for the best. In the light, we could see our hands were swollen from all the mosquito bites and scrapes and cuts.

As we walked into the Miskito Indian town, we were surrounded by villagers. The head man, Garcia Rodriguez, told us that his militia had seen two Colombians on the beach with bags full of cocaine and a shotgun. He'd sent his men to search the beach. They found us and assumed we were the Colombian drug smugglers. They had loaded up our canoe with our equipment and towed it to the village.

We told our version of the story. We knew we had to be very diplomatic and didn't want to raise tempers or show anger, but we didn't want to become victims either. Still, we're in a Third World country, an Indian town, in the middle of nowhere, and these people could do anything to us they wanted to.

Garcia said he was the chief of the Miskitos, possessing a treaty signed by the British in 1915 giving him control over all Miskito Indians and their lands, and his law states any vessel must get clearance from him. We hadn't done that. But because we were English, we showed him our letter from the British consulate and once he saw the stamp, the same seal as on his precious treaty, he listened to us. Luckily, Garcia's Miskitos felt they had more allegiance to England than to the rest of Nicaragua.

After our lengthy explanation of our journey, the chief declared everything a misunderstanding.

They took us to our canoe, and what a feeling of relief we felt when saw it and all our equipment. We did an inventory, discovering some items missing, but nearly everything was intact although a little waterlogged. Our wallets were returned with nothing missing.

Garcia insisted we stay and recuperate at his house. We saw little choice as the condition of our hands meant we couldn't paddle for days. Once there, we stuffed ourselves with turtle, rice, bread, and Kool-Aid. Our only aggravation at that point was the chief insisting we had to pay for gasoline, flashlight batteries, and other expenses his militia had incurred, about $30 in all. We joked that maybe we could pay for the bullets they shot at us as well.

Our situation was so ironic it was laughable. We were staying in house of the man who had given the orders to shoot us. They fed us, gave us a roof to sleep under, and had even become our friends.

After a few days, we continued on down the coast, deciding this canoeing was not worth our lives. Why are we doing this? We're just doing this to meet people, to have an adventure, not to dodge bullets and be robbed and hassled. Let's just think about this, so we discussed taking measures to insure we wouldn't have a repeat. Colombia would be one of them.

We spent 16 days in Cartagena in September, resting and making repairs. The city proved to be everything we'd heard, beautiful and relatively safe. But all the people we met warned us about drug smugglers and Guajira Indians, all of whom would kill us. No one gave us a chance of getting to Venezuela. We called the British Embassy and their advice was to stop the expedition immediately because a British diplomat had been kidnapped just that week by terrorists. That wasn't what we wanted to hear. Stopping never entered our minds.

We decided to avoid the dreaded Guajira Peninsula altogether. We could portage across the peninsula, eliminating 210 miles of paddling around a very exposed area, and eliminating the danger of running into smugglers and thieves and murderers. But the portage would mean pulling a 500-pound canoe across 75 miles of desert.

We had a boat trailer modified so we could pull it, then hired an armed guard from a private security company to escort us across the desert. The four-day walk eliminated two weeks of paddling, but it turned out to be the portage from hell.

We don't know how hot it actually was, but we never sweated so much in our lives. We stopped for water every fifteen minutes and couldn't walk a full kilometer without a break. Neil was dizzy, headachy, and at times could hardly breathe, obviously rapidly approaching heat exhaustion. Our armed guide was of little help. His mileage calculations were always wrong, he never knew where the rest stops were, and he didn't even have sense enough to wear a hat in the godforsaken heat. The one time we thought we were about to be robbed, he disappeared. Luckily for us, the men we thought were thieves turned out to be plainclothes policemen who had their colleagues continually check on us.

At the end of the first day, after twelve hours of walking, we camped next to a family's house. They invited us in for dinner but Neil was so exhausted he was cramped up, shaking, and couldn't even eat. Chris watched a Colombian football match on TV.

Before we left the next day, a police car pulled up and one of the men asked us if there was anything we wanted. We said, "Cold Pepsi. Please, cold." A little later a truck driver pulled up behind us with a bottle of Pepsi and said the police told him to give it to the first canoe he saw on the highway. That must have been a first.

Police continued stopping by four or five times a day to make sure we were OK. They even took photos of us portaging.

When we crossed into Venezuela, a man at customs inspection kept trying to sell us rubber frogs, waving them in our face. The portage had frayed our nerves at that point and Chris screamed at the man, demanding to know why anyone crossing the border would want to buy a rubber frog.

But we had crossed the peninsula successfully, and we continued along the coast until the end of December when we paddled into the Caribbean so we could spend Christmas in Trinidad.

While there we visited the British Embassy, a fine looking building without fine people. It took forever just to get past security, then the officials showed little or no interest in our expedition even though we had already been written up in the local newspaper. We had to speak through a thick piece of glass, no one was interested enough to speak to us in person. In the lobby was a large photo of Allison Hargrave, an Englishwoman who died climbing K2. If you fail, you're a legend. We left the embassy depressed and disappointed with our homeland. For some strange reason, we're still proud to be British but don't know why.

As 1996, our final year afloat, began we entered the Orinoco River, ecstatic to be out of the surf finally even though we knew we had 1,000 miles of upriver paddling ahead of us. For 16 months we'd worried about surf and weather. No more.

We saw our first toninos on the Orinoco, ugly pink things that look like Elephant Man dolphins. We didn't look much better. We both had multi-colored brolleys up for shade, music by Cat Stevens or Phil Collins or Hootie and the Blowfish or Van Morrison or Bob Marley blasting from the canoe. Chris would read our Spanish dictionary as Neil made lunch in an eddy current. Our river coffee had become T-shirt coffee, because regular filters were too slow. T-shirt coffee is an acquired taste, a little salty and sweaty. When we passed people, they would laugh and laugh. We were a sight.

The river bank became a ten-foot vertical wall of green with a canopy of trees and long vines reaching into the water. The sky was abundant with squawking macaws. This was an area previously untouched by gringos. We were in paradise, if it hadn't been for the biting blackflies, mosquitoes, fire ants, and killer bees.

In March we made one of our proudest accomplishments, paddling up the Artures Rapids on the Orinoco near Puerto Ayachucho, Venezuela. They were certainly the worst rapids of the entire trip, a maze of rocks and islands, and both Don Starkell and Verlen Kruger had portaged around them. We paddled.

In May we crossed the Equator and we both felt physically and mentally tired. Part of that was because we could see the end of our journey just a few months away. It felt like the challenge and the sense of urgency were gone; no new surprises waited around the corner. Perhaps we'd traveled too long and seen too much.

But we hadn't seen it all. In June, on the Amazon, the radio batteries were dead, disappointing Chris who wanted to listen to an English football game that afternoon. We saw a couple of small huts, mostly just three-sided, built up from the riverbank on stilts, and decided to stop and ask for water.

Our first surprise was that the small community was Japanese. What they were doing in the middle of the Amazon jungle we never did learn, but even though they were living in what looked like primitive conditions, they had a power generator. And a satellite TV dish. And they were big football fans, watching the England vs. Spain match Chris had so wanted to hear. What a strange situation—we're seated in a bright blue room, in a wooden hut in the middle of a jungle watching a football game live from England in a community of Japanese people on the Amazon River. England won, by the way, after a penalty kick.

As we paddled on, we averaged 40 to 50 miles a day until by the end of July we were so close to the ocean that we had to deal with tidal flow coming up the river. The banks were sheer mud for what seemed like miles, so we slept in the canoe a lot. As we neared Belém, we wanted a decent night's sleep so we could be fresh on our final day and enjoy our triumph.

We'd almost given up hope of a dry camp on our last night on the river, the last night of the trip, when Chris begged God for help. Suddenly, the mists parted and we were dwarfed by the Virgin Mary. This large statue of the Virgin looked down on us from a hill—a dry hill. We pulled up and camped out by her feet, falling asleep to the glow of lights on the horizon from Belém, the Portuguese name for Bethlehem.

On August 1, 1996, we arrived in Belém. We made it on our own, against the odds, and there was no doubting our joy, but it seemed strange. Canoeing had been our lifestyle for three years and now we didn't have to think about paddling the next day.

When we began in Medicine Hat, if we had known everything that we know now, if we had known we would become the British Canoe Expedition, that we'd have all these information sheets printed up in Spanish, that we'd be written up in dozens of magazines and newspapers in several countries, if we had known we'd be filling several diaries, if we had known we'd set a new world's record, we'd have laughed. We might have never done it. We certainly would have had a completely different outlook. We're glad we didn't know that. If we had, we would have been under more pressure. We would have had to be more serious, and we wouldn't have experienced half the things we did.